THE AMERICAN REVOLUTION: A SHORT HISTORY

Mary A. Y. Gallagher

Brooklyn College and Queens College of the City University of New York

AN ANVIL ORIGINAL
under the general editorship of
Hans L. Trefousse

KRIEGER PUBLISHING COMPANY
MALABAR, FLORIDA
2002

Original Edition 2002

Printed and Published by
KRIEGER PUBLISHING COMPANY
KRIEGER DRIVE
MALABAR, FLORIDA 32950

Copyright © 2002 by Mary A. Y. Gallagher

All rights reserved. No part of this book may be reproduced in any form or by any means, electronic or mechanical, including information storage and retrieval systems without permission in writing from the publisher.
No liability is assumed with respect to the use of the information contained herein.
Printed in the United States of America.

FROM A DECLARATION OF PRINCIPLES JOINTLY ADOPTED BY A COMMITTEE OF THE AMERICAN BAR ASSOCIATION AND A COMMITTEE OF PUBLISHERS:
This publication is designed to provide accurate and authoritative information in regard to the subject matter covered. It is sold with the understanding that the publisher is not engaged in rendering legal, accounting, or other professional service. If legal advice or other expert assistance is required, the services of a competent professional person should be sought.

Library of Congress Cataloging-in-Publication Data

Gallagher, Mary A. Y.
  The American Revolution : a short history / Mary A. Y. Gallagher.
    p. cm.
  "An Anvil original."
  Includes bibligraphical references (p.) and index.
  ISBN 1-57524-073-4 (pbk. : alk. paper)
    1. United States—History—Revolution, 1775–1783. I. Title.

E208.G16   2001
973.3—dc21   2001029280

10 9 8 7 6 5 4 3 2

THE ANVIL SERIES

Anvil paperbacks give an original analysis of a major field of history or a problem area, drawing upon the most recent research. They present a concise treatment and can act as supplementary material for college history courses. Written by many of the outstanding historians in the United States, the format is one-half narrative text, one-half supporting documents, often from hard to find sources.

CONTENTS

Acknowledgments vii
Introduction ix

PART I—The American Revolution: A Short History

1. The Rise of Nation-States and Empires: 1500–1750   3
2. War for Empire and Its "Deadly Fruit": 1750–1770   8
3. Fragile Tranquility: 1771–1773   26
4. "Neither Dependent nor Independent": 1774–1776   42
5. Independence, Alliance, and the Experience of War: 1776–1780   63
6. Experimenting with Confederation: 1781–1783   84
7. Experimenting with Republican Ideology in the Postwar Period: 1784–1787   103
8. Conclusion and Epilogue   120

PART II—Documents

1. Benjamin Franklin's "Short Hints" for Establishing a Union of the Colonies   125
2. The Petition of Anson County, North Carolina   127
3. Address of the Virginia House of Burgesses to the House of Lords   129
4. Resistance to the Stamp Act   132
5. Phillis Wheatley's Poem to Lord Dartmouth   134
6. "Novanglus" Attacks Corruption in Government   136
7. Joseph Galloway's Plan of Union   139
8. Congress Addresses the Iroquois   140
9. George III Addresses Parliament   144

10. *Common Sense*	146
11. The Declaration of Independence	149
12. The Articles of Confederation	153
13. A Plan of Treaties	160
14. The Army Celebrates a Thanksgiving at Valley Forge	162
15. Women's and Loyalists' Experience of the War	164
16. The Fort Wilson Riot	166
17. "An American" Argues the Case for an Unregulated Economy	167
18. Mutiny in the Connecticut Line	171
19. Congress Approves a Tax on Trade	176
20. Thoughts on the Characters of American Ministers	178
21. New Instructions for the American Peace Commissioners	180
22. Political Arguments Against the Impost	182
23. The Superintendent of Finance Resigns	186
24. Congress Confronts a Growing Crisis	187
25. "Lucius" Attacks the Financier	188
26. David Ramsay's Account of the Newburgh Affair	191
27. Mercy Otis Warren's Account of the Newburgh Affair	194
28. The Society of the Cincinnati	197
29. A Plan for a Temporary Government of the Western Territory	201
30. Billey Stays in Pennsylvania	204
31. Who Qualifies as a Voter?	205
32. Lord Sheffield's Observations on the Commerce of the American States	208
33. "Governments as Imperfect as Ours Are"	210
34. Proceedings of the Convention Held in Hampshire County, Massachusetts	213
35. A Report on Shays's Rebellion	215
Bibliography	219
Index	225

ACKNOWLEDGMENTS

I would like to express my deep appreciation to Valerie Yow, Ross Gelbspan, Donald F. Gerardi, and Elizabeth Miles Nuxoll, friends, writers, and fellow historians, who read and commented on this manuscript. I would also like to acknowledge my debt to Marshall Smelser, E. James Ferguson, and Clarence L. Ver Steeg, who, as teachers or mentors, informed and enriched my understanding of the American Revolution. Thanks are also due to Hans L. Trefousse, general editor of the Anvil Series, who suggested this project to me and shepherded it through to conclusion. Finally, I thank my husband, Philip F. Gallagher, and my daughter, Hanna Alix Gallagher, for their honest opinions and for supporting this and all my professional endeavors.

INTRODUCTION

Why was there an American Revolution? Because a series of events we call by that name happened, it is easy to assume that thirteen British North American colonies, and only those thirteen, were inevitably destined to declare their independence in 1776 and to establish the United States. This overlooks how difficult it is to start and to sustain movements that fundamentally change political, economic, or social frameworks. Thomas Jefferson observed in the Declaration of Independence that men were more disposed to suffer evils than to right them. He and many other Americans were well aware that challenging the system carried with it the risk of bloody conflict and an uncertain future.

What was it, then, that persuaded average people who enjoyed a standard of living far better than their European counterparts to rebel against the government many of them had prospered under? What had happened that made this government no longer a good "fit?" William Franklin, Benjamin's son, Governor of New Jersey (1763–1776), argued that Britain's constitution had never taken the colonies into account, and that it had to be modified to provide them with a government based on "principles of Liberty." William chose to remain loyal to Great Britain. His father, however, played an important role in guiding the American search for a government that would serve common needs, accommodate local interests, and raise revenue in a manner suited to their circumstances and for purposes they were willing to support. Americans evolved, tried, and rejected many governmental formulations on the state and national level before they ratified the United States Constitution in 1788. Documents in this volume will illustrate how they attempted to balance the principles of liberty and republicanism against their desire for order, effectiveness, and respectable standing in the world of nations.

American prosperity depended heavily on trade. In the days before citizens' income could be easily calculated and taxed, commerce was the best source a government could tap for revenue. The most obvious trigger of the conflict that led to independence was the British Parliament's decision, made after the French and Indian War (1763), to raise revenue from the colonies by directly taxing their trade. This was a dramatic departure from previous practice. Duties paid in the thirteen colonies prior to that time had been imposed primarily to enforce a system of imperial regulations called mercantilism.

Mercantilism was not intended to prevent colonies from prospering. It attempted to shape their economies so that they complemented the economy of the motherland by providing needed raw materials and purchasing its manufactures. It was also designed to ensure that the motherland derived primary benefit from their trade. Mercantile or navigation acts mandated that the most prized commodities the colonies produced could be shipped only on vessels built within the empire and sold only to the motherland. They guaranteed that the island kingdom would have the strategic resources, skills and manpower required to maintain itself as a major maritime power. While American produce had privileged status in Britain, it often sold for less there than it would have brought on the open market. Colonial products were also generally less valuable by bulk than the goods colonial consumers obtained from the motherland. Therefore, the colonies had to pay the difference in specie—gold and silver coin—that was always in short supply in North America because the balance of trade favored Britain overwhelmingly.

If, as historian E. James Ferguson has said, "much of the history of Revolutionary America proceeds inexorably from questions of government finance, taxation, and debt payment,"[1] what did Britain fail to consider when it decided to raise revenue from the colonies to cover the expense of their administration and defense? What convinced ordinary folk that Britain's plans to tax the colonies were unconstitutional and destructive of their liberties? Before the conflict erupted the colonists generally agreed that Britain had the right to regulate trade for the general good of the empire. They took issue with parliamentary taxation because they firmly believed that only representatives they had elected had a right to pass laws whose purpose was to raise revenue from them. When British ministers insisted that Parliament was within its rights to tax them directly and attempted to enforce its will, the colonists protested that they were being oppressed by a tyrannical central government that ignored both their concerns and the substantial contributions they made to imperial well being. They also complained bitterly that the taxes imposed by Parliament had to be paid in specie—colonial legisla-

[1] E. James Ferguson, *The Power of the Purse: A History of American Public Finance, 1776–1790* (Chapel Hill: University of North Carolina, 1961), xvi.

tures levied taxes in paper money or in goods produced locally. Spokesmen from plantation colonies that shouldered more of the burdens and received fewer of the benefits from the navigation acts complained that they were burdened both by trade restrictions and taxation.

The interrelated focal points of the conflict were, thus, executive tyranny, parliamentary taxation, specie shortages—an irritating symbol of colonial economic and political dependence on the motherland—and, in some colonies, mercantilism itself. The narrative that follows will attempt to show how these issues generated the revolt against British authority and how Americans continued to struggle with them as they attempted to define and institute a new form of government that would fit their ideals, suit their needs and "effect their safety and happiness." Documents in this volume will illustrate how problems related to taxation by a central government, commerce, and currency affected all levels of colonial society before, during, and after the war for independence.

Although social discontent existed in the thirteen colonies, social protest was more directed against colonial or state legislatures and local elites than against Great Britain. American discourse about taxation and executive power was, however, embedded in a broader discussion of natural and contractual human rights. This compelled those who were better positioned in the new order to confront the moral dilemmas they had created by refusing to admit disadvantaged groups to equal rights and full citizenship. Documents that attest to the concerns of slaves, women, Indians, and whites burdened by debt show that the American Revolution was a multilayered event that served some of its constituents much better than others. Those excluded from full participation in the political process and from economic opportunity made their voices heard through riots, mutinies, and internal rebellions that eventually forced the new power structure to respond to their demands to some degree.

The decision to seek independence was the first of many that Americans would be forced to make. What kind of a government and society did they want to create or protect? How could they fashion a union out of thirteen colonies that jealously guarded their own individual sovereignty? How could resistance to Britain be organized so that it could sustain itself without destroying the principles it espoused? What principles really mattered? History provides many examples of revolutionary movements that produced only chaos or a return to systems little different than those they had recently overthrown. Was this the case with the new states and the new nation? What can we learn about what the Revolution was and became from the records its participants created as they engaged in their act of rebellion?

PART I

THE AMERICAN REVOLUTION: A SHORT HISTORY

CHAPTER 1

THE RISE OF NATION-STATES AND EMPIRES: 1500–1750

The Growth of Effective National Government. The war for independence is best understood when we see it in a broader chronological and geographical context. Western Europe did not develop the resources and infrastructure needed to support centralized governments until the sixteenth century. The medieval economy in western Europe was based largely on agriculture and the processing of local products. In the early modern period better roads and bridges allowed information and goods to circulate faster, more widely, and more securely. Foreign trade gradually came to represent a greater and more significant proportion of economic activity. New, more encompassing political systems began to be created to support and to draw benefit from economic and technological advances.

Government, Revenue, and War. Premodern European governments financed war by obtaining gifts and loans from wealthy subjects and institutions. Once the volume of trade began to grow, they began to impose indirect taxes on commerce. A few years after Columbus's discovery of America, gold and silver from Spain's new colonies diffused rapidly throughout Europe where it financed wars that were fought with larger and larger armies and on a more global scale. America's treasure prompted Spain to create an administrative structure that would enable her to control and defend her American colonies and funnel revenues to the crown. During this same period, French kings extended the reach of royal government to the provincial level where it had never been a major force before, and this enabled it to tap domestic sources of wealth more effectively. Wars compelled nations to develop systems that could assemble the vast resources required. In some instances, however, the stresses they generated brought new groups to power and challenged established structures in unexpected ways. England is a case in point.

War and Taxation in England. English kings had begun to consolidate their power before the age of discovery. Throughout most of the sixteenth and early seventeenth centuries, England held herself apart from the wars that devastated continental Europe. Levels of taxation were modest as the island kingdom had less need for a standing army to defend it against invading enemies. By the middle of the seventeenth century, however, the Stuart monarchs had antagonized Parliament by their claims to rule by divine right, by their fiscal maneuvers, and by their harassment of religious dissenters. Under Oliver Cromwell's leadership, England moved inexorably toward civil war (1642–1646), and then to regicide (1649). During his command (1642–1658), the English army grew as large as other European armies. Cromwell used it to conquer Ireland and Scotland. He also waged a fierce war against Dutch commercial dominance, followed it with a contest against Spain, and won victories in Europe and in the West Indies.

From Cromwell's time onward, England had a standing, or permanent, army. The cost of the new military establishment tripled the national budget and introduced the English people to unaccustomed levels of taxation. England continued to battle the Dutch for control of maritime trade and North American territory during the third quarter of the seventeenth century. Parliament passed navigation acts to ensure that English sea power, merchants, and manufacturers grew stronger at the expense of their competitors and that government revenues from trade increased. The struggle against the Dutch was barely decided in England's favor when, in 1689, she began to challenge French power on the European continent. Related campaigns for control of Caribbean plantation colonies, the Ohio Valley, and the fur trade in North America were waged intermittently thereafter and involved Indian allies on both sides.

The English Colonies in North America. Englishmen began to establish settlements in North America early in the seventeenth century. They found no large native populations to exploit and no gold or silver deposits that could be mined to finance foreign wars or an enlarged bureaucracy. Instead, they farmed, fished, traded with the Indians, absorbed England's dissident and surplus population, and bought her merchandise. Because they had no precious minerals and because England was in political turmoil, they were left to govern themselves with little interference throughout their formative years. The monarchy was restored in 1660, and, after another Stuart monarch was driven from the throne by the Glorious Revolution in 1688, England began to achieve a new political consensus about the respective roles of king and parliament. The new royal couple, William of Orange and his wife, Mary, accepted a bill of rights that specified the civil liberties guaranteed to Englishmen as a condition for their accession to the throne.

English Political Values. "Republican" values that emerged from the seventeenth century struggles between king and parliament took root in America. The republican tradition maintained that the monarchy's power was limited by England's ancient constitution, common law, and statutes passed by Parliament and that charters were sacred compacts that the king could not abrogate. Republican thinkers were convinced that high taxation and a standing army in peace were hallmarks of despotism. They believed that government was made legal by the consent of those entitled to vote and that it should protect their civil and property rights. Broad exercise of the franchise in the colonies and the control assemblies exercised over taxation made for representative institutions capable of challenging the authority of governors sent over from England. Republicans prized their right, if accused, to be tried in their neighborhood by a jury of their peers. Although there was comparatively little corruption in colonial politics by eighteenth-century European standards, republican theorists warned of the need to be vigilant against "influence" that might lead to the domination of government by self-interested, power-hungry individuals. Only an independent, involved, and "virtuous" citizenry, they insisted, could prevent government from degenerating into corruption and tyranny. An active press, widespread literacy, and sermons on political issues also contributed to a politically active, well-informed population.

When Britain embarked on a program of imperial reform in the course of the eighteenth century, Americans were quick to invoke republican ideology to explain their resistance to innovations to which they objected. The colonists were absolutely convinced that they had surrendered none of the rights of Englishmen when they emigrated to the New World, least of all their right to be taxed only by representatives they themselves had elected. They had become accustomed to managing their own affairs without interference and were adept at circumscribing the power of governors and frustrating attempts to regulate their economic and political activities.

Administrative Reforms and Imperial Struggles. The Treaty of Utrecht (1713), brought a temporary halt to hostilities between Britain and France but it paved the way for future conflict in North America by allowing the French and English to trade with each other's Indian allies. Spain and the trans-Appalachian region from the St. Lawrence River to the Mississippi became more and more involved in the contest as Britain's colonies began to experience dynamic population growth. Settlers pressed into lands claimed by Indians and by rival European powers. The colonies' trade with England grew substantially and convinced Americans that they were making an important contribution to imperial wealth and power by providing Britain with raw materials and by buying her manufactures. By mid-century Britain and France were aggressively contesting for control of the Ohio Valley. While France felt little need to modify the system of government in place in Canada since the 1660s, constant threats against each other's colonies made Britain and Spain determined to improve the administration of their colonies.

Once its internal political struggles were resolved, the English government made earnest efforts to systematize both its domestic and its colonial administration. In 1696 it took two major steps to tighten its control over its colonies. Parliament passed a new navigation act that created admiralty courts (courts without juries) in America to enforce trade legislation. The king established the Board of Trade and assigned it major responsibility for colonial administration and policy making. It gathered information about the colonies, reviewed all legislation passed by their assemblies, recommended persons to fill administrative posts, drafted their instructions, and suggested measures to promote trade. The effectiveness of the Board varied according to political circumstances. George Montagu Dunk, Earl of Halifax, who was appointed president in 1748, provided it with dynamic leadership. Halifax was well aware that Britain had less control over its colonies than its European rivals did. He was determined to supervise them more closely, defend them more effectively against the incursions of rival powers, and expand their potential more fully.

Problems with Paper Money. One of the endemic problems Halifax had to confront was directly related to the mercantile system: specie shortage in the colonies. No gold or silver was mined or minted into coin in the American colonies, and Britain sent none in their direction. Specie earned in the West Indies trade circulated in port cities but, since the colonies' balance of trade with Britain was unfavorable, it was quickly rerouted to Britain to pay for manufactured goods. The lack of a reliable currency hampered economic development and depressed the colonists' earnings, especially those on the lower rungs of the economic ladder. Colonists dealt with the problem by creating different types of paper money that could be used for daily business transactions. The most troublesome kind was paper issued by colonial legislatures in the form of tax anticipation notes (government-issued IOUs), and declared to be legal tender, that is, money that had to be accepted at face value in payment of public and/or private debts. If a colony overexpanded the money supply by issuing more notes than it planned to collect in taxes in a reasonable period of time, or if the total amount of money in circulation was far greater than was necessary for trade, the notes would depreciate—their *real* value would fall below their face value because there was not enough demand for them. Severe depreciation threw the economy into disarray.

During the course of the wars that continued intermittently throughout the eighteenth century, the New England colonies, which were most heavily involved in the struggles, issued many more notes to supply and pay their soldiers than they could absorb back through taxation. Several times during the eighteenth century, Parliament granted cash subsidies to compensate colonies for debts they contracted to support military operations against the French. These grants were as much designed to satisfy British merchants who did not want to have to accept payment for debts in depreciated paper money as they were to help colonial governments take their notes out of circulation.

Nevertheless, some colonies continued to issue excessive amounts of paper money and British merchants continued to complain about it. In 1751, Parliament passed a currency act that prohibited the New England colonies from issuing any more notes as legal tender and ordered them to withdraw all paper money then circulating on schedule. Where and to the degree that the law was enforced, ordinary people were forced to barter to obtain necessities, saw their wages contract, and found it more difficult to pay their debts. More important, the money problem contributed to the stresses that eventually exploded into revolution.

CHAPTER 2

WAR FOR EMPIRE AND ITS "DEADLY FRUIT": 1750–1770

Colonial Disunity Hampers Relations with the Indians. As her struggle against European rivals focused more intensely on North America, Britain called on her colonies to supply more manpower and resources—with mixed results. Her ability to wage war effectively was compromised because the colonies competed amongst themselves for control of the fur trade and Indian lands and often refused to unite against a common enemy. This created serious difficulties with the League of the Iroquois, or Six Nations, Britain's most important Indian allies west of the Hudson River. Since their attitude could mean the difference between success and failure, the Board of Trade was determined to repair relations with them before full-scale hostilities with France began.

The Albany Plan. In September 1753 the Board directed the governor of New York to invite New Hampshire, Massachusetts, New Jersey, Pennsylvania, Maryland, and Virginia to send delegates to prepare for a conference with representatives of the Six Nations. Such a meeting, it believed, would show that the British colonies were united, concerned about Indian grievances, and willing to support their allies. The colonial delegates were to meet at Albany in June, 1754. Virginia and New Jersey did not participate. Connecticut and Rhode Island were added to the list of invitees and they agreed to attend. Massachusetts, which had taken a leading role in organizing the New England Confederation in the seventeenth century, specifically instructed its delegates to propose forming a confederation that would coordinate colonial defenses and promote their interests in peace as well as war. Instructions given to the other delegations, including Pennsylvania, however, mentioned only joint arrangements designed to promote a positive relationship with the Indians.

The Albany commissioners went beyond the limits of their instructions. Shortly after the conference began, they unanimously decided to consider whether it would be advisable for the colonies to form a union for their security and defense. On his way to Albany, Benjamin Franklin, a delegate from Pennsylvania who had already decided that a cooperative intercolonial organization would be advantageous, jotted down some "Short Hints" for a union of the northern colonies. (*See Doc. No. 1.*) They were discussed at the conference, and formed the basis of the Albany Plan.

The Albany Plan called for a president general appointed by the crown and a grand council chosen by the colonial legislatures to share responsibility for managing relations with the Indians and for providing for frontier and naval defense. Although it focused on Indian affairs, the plan touched on fundamental issues regarding the colonies' relations with Great Britain and with each other: how power would be shared between and among them, and how a common revenue could be raised in the colonies. What it suggested was very controversial: a central government located in America that had more power than either the colonies or Britain were willing to accept—including the power to make laws and levy general taxes. The plan also proposed a system of representation proportioned to the wealth of the individual colonies, a rotating seat of government, and a common navy. Some of these issues, unresolved, became the grounds that shaped the Revolution. Some were dealt with as the colonies searched for an appropriate constitution for an independent government. Others, how to apportion representation in the colonial legislature, when and where it would meet, what powers it would enjoy, how it would function, and how a federal union could be formed, remained unsettled until the Constitution of 1787 was ratified.

A majority of the conference delegates approved the Albany Plan on July 10, 1754, and sent it to the colonial assemblies and to the Board of Trade. It was not received favorably anywhere. The delegates had concluded that union would have to be imposed by an act of Parliament since they could not imagine that all colonies would accept it voluntarily. The colonies, however, objected strongly to the slightest hint that Parliament had the power to supersede or alter their charters in any way, and they were far from ready to sacrifice their individual interests or revenues for the common good. The Board of Trade was determined to administer the colonies from Britain and this brought discussions about an American-based defensive union to an abrupt end.

Dismissal of the Albany Plan by all parties in 1754 was a striking measure of how difficult it would be to find a formula that would accommodate the colonies' widely different economic and political interests. Even though it failed to win approval, the plan was an important evolutionary marker in the constitutional development of the new nation. It was the first attempt by delegates from a majority of the colonies to develop a federal structure. Years later, Franklin still believed that if the crown and colonies had accepted "something like it," independence might have been postponed for a century or more, and the sufferings and distress of war might have been avoided.

War Against France. A contingent of troops from Virginia under Lieutenant Colonel George Washington began skirmishing with the French in the Ohio Valley in April 1754, several months before the Albany Conference began. Two years later hostilities between the two powers had spread to Europe, the Caribbean, Africa, and the Far East. The war went very badly for Britain at the start. The government reacted to defeats in North America by sending more soldiers and a new commander, John Campbell, Earl of Loudoun. Loudoun was determined to wring more financial support and manpower out of the colonies and to impose European professional standards on the troops raised there. He also endeavored to prevent any colonial trade that might benefit the enemy. Sweeping embargoes imposed at his insistence disrupted long-standing patterns of colonial commerce with foreign possessions in the Caribbean and neutral European nations. Effective enforcement deprived the colonies of markets for their produce and destroyed their ability to earn the cash they needed to pay the war taxes—the West Indies paid for a portion of their purchases in silver. The economy was further damaged when recruiters took men away from a labor-short economy and onto battlefields far from home. Many never returned.

Americans were asked to support the war at unprecedented levels when they were least able to do so, yet given little voice in planning operations. Loudoun's high-handed, coercive methods antagonized colonial assemblies that had grown increasingly powerful and self-confident over the years and they generated mass protests unrivaled in number and intensity until the Stamp Act. The experience taught the colonists to fear and resist taxes, impressment of men and supplies, and compulsory quartering of soldiers. It also made them question whether such measures were constitutional. The British learned to suspect the Americans of disloyalty and believed they were trying to evade their responsibilities.

In 1757, after a series of military disasters, Britain turned to a new prime minister and strategist, William Pitt (the elder). Pitt quickly reorganized priorities, committed more British resources to the struggle in North America, and demonstrated more sensitivity to colonial sensibilities. By 1759, he had 200,000 soldiers in the field in various theaters, and 120 ships of the line at sea. Many of these were assigned to prevent the French from supplying their forces in Canada. Pitt's efforts quickly turned the tide of war in Britain's favor. By early 1763, France was soundly defeated and forced to accept a peace settlement, the Treaty of Paris, in which she ceded Canada to Britain and Louisiana to Spain. From Spain, France's ally in the conflict, Britain obtained East and West Florida. British victory did not, however, come cheaply. By 1760, Englishmen were paying more and more of their income, up to 20 percent per capita, in taxes—double or triple the amount paid by the French. By the end of the war, they could not easily be squeezed for more. The fruits of victory were not immediate or ample enough to defray the costs of administering and defending the newly conquered territories. Nor did they suffice to pay off the monstrous war debt that carried an annual interest of over £4.4 million.

War and the Colonial Economy. During the war, some areas had benefited from military spending. The prosperity was not, however, equally distributed and it did not last. Its companion was economic dislocation. Port cities like New York and Philadelphia that served as supply bases for the armed forces profited the most. As soon as the troops or ships moved to another location, however, good times gave way to depression. After the war, some sectors of the economy rebounded. Grain producers and exporters in the middle colonies and shipbuilding centers in New England showed gains, some of them substantial. More commonly, however, changed patterns of trade, contraction of credit and new imperial regulations caused bankruptcies and distressed commercial middlemen and artisans. This in turn triggered substantial unemployment and lowered wages and property values. Many ordinary people lost all sense of security about their economic futures. Colonial governments were compelled to levy heavy taxes to pay off debts they had incurred for the war effort and to provide for widows, orphans, and indigents.

Trouble on the Frontiers. What the colonists seemed to want most after the war was a government that demanded less of them than it had during the conflict and that would open up lands that the French presence had denied them. Neither materialized. As soon as circumstances permitted, eager settlers headed for the frontier. The ink was barely dry on the Treaty of Paris when Ottawa, Seneca, and Delaware Indians in the Great Lakes region attempted to turn back the tide of settlement by attacking every British post in the region. Parliament responded by closing lands west of the Appalachians to settlement. It announced its intention in the Royal Proclamation of October 7, 1763, and assigned over a dozen regiments of British troops to keep settlers east of the mountains and to prevent them from cheating the Indians in trade. This offended both land speculators and settlers, who were convinced that the British government was more sympathetic to the concerns of "savages" than their own.

In December, when their colony's government proved unwilling to expand frontier representation in the Assembly and to allocate sufficient resources to defend their settlements, Pennsylvania frontiersmen murdered peaceful Indians and marched against Philadelphia to protest the government's indifference to their interests. Discontent surfaced several years later in North and South Carolina. Angry frontiersmen, called Regulators because they wanted a more effective and honest government, complained bitterly about the high cost of justice, a system of taxation that was especially burdensome to back country folk, a severe shortage of money, and other grievances. (*See Doc. No. 2.*) Underrepresentation in the Assembly and the legislature's record of ignoring their concerns added to the Regulators' frustration and led them to arm themselves against the government. Disturbances continued until May 16, 1771, when North Carolina Governor William Tryon led a force that subdued an army of several thousand frontiersmen, but not the anger of those who survived the bloodshed. Seven Regulator leaders were executed. Thereafter, most of those involved in the movement signed oaths of allegiance to the government and accepted pardons that brought a temporary halt to conflict and bloodshed in the Carolina back country.

The Cost of Empire. As the glory of the victory faded, Britain confronted the enormous war debt and the challenge of administering a larger, more diverse empire in North America. It did not ask the colonies to take on a share of the war debt, but it very much wanted them to begin to cover some of the expenses for the soldiers stationed in America and more of the cost of their own government. The necessary revenue, it decided, could be raised by levying taxes on colonial trade.

Convinced that its position was reasonable, the government never seriously questioned whether there was enough specie in the colonies for them to pay the taxes without considerable hardship.

Taxing Trade: The Sugar Act. In a busy two weeks in April, 1764, Parliament approved a pair of measures proposed by Prime Minister George Grenville that alarmed the colonists and increased the economic strain the war had brought. The Sugar Act, passed on April 5, actually lowered the duty on molasses the colonists imported from foreign West Indian islands from 6 to 3 pence per gallon. The ministry, however, planned to collect it in full—something it had never succeeded in doing before. The act raised duties on other foreign goods the colonies imported. Both the duties and fines for noncompliance had to be paid in specie. There were also additions to the list of "enumerated" articles the colonies could export only to Britain or her possessions. This cut sharply into colonial profits on goods they had previously exported directly to Europe. Taken together, the provisions attacked branches of trade, especially the foreign West Indies trade, that would have had to be expanded to facilitate paying the tax in specie. Most disturbing of all, however, was the fact that the stated purpose of the act was not to regulate trade but to raise revenue.

Customs officials were put on notice that they would be required to collect duties in full. They were also given financial incentives to confiscate property and win convictions against merchants who tried to avoid paying. A vice admiralty court was established in Halifax, Nova Scotia, where charges of customs evasion were to be referred. Admiralty courts functioned without juries—the ministry had learned from experience that neighbors who sat in judgment of their peers rarely convicted them of smuggling. The colonists, however, considered jury trials as a bastion of defense against tyranny and were deeply alarmed by this apparent disregard for their civil rights. Then, on April 19, Parliament passed a new currency act that extended the Act of 1751 to all the remaining colonies. To the degree that it was enforced, it further intensified the "money squeeze."

The northern states, where West Indian molasses was distilled into rum, were most seriously affected by the Sugar Act. New England had also experienced the heaviest burdens of the recent wars and it depended more on commerce to earn money to pay its debts to British merchants. Its early settlers had fled England when the struggle against the Stuart kings was provoking protests against enlargement of the central government's powers, suppression of civil rights and establishment of a standing army. Their descendants were especially sensitive to the fact that the Sugar Act was a revenue measure that changed the rules of the imperial game, even though on the surface it looked like earlier duties that had been imposed to regulate trade. They saw the current ministry's actions in the sinister light of past struggles. Then and later they voiced suspicions that Americans were about to be forced to pay for a large bureaucracy that existed only to oppress them and for a military presence whose real purpose was not to defend them against foreign enemies but to suppress American liberties. Colonial assemblies in New England passed resolutions that claimed that the Sugar Act was unconstitutional because it taxed them without their consent. Merchants in New England and New York began to boycott British goods.

The Stamp Act. Low on the list of revenue proposals Grenville presented to Parliament in 1764 was a resolution that stated that it might be "proper" to charge stamp duties in the colonies. At the time, Grenville was testing the waters. He wanted to determine whether Parliament was prepared to assert its right to raise a revenue in this fashion, to measure reaction to it in the colonies, and, supposedly, to allow them to suggest alternatives. Agents representing Massachusetts and Virginia clearly believed that the colonies might be allowed to substitute self-imposed taxes for a stamp act and so informed their respective assemblies. Later, however, Grenville made it plain that he did not intend to allow the colonies to devise self-taxing alternatives by evading questions about just how much they were to be asked to raise. He was determined to ease the colonies past their preference for "granting" revenues in response to royal requisitions and to assert Parliament's right to tax them directly. Soon after the Virginia legislature learned about the proposal, it immediately challenged Parliament's right to tax the colonies without their consent. (*See Doc. No. 3.*) Grenville ignored Virginia's arguments and tried instead to persuade them to accept in advance whatever measure Parliament eventually passed.

Spokesmen for America failed to marshal enough opposition to prevent Parliament from approving the stamp tax by a large majority. Fears first awakened by the twin acts of 1764 were driven even more deeply into the colonial psyche when the king signed the Stamp Act in March 1765. Its prologue asserted that it was "just and necessary" to raise a "further revenue" from America. The Act required the colonists to use stamps on legal, academic, commercial and real estate documents, licenses, public appointments, wills, articles of apprenticeship or indenture, pamphlets, advertisements, calendars, almanacs, playing cards, and dice. As with the Sugar Act, the duties were to be paid in specie. British commissioners would administer the act but would select officers to implement it in the colonies. The fact that the monies raised were to be held in a separate account to fund the defense of the colonies did not sweeten the pill because the colonists believed troops were needed only on the frontiers and not in the cities where many of them were stationed.

Housing British Soldiers in America. Even before it passed the Stamp Act, Parliament began to deal with another sensitive problem, how to house and supply British troops where there were no barracks or taverns to accommodate them. Anticipating strong objections if soldiers were billeted in private homes, Parliament passed a Quartering Act (1765), which ordered that they should be assigned to unoccupied buildings. It required colonial assemblies to pay for heat, light, bedding, beer, and other incidentals. This, of course, meant that colonies with the largest troop concentrations would have to tax themselves more heavily to meet their obligations.

The British Army, commanded by General Thomas Gage, was then headquartered in New York. Its legislature agreed to provide some but not all the supplies required, but it also let it be known that it considered the Quartering Act unconstitutional. When the ministry rebuked it for protesting, New York refused to vote any supplies at all. Gage wrote privately to Viscount Barrington, British Secretary at War, that the colonists were moving rapidly towards "independency," and he recommended that Britain act assertively to convince them that they were still dependencies of Britain.[1] To punish the defiant assembly, Parliament passed the New York Restraining Act, which instructed the governor not to sign into law any bills the legislature passed until it met its obligations to the troops in full. The assembly conceded for the moment and voted enough money to cover all the supplies before the act went into effect, thereby

---

[1] See John Shy, ed., "Confronting Rebellion: Private Correspondence of Lord Barrington with General Gage, 1765-1775," in Howard H. Peckham, ed., *Sources of American Independence: Selected Manuscripts from the Collections of the William L. Clements Library, 2 vols.* Chicago: The University of Chicago Press, 1978), (hereafter, Gage-Barrington Correspondence), 1: 28.

preserving its right to function. Parliament's attack on a colonial legislature did not go unnoticed by the other colonies, nor did it stop the New York legislature from subsequently condemning the Restraining Act as unconstitutional. In the years that followed, other colonies also refused to comply in whole or in part with the Quartering Act, which remained an irritant despite revisions designed to make it more palatable.

The Rights of Colonists and Englishmen. These measures raised issues that had never surfaced before. As had the Virginia Burgesses, colonial spokesmen everywhere insisted that colonists were first and foremost Englishmen who had lost none of their rights by emigrating to the New World. They also asserted that they were not and could not be represented in Parliament and therefore could not be taxed by it. Spokesmen for the British government, however, argued that the colonies were as fully represented as the large majority of Britons who were not eligible to vote for members of Parliament. They paid no heed to arguments that Americans returned the wealth they generated by purchasing more and more British goods. They held that the colonies were part of an imperial system and thereby bound to sacrifice some of their interests to the good of the whole in return for the benefits they received from it. They asserted that the government was only asking for modest support from those who stood to gain the most from the costly triumph over France. Britain's unprecedented attempt to raise revenue directly from the colonies without their consent touched off turbulent struggles throughout the rest of the decade. The herculean effort to crush French power in North America produced a victory that neither motherland and nor colonies could savor. Instead, as historian David Ramsay noted, the "calamities" of the recent war nourished the germ of another war "which soon grew up and produced deadly fruit."[2]

The colonies challenged the British ministry even more explicitly and overtly after the Stamp Act was approved. The first official response to it came from Virginia's half-empty House of Burgesses in May 1765. Patrick Henry, a newly elected delegate, pushed through a series of resolutions stating that Virginians were bound to pay only those taxes passed by representatives they themselves had elected. A fellow delegate, Richard Bland, did not support Henry's resolutions because he be-

---

[2] David Ramsay, *The History of the American Revolution*, 2 vols. (Indianapolis: Liberty-Classics, 1990), 1: 53.

lieved they tended toward independence. Nevertheless, he expressed his own strong views about colonial rights in an *Enquiry into the Rights of the British Colonies.* Bland went so far as to assert that no "new" law of any kind could bind the colonies if it was passed without the "concurrence" of their representatives. He also asked why the trade of the colonies should be taxed or restrained in ways that British commerce was not, and argued that both should be "equally free." Other towns and colonies passed their own resolutions opposing the Stamp Act. Massachusetts called for all colonies to send representatives to a special convention to "consult" about coordinating a response. The Stamp Act Congress met in New York in October 1765 and again challenged Parliament's right to tax the colonies on constitutional grounds. It also complained that the duties charged were "extremely burthensome," and pointed out that it would be virtually impossible for the colonists to pay them since they were to be collected in specie. Colonial merchants organized boycotts of British goods, and urged British merchants with whom they dealt to press for repeal.

Protests made through these legal avenues were immeasurably strengthened by the common folk, who did not wait for their representative bodies to act but formed themselves into groups called "Sons of Liberty." These men, mostly artisans, mechanics, lesser merchants, and a sprinkling of radical intellectuals, organized street drama, threats, and overt violence to convince those who had agreed to distribute stamps or were suspected of being Stamp Act supporters that their personal safety could not be guaranteed. (*See Doc. No. 4.*) One by one, stamp agents resigned. When the time came for the act to go into effect, there was no one to sell the stamped paper. Governors had to look the other way as commercial transactions and legal proceedings were recorded on unstamped paper. The people had gained an early, relatively easy victory in their struggle against a government whose tax they branded as an unconstitutional attempt to deprive distressed but loyal subjects of their property. They had also successfully executed an important function of local government, police power, and established themselves as players in the oncoming struggle.

Even before the Stamp Act Congress met in New York, a new ministry headed by the Marquis of Rockingham had replaced the Grenville ministry. It had to choose between attempting to amass enough force to coerce the colonists into compliance or finding a way to rescind the act without losing face. Neither alternative was attractive or easy to achieve.

American resistance had stiffened Parliament's determination to make the colonies submit to its authority, but British merchants, worried about the economic impact of a trade boycott, pressed for conciliation. The ministry expected that Parliament would refuse to rescind the act. Repeal, it anticipated, would encourage the colonists to believe that they had established their claim that they could only be taxed by their own legislatures.

The Declaratory Act. To get around this difficulty, Rockingham proposed a Declaratory Act that proclaimed that Parliament had the right to legislate for the colonies in all cases whatsoever. Although Rockingham clearly intended "all cases whatever" to include taxation, the act was carefully worded to avoid any specific mention of it. William Pitt was one of the few who did not see either the wisdom or the expediency of the ministry's position, which he considered a "delusion that may lead to destruction." In a speech of January 14, 1766, on repeal of the Stamp Act Pitt drew a clear line between taxation and legislation. Parliament, he said, should assert its right to legislate. He also argued, however, that it should accept the American position that only colonial legislatures could tax colonists. At this point in time, the colonists would probably have welcomed a settlement on this basis. Neither the ministry nor Parliament, however, was willing to stay with the requisition system in order to avoid conflict over the right to legislate for the colonies. Instead, the controversy continued and the colonists pressed the logic of their position further and further until they unequivocally denied Parliament's right to either tax or legislate for them.

With the Declaratory Act strategy in place, the ministry used pressure from British merchants, economic unrest in Britain, and testimony of expert witnesses like Benjamin Franklin to convince Parliament to repeal the stamp tax. On March 18, 1766, the king approved both the Repeal and the Declaratory Acts. Several months later, Parliament lowered duties on foreign molasses imported into the colonies to a penny per gallon, the same rate charged on molasses from the British West Indies—the colonies paid without complaint. Americans celebrated the Repeal Act as though it meant that Parliament would never again try to tax them and generally ignored the declaration that accompanied it. The ministry was pleased to be rid of a tax it could not collect and congratulated itself that Americans did not challenge the reaffirmation of its power to make laws that bound the colonies "in all cases whatever."

Both sides were soon forced to confront the reality they had chosen to overlook.

The Townshend Acts. A few months later, Rockingham was replaced as prime minister by Pitt, who was frequently ill and unable to function. Charles Townshend, Chancellor of the Exchequer, took over the task of designing a system of colonial revenues that could actually be collected. He gave his name to a new act whose stated purpose was once again raising revenues, not regulating trade. The tax would be levied by Parliament without the colonies' consent. Its revenues were to be used to pay the salaries of colonial administrators—and thereby free governors and judges from their dependence on colonial legislatures. If there was any surplus, it would be applied to the cost of defense.

Townshend tried to be subtle. He sidestepped the colonists' opposition to taxes collected "internally" by proposing a series of import duties on tea, paint, glass, lead, and paper that would be collected at customs houses before the goods were retailed. He offset the bite the tea duty would take out of colonial pockets by arranging a lower overall price for it even with the duty included. This, he hoped, would establish Parliament's right to tax the colonies. It would also enable the British East India Company to sell off the huge inventory it had accumulated because Americans had been buying their tea from otherwise respectable merchants who illegally imported (smuggled) cheaper foreign teas. Townshend's efforts to sweeten the tax pill were offset, however, by provisions of the act that authorized customs officials to forcibly enter homes, shops, or warehouses to search for and seize prohibited goods or merchandise on which duties had not been paid. The Townshend Acts became law on June 29, 1767. Parliament created an American Customs Board to insure that the duties would be collected.

The Townshend Acts set off another extended debate that Townshend himself did not live to witness. It again explored whether the colonies were, could be, or had to be represented in Parliament and whether Parliament had the right to tax them, legislate for them, and to regulate their trade. In November, 1767, just as customs officials were arriving in Boston, John Dickinson, a Philadelphia lawyer, wrote fourteen essays entitled "Letters from a Farmer in Pennsylvania to the Inhabitants of the British Colonies," which appeared in a Pennsylvania newspaper and were widely reprinted thereafter. The "Farmer" conceded that Britain had the right to regulate colonial trade to promote the best interests of the British Empire as a whole. He rejected out of hand, however, any suggestion that Parliament had the right to impose duties to raise revenue. He pointed out that paying any such duties, however light, would acknowledge Parliament's right to tax the colonies. Once Americans conceded this, he suggested, heavier duties would inevitably follow. There was further danger. Two of the taxed items, paper and glass, could be imported only from Great Britain. This made it abundantly clear that the purpose of the acts was revenue and not regulation of trade. Since only trifling amounts of paper and glass were produced in the colonies, Americans would have to either pay the tax or do without. Dickinson left the colonists with an important question to consider: "Whether the parliament can legally impose duties to be paid *by the people of these colonies only* FOR THE SOLE PURPOSE OF RAISING A REVENUE, *on commodities which she obliges us to take from her alone;* or in other words, whether the parliament can legally take money out of our pockets without our consent."[3]

The colonists got the point. They did not act as quickly or with as much unity as they had during the Stamp Act, but they used each successive assertion of authority by the British government to build quasi-governmental structures for cooperative action and effective resistance. Imperceptibly, opponents of ministerial policy formed themselves into groups that came to rival or dominate the established colonial governments. Town meetings and colonial assemblies sent off protests and petitions for repeal of the acts. After delegates from more remote areas returned home, a rump Massachusetts legislature approved and sent out a circular letter in February 1768 that urged the other colonies to make a common stand and to keep each other informed about their positions and intentions. On April 21, 1768, Lord Hillsborough, the Secretary of State for the American Department, instructed Governor Francis Bernard to order the legislature to rescind the letter, which he considered a flagrant challenge to the authority of Parliament. Hillsborough also ordered governors of the other colonies prevent their legislatures from acting on the Massachusetts circular.

Opposition to the Townshend Acts was not limited to legislators. Ordinary citizens were concerned and involved. Customs officers stationed in the colony feared the consequences of doing their duty and asked for

---

[3] John Dickinson, *Letters from a Farmer in Pennsylvania, to the inhabitants of the British Colonies,* introd. R. Th. H. Halsey (New York: The Outlook Company, 1903), 26.

force to back them up. Hillsborough had already ordered ships and soldiers to Boston before inspectors seized the *Liberty*, a sloop belonging to John Hancock, a prominent merchant, for failing to pay duty on all the goods aboard. On June 10, 1768, Bostonians attacked the customs officers, who fled, first to a warship and then to Castle William, an island in the harbor.

Not long after, Hillsborough's letter ordering the assembly to rescind its circular letter on the Townshend Acts reached Boston. The Massachusetts Assembly refused to comply, and Governor Bernard dissolved it. When Bernard announced in early September that British troops would soon arrive, a Boston town meeting demanded that he call the legislature back into session. When he refused, Boston invited the other Massachusetts towns to send delegates to a convention on September 22. The convention petitioned the king to redress its grievances, and advised the towns to make military preparations to repel a "French invasion." It also kept itself in session to prevent any imprudent response to the arrival of the troops. The first soldiers landed on October, and marched "sword in hand" through Boston. They met no resistance. Gage arrived soon after, and saw to it that the troops were housed in the state house and in unoccupied buildings throughout the city. This put the soldiers in daily and—as events would prove—dangerously close contact with the civilian population. British authorities, however, mistakenly hoped that their show of force had convinced rebellious Bostonians that resistance to royal authority was futile.

A newly elected legislature met in the spring. It refused to rescind the circular and proclaimed that no man could be justly taxed or bound to obey any law to which he had not consented in person or by his representative. For good measure, it also demanded the removal of Governor Bernard and all the military forces, and refused to vote supplies for the troops. By denying Parliament's right to legislate for the colonies, Massachusetts defied the Declaratory Act and took the first step across a new Rubicon in the direction of independence, a direction from which it did not depart.

Some colonies had already endorsed the Massachusetts position before Hillsborough's instructions of April 21, 1768, arrived. Some met unofficially afterward, but no equivalent to the Stamp Act Congress materialized. The most vigorous response came from Virginia, which took advantage of some special circumstances—Lieutenant Governor Fauquier had called the General Assembly into session on the last day of March and then died. This left the delegates free to act without fear of being dissolved. They quickly prepared letters to the King and both houses of Parliament that restated all the arguments they had made in 1764 against the Stamp Act. They claimed that they had never challenged Parliament's right to regulate trade for the good of the Empire, but pointed out that the Stamp and Townshend Acts were both revenue measures, not trade regulations. They complained further that the Townshend duties fell not on foreign but on *British* goods that were necessities of life. They informed Parliament that its earlier threat to suspend the New York legislature had alarmed all the colonies. Finally, they protested that the Quartering Act amounted to another instance of taxation without representation.

The Townshend Acts also set off a new round of economic retaliation. Boston merchants claimed that the duties discouraged trade, drained off scarce specie, and increased their indebtedness to British merchants. In March 1768 they voted to boycott British goods for a year—if supported by merchants in other colonies. New York complied in August, but Pennsylvania merchants, many of whom had close ties with British houses or were opposed to confrontational tactics for religious reasons, were slow to cooperate. Boston and New York had to begin without them. Philadelphia joined in March 1769. Several months later, most merchants in Charleston, South Carolina agreed to boycott a list of items that included slaves. Supporters of the boycott ignored protests that coercion violated liberty of conscience and published the names of merchants who refused to join.

Some ports did not enact boycotts until well into 1769. Some never did. Merchants found it difficult to agree on which items they would refuse to import, on how long the ban would remain in effect, and on the terms on which it would be lifted. They were not always able to hold signatories to their pledges. Merchants' livelihoods were at stake for the second time in a very few years, and boycotts tended to enrich wealthier entrepreneurs who could afford to stockpile goods before they went into effect. Smugglers benefitted at the expense of those who were engaged in legal trade. Enforcement was a problem everywhere. Unity was difficult to achieve and the message delivered to the British was far from unequivocal. In some instances, it took pressure from local politicians or from artisans and mechanics to convince the merchants to sign on.

The Townshend tax did not cure Americans of their passion for tea. Most of the tea drunk in New York and Philadelphia was smuggled. Not so in Boston, which imported almost 400,000 lbs. of it legally from Britain. Enough revenue was collected there to cover the salaries of Massachusetts judges and governors. Although the boycott on other items was not completely effective, it reduced imports from Britain. In 1769, New York took goods valued at only a sixth of what it had bought the previous year. Pennsylvania and New England cut their imports by about half. Men and women of all classes vowed to substitute homespun goods for British cloth. Several colonies considered using bounties to encourage local industries.

Parliament, under pressure from British merchants, began to consider whether the Townshend Acts were worth the trouble and economic distress they were causing in Britain. Agents who looked after the interest of individual colonies in Britain were told that repeal would be made easier if there were no embarrassing acts of resistance in America. On May 13, 1769, Lord Hillsborough informed the governors that, while the British government still claimed its right to legislate for the colonies, it did not plan to levy any further taxes on them for revenue. Hoping to weaken the trade boycott, he took the unusual step of notifying the colonies that, at its next session (January 1770), Parliament would consider repealing all the Townshend duties except the tax on tea. Americans ignored hints that their good behavior would facilitate repeal. Boston merchants suspected that the government had announced that the Townshend Acts might be repealed as a way of breaking up the boycott—and so they renewed it for another year. Incidents in other colonies further fed parliamentary fears that any concession to the Americans would incite the colonies to demand more.

Nevertheless, since the current ministry favored eliminating all the Townshend duties except the tax on tea, the repeal process went forward. On March 5, 1770, the House of Commons took up a petition from London merchants that complained about the adverse effects of the trade boycotts. Lord North, the new chancellor of the exchequer, used the occasion to argue that the duties on all commodities except tea were bad taxes and ought to be removed on that ground alone. He spoke against repealing the duty on tea, however, because he feared it would incite the Americans to demand repeal of the Sugar Act as well. Some members replied that very little revenue was raised by the tea tax, and only repeal of all revenue measures would calm the colonies. Hard-liners advocated keeping all the duties to establish Parliament's right to impose them and the colonies' obligation to obey. North carried the day.

After an attempt to repeal all the Townshend duties was defeated, repeal of all the duties except tea passed by a comfortable margin.

As the British ministry had anticipated, repeal of all of the Townshend Duties except the tea tax created problems for the nonimportation associations. In Boston, news that the tea tax had been retained led its merchants and tradesmen to maintain the boycott and to ship back to Britain imported goods they had held in storage on the hope that all duties would be repealed. Merchants in other cities, however, were tempted to end the boycott on everything but tea. Philadelphia tentatively adopted this approach, but consulted New York and Boston to see if they would concur. New York took elaborate steps to poll its citizens and, despite opposition from the Sons of Liberty, eventually adopted that policy. Although Boston stood firm against lifting the boycott, belief that many of her merchants cheated deprived her position of weight. By fall, Philadelphia lifted the boycott on all goods but tea. Charleston and smaller ports dropped it completely.

The Boston Massacre. Benefits from Parliament's decision to repeal most of the Townshend duties had already been compromised by tragedy in Boston. The misguided decision to station troops in the center of the city made confrontation there inevitable. Tensions mounted in February 1770, when a customs informer besieged in his house by an angry crowd shot and fatally wounded a young boy. Agitators routinely wrote up the disorderly conduct, provocative behavior, and petty crimes committed by the soldiery and their accounts were widely republished. Reports circulated that British officers had offered to reward slaves for robbing and murdering their masters. Several days before the event that became known as the Boston Massacre unfolded, rope makers and soldiers brawled over an insult offered to a soldier seeking part time work.

On the very day that Commons voted to repeal most of the Townshend duties, the ringing of alarm bells brought a taunting crowd into the streets around the Customs House in Boston. It pelted snowballs and chunks of ice at a sentry and a handful of soldiers sent to assist him. In the chaos and confusion the soldiers panicked and fired into the crowd, killing five and wounding six. The city erupted in protest. The next day, a town meeting demanded that the soldiers be withdrawn from the city to Castle William and left Governor Hutchinson no alternative but to agree. The eight soldiers involved in the massacre and their Captain, Thomas Preston, were arrested and jailed. Popular opinion demanded speedy trials, but cooler heads prevailed to postpone them until passions calmed and justice could be done.

By 1770 Parliament had reached a consensus that it would compel its North American colonies to contribute to the costs of imperial administration. The ministry also decided to wean them from the outmoded and inefficient method of raising revenue by requisitioning their legislatures for men and supplies. In its place it intended to impose a system better suited to the needs of modern imperial government: taxes levied by Parliament and collected in specie. The attempt to make the new system work tore the empire apart. The same tax and revenue issues would, in the near future, trouble the union the colonies eventually forged among themselves. This, however, was unanticipated and temporarily hidden from view as both parties to the struggle retreated from confrontation and hoped the issues that divided them would be resolved.

CHAPTER 3

FRAGILE TRANQUILITY: 1771–1773

Fragile Tranquility. "The quiet that Great Britain now enjoys must give satisfaction to every well-wisher of his country, and I have the pleasure to tell your lordship, tho' America before followed her example in popular tumults and riots, she now pursues her more laudable example in preserving domestick tranquility. . . . I hear of no ill humour any where at present."[1] So said General Thomas Gage, commander in chief of British forces in America, on January 17, 1771. Gage was writing from New York to the Viscount Barrington, British Secretary at War. The previous month, a legal team headed by John Adams had won the acquittal of Captain Thomas Preston and six of the eight soldiers involved in the Boston Massacre. The remaining two had been convicted of manslaughter, branded on the thumb, and released. Trade between Britain and her colonies had virtually returned to normal and the tax on tea, a beverage as widely consumed as soft drinks are today, was still in place.

The political situation in Britain had also improved, and this allowed the North ministry to adopt a more relaxed attitude toward the colonies. In August 1772, the pious William Legge, Lord Dartmouth, replaced Hillsborough as Secretary of the American Department. Americans from Benjamin Franklin to slave poetess Phillis Wheatley hoped that the appointment signaled a turn toward conciliation. (*See Doc. No. 5.*) Dartmouth agreed to recognize colonial agents whose appointment had not been approved by the governor in council, something Hillsborough had steadfastly refused to do. He also granted all colonies the right to issue paper currency that would be legal tender for the payment of public debts.

The *Gaspée* Incident. These concessions were welcome and hopeful. They did not, however, address the colonies' concerns about parliamentary taxation and curtailment of civil rights. Nor did they resolve the most intractable problem for the motherland, enforcement of the trade laws, which colonists took every opportunity to defy. One of the more brazen incidents which peaked British ire transpired when the

[1] Gage-Barrington Correspondence, 1:89.

schooner *Gaspée* grounded off the coast of Rhode Island in June 1772, while pursuing a suspected smuggler. A raiding party whose members ranged from leading merchants to lower class artisans boarded her, wounded her commander, took off her crew, and burned her. A commission of inquiry was established to identify participants and bring them to justice. It was authorized to bring charges of high treason and to send the accused to England for trial. This outraged the local citizenry, and they refused to cooperate in any way. Stephen Hopkins, who had been a delegate to the Albany Conference and served as governor for several years, used his position on the Rhode Island superior court to obstruct arrests. Joseph Wanton, current governor and native son who eventually became a loyalist, discredited the only two witnesses who appeared to testify before the commission. General Gage believed he was no more eager to see the participants prosecuted than anyone else in the state. A handsome reward was offered for information that would lead to identification and conviction of the perpetrators of the attack. No one came forward and the culprits were never brought to justice.

British authorities took the *Gaspée* incident as one more proof that Americans would never convict their fellows of crimes against the revenue acts. American propagandists spread outrage at the government's attempt to bypass local justice systems. In distant Virginia, the House of Burgesses decried the authorization to remove suspects to Britain for trial as evidence of tyranny and oppression. They appointed a committee to gather "early and Authentic" information about any decisions the British government made that threatened the constitutional rights of the colonies and planned to share their findings with their sister legislatures. In the months that followed, most of the other colonies appointed similar committees.

Salaries for Massachusetts Officials. Rhode Island was not the only scene of trouble. Constant agitation in Massachusetts convinced the ministry it would have to revise the colony's charter to make its government more accountable to the crown and less amenable to local pressure. First, it decided to use revenues from the tea tax to pay the salaries of the governor, lieutenant governor, and supreme court justices so they would not have to depend on the legislature to vote funds for them. Republican thinkers were convinced that one of the people's principal defenses against tyranny was control over administrators' salaries, and they were determined to oppose this innovation. Governor Thomas

Hutchinson, who, John Adams later suggested (*See Doc. No. 6*), had long been plotting to persuade the ministry to reorganize colonial administration and to pay his and other salaries from taxes imposed on the colonies, refused to call the legislature into session to discuss the issue in the fall of 1772. A Boston town meeting then took matters into its own hands. Its correspondence committee urged Massachusetts towns to consider how their rights had been attacked. It denied that Parliament had any right to tax or legislate for the colonies and charged the ministry with plotting to deprive Americans of their civil liberties. Many towns were receptive to its suggestions and joined the chorus of protest.

Hutchinson answered the committee's arguments in an address to the legislature in January 1773. Where it had claimed that the colonists had forfeited none of their rights as Englishmen by migrating to America, he replied that America had been settled on the presumption that the colonies would remain subject to Parliament's authority. He admitted that colonial legislatures had exercised broader legislative powers than any "corporation" in Britain and acknowledged that Parliament had rarely intervened in colonial governance. He remarked, however, that this did not justify the increasing frequency and insistence with which Parliament's right to legislate had recently been called into question. Hoping that he could convince the assembly to publicly agree, he argued that the rights of Englishmen were *not* the same in all parts of the empire and that settlers *had* relinquished some of their rights by moving from England. The colonies, he insisted, had to recognize Parliament's authority unless they wished to declare their independence from Britain for there could not be two independent legislatures in one state.

Hutchinson badly miscalculated the effect his speech would have—neither branch of the legislature reached the conclusions he wished them to draw. His council denied that Parliament had total authority over the colonies, especially in matters of taxation. The lower house proclaimed its allegiance to the king but boldly denied Parliament's right to tamper with its charter or to legislate for the colonies. Parliament's authority, the House said, was and always had been limited to the British Isles. Popular reaction strongly supported these positions. The lower house further challenged Parliament's authority by calling on the judges to refuse to accept "unconstitutional" salaries from the crown. Although it took considerable pressure on one of them (Hutchinson's brother), four of the five judges capitulated. Only Chief Justice Peter Oliver,

Hutchinson's brother-in-law, decided to take his salary from the crown. For this, he was summarily impeached by the lower house. Hutchinson refused to approve the impeachment.

The controversy goaded Massachusetts agitators to embarrass the governor. In June 1773 they released copies of letters Hutchinson and Lieutenant Governor Andrew Oliver had written to a British treasury official that Benjamin Franklin had surreptitiously obtained. Hutchinson suggested, as he had in his address to the Massachusetts legislature, that the American colonies could only be kept within the empire if some of their rights as Englishmen were restrained—and he recommended doing this for their own good. Soon after the letters were made public, the lower house asked the ministry to remove Hutchinson and Oliver from office for having spoken falsely about the colony and given bad advice regarding them.

Trouble over Tea. The salary controversy in Massachusetts was a mere prelude to a decision by the British government that brought this period of relative tranquility to an abrupt end. The decision had as much to do with surplus tea the British East India Company had accumulated as it did with affairs in the colonies. Taxed tea was being sold in all ports except New York and Philadelphia, but in amounts far smaller than expected. The ministry concluded that customs officers had been intimidated into admitting large quantities of smuggled tea. Pressure for some sort of action was building in Britain as the tea piled up in East India Company warehouses at the rate of about four million pounds per year. Some suggested that the surplus would evaporate if the tax on tea sold in America were removed. Lord North, however, was opposed to this on principle and because he did not want to forego the revenue that was paying the salaries of governors and judges there.

As Townshend had done before him, North attempted to minimize colonial opposition to the tax by holding down the price consumers would pay for the tea. He persuaded Parliament to rebate all the import and export duties the East India Company paid on tea in England, thereby lowering its wholesale price. The Company, which had previously auctioned its tea to both British and American merchants for resale in America, now decided to retail it solely through its own agents in the colonies. The new monopolistic arrangement would allow the Company to undersell smugglers while guaranteeing the colonists cheap tea if they paid a tax on it. It also, however, deprived American retailers of a valuable line of business, and threatened the interests of those who dealt in smuggled merchandise.

The Act became law in May 1773, and the tea began to arrive in America in the fall. New York and Philadelphia, whose merchants had been more heavily involved in smuggling tea than those in Boston, were the first cities to react. Sons of Liberty in both sprang to action. Company tea agents were treated as the stamp agents had been—they were urged to resign and threatened with violence if they did not. The *Polly*, the first tea ship to reach Philadelphia, returned to England without attempting to unload its cargo. It arrived there shortly after news of the events at Boston reached Britain.

Once again, special circumstances made for violent conflict in Boston. The tea tax was paying Governor Hutchinson's salary. Two of the five tea agents were his sons. After a press war failed to bring about their resignations, local patriots organized town meetings and attacked their homes. All of them refused to resign, and put themselves out of reach by moving to Castle William. When the *Dartmouth*, *Eleanor*, and *Beaver* sailed into Boston harbor with 114 cases of tea each, the stage was set for confrontation. Hutchinson was determined to land the tea. He refused to allow the captains to leave port without obtaining clearance from the customs house stating that the tea duties had been paid, and he had a warship ready to intercept them if they tried to sail without it. The Boston town meeting was determined to prevent the tea from being landed. A crowd of men became Narragansett Indians for an evening, boarded the ships, and dumped 90,000 pounds of tea into the sea. They used extreme care to insure that no other merchandise was damaged in any way.

The ministry regarded the destruction of the tea as the latest in a series of increasingly brazen provocations. Its outrage was unbounded. British friends of the colonies were also angered and alienated. Franklin, who appeared before the Privy Council as agent for the Massachusetts legislature to present its petition for removing Hutchinson and Oliver from office, was the first to feel official wrath. He was subjected to a blistering attack that clearly demonstrated that the government's patience with the colony was at an end. Then, he was summarily removed from his position as Deputy Postmaster General for America for his role in the publication of the letters from Hutchinson and Oliver.

Four Coercive Acts. The colony of Massachusetts was next, and its punishment was even more severe. Between March 25 and May 20,

1774, Parliament expressed its pent-up anger in four Coercive Acts that were designed to establish its authority over the colonies definitively. The Boston Port Act claimed that British subjects could not safely carry on trade there nor could the king's customs be collected. The Act closed the customs house and shut the port to commerce until the "ill-affected" Bostonians paid for the tea they had destroyed and compensated those who had suffered in the disturbances. Only supplies for British forces and food and fuel for the "necessary use" of the people of Boston could be landed. This bit of mercy hardly offset the loss of livelihood suffered by many inhabitants whose occupations depended on trade.

The Massachusetts Government Act struck at the colony's government and charter. First, it revoked the House of Representatives's power to elect the twenty-eight members of the governor's council. Election by the House, Parliament said, had not contributed to promoting the internal welfare, peace, and good government of the province. Instead, it had obstructed and defeated the execution of the laws and encouraged the "ill-disposed" to openly resist authority. Effective August 1, 1774, council members would be appointed by the king and would serve at his good pleasure. The governor would appoint judges and sheriffs. Parliament then moved to suppress popular challenges to British authority. No town meetings, it ordained, could be held without the written consent of the governor unless their purpose was to elect constables and other local officers. Town meetings could consider only those agenda items the governor approved. The court system did not escape notice. Jurors, formerly elected by the freemen of Massachusetts, would now be appointed by the sheriffs who were appointed by the governor. Parliament had threatened the New York legislature with the Restraining Act in 1767, but the colony had gestured appropriately and been spared. There was no room for maneuver here. Massachusetts would pay the full price for its defiance: its charter was set aside and the crown assumed substantial control over its government.

Parliament also decided to provide extra protection for officials involved in suppressing the riots and disturbances for which Massachusetts had become notorious. Magistrates, it reasoned, might be afraid to use force against protestors because they feared they would be prosecuted by "persons who do not acknowledge the validity of the laws." The Administration of Justice Act allowed any officer charged with a capital offense in the course of doing his duty to have his case heard in another British colony or in Great Britain itself if the governor judged that he could not obtain a fair trial in Massachusetts. Fourth and finally,

Parliament passed a new and very much more offensive Quartering Act applicable to all the colonies. It provided that, where barracks were not available, troops could be billeted in private buildings.

The Quebec Act. On the very same day that Parliament passed the Massachusetts Government Act it also established a government for the province of Quebec. Here, too, there was much to alarm the thirteen colonies. The Quebec Act truncated their claims to lands granted in their charters by extending Quebec's boundaries along the St. Lawrence, Great Lakes, and Ohio River to the Mississippi. Furthermore, instead of basing the new Quebec government on a British model, Parliament adopted the authoritarian French system in place there before 1763. Quebec would be governed by a council that was appointed, not elected. The laws it passed were subject to the veto of the king's governor. It had no powers to levy taxes or duties except to provide funds for public roads and buildings. There would be no representative assembly and no juries for civil trials. Parliament also threw religion into the mix. The Act conceded free exercise of religion to Quebec's Catholics and promised state support for their clergy.

Colonial Reaction to the Coercive and Quebec Acts. By punishing the Bay Colony so severely, Parliament had hoped to convince the other twelve colonies that the only safe course to follow was to recognize its authority. Although Parliament did not intend the Quebec Act to be considered a repressive measure, anxious colonists compared it with the Coercive Acts and concluded that together they constituted the first phase of a broad attack on colonial self-government. They appeared as such on the list of grievances against the king in the Declaration of Independence. Toleration and state support for Roman Catholicism in Quebec suggested, as had earlier attempts by Anglican churchmen to have a bishop appointed for the colonies, that the government intended to increase its authority over churches that had previously been under local control.

Many colonists believed that Parliament's attack on Massachusetts could not be allowed to go unanswered. They turned to familiar patterns of response. Mob action in Massachusetts closed courts and persuaded royal appointees not to accept their new positions. Correspondence committees in all the colonies involved more and more people in opposition to British policy and marshaled support and sympathy for suffering Bostonians. Some suggested another boycott; others, an intercolonial congress. Merchants did not want another boycott. Boston traders even considered paying for the tea to get their port reopened and some Philadelphia merchants agreed they should, but the people would not hear of it. It was easier to win support for an intercolonial congress —a conference, not a legislature—which would take on the task of designing a unified response to the Coercive Acts. In one manner or another, all the colonies except Georgia managed to elect representatives to the gathering, scheduled to be held in September, 1774.

The First Continental Congress Convenes. Delegates began arriving in Philadelphia at the end of August. Their diaries and letters give details of their travels, comment on how elegantly they were received, recount their first impressions of other delegates, and show their excitement and awareness of the responsibility with which they had been entrusted. The Congress opened its first session on September 5. The delegates' political and ideological differences were evident almost immediately. Minor points to be settled—where they would meet, who their presiding officer would be, and who would take the minutes— revealed more serious ideological differences beneath.

Some of the more radical members of the Massachusetts, Virginia, and South Carolina delegations had become acquainted through prior correspondence or in the days before Congress convened. Before the first session they had already laid the groundwork for settling some of these questions. Although Joseph Galloway, conservative Speaker of the Pennsylvania Assembly, offered them the State House for their deliberations, the delegates chose to sit in Carpenter's Hall, home to Philadelphia's artisans. Then, they elected Peyton Randolph, Speaker of the Virginia House of Delegates, not Galloway, to preside over the meeting. These two moves deprived Galloway of any special advantage he may have hoped to gain and made it easier for radicals to thwart his agenda— reconciliation with Britain and approval of his plan for an imperial constitution. In another surprising move, Pennsylvania Son of Liberty Charles Thomson, whose election to the Pennsylvania delegation Galloway had successfully opposed, was chosen as secretary to the Congress over the discreet objections of some of the more conservative delegates. Finally, to provide an environment for honest discussion of extremely sensitive issues and to preserve an appearance of unity, the delegates agreed to keep their deliberations secret until Congress published them at the end of the session. They also agreed to record only those resolutions that passed in the affirmative.

Congress Confronts Questions about Government in Massachusetts. Even with radical leaders John and Samuel Adams away in Philadelphia, things were not quiet in Massachusetts. Not long after it went into session, Paul Revere, riding express from Massachusetts, presented Congress with a letter from a Boston committee asking for advice about how to respond to suspension of the Massachusetts legislature and military preparations by the British army. Revere also brought the resolves that Suffolk County had adopted on September 9 in response to the Coercive Acts. They defiantly urged the colonists not to recognize any officials appointed under the Massachusetts Government Act. They called for retaliation against British trade and manufactures, nonpayment of taxes, and military preparations if the Coercive Acts were not repealed. Thus confronted, Congress was forced to choose between supporting the suffering citizens of Boston or allowing them to set their own course. It endorsed the resolves as "firm and temperate" even though it hoped that there would be no provocations from Massachusetts to complicate efforts to reach an accommodation with Britain.

Several weeks later, Revere appeared again to announce that General Gage had seized military stores that the colonists had stocked at Cambridge and had fortified the isthmus between Boston and the mainland. Rumors that the British navy was bombarding Boston brought out local militia units and sent those who had accepted appointment under the Massachusetts Government Act scurrying into hiding. Early in October, the Massachusetts House of Representatives called itself into session in Salem, resolved itself into a provincial congress, elected John Hancock its president, and began governing all parts of the colony not under the direct control of General Gage. It drew up plans for defending the colony, called up the militia, began collecting taxes into its own coffers, and sent messengers to neighboring colonies to ask for their cooperation and support. In fact if not in theory, most of Massachusetts had an independent government.

Congress Decides on Procedures. The first major organizational issue the Philadelphia Congress faced was whether to give each colony a single vote, or whether, as had been proposed in Franklin's

"Short Hints" and the Albany Plan, voting strength should be proportioned to population and wealth. Discussion became so heated that it threatened to break up the Congress before it had even begun to deal with more substantive issues. Finally, since there was no way to accurately measure wealth or population, it opted for one vote per colony.

Once this divisive issue was out of the way, the delegates had to face the overriding issue they had come to discuss: could the colonies find common ground on which to stand before king and parliament, and how should that ground be defined? Would the radical members of the Massachusetts, Virginia, and South Carolina delegations who were so ready to challenge British prerogatives prevail, or would the more moderate delegates from New York and Pennsylvania, caricatured as "Hutchinsonians" by John Adams, carry the day? The delegates began to assess as a group what most offended them about the government's policies. Would they continue to profess loyalty to the king while trying to define a mutually acceptable place for themselves within the British Empire or would they decide that their only realistic option was a course that moved them toward confrontation? Within a week, Congress had appointed two major committees, one with twenty-four members, the second with twelve. They sat concurrently, and reported alternately to the body as a whole. The division of functions represented the two interrelated but not always complimentary forces that slowly but inexorably drew the colonies to the precipice of independence: a determination to defend political and civil rights, and a determination to remove obstacles to economic opportunity.

The Committee on Colonial Grievances. The committee of twenty-four, two delegates from each state, was charged to formulate a statement of the rights of the colonies, to enumerate where they had been violated, and to suggest how to obtain redress. It was not easy for the delegates to agree on which acts of Parliament they most objected to, or to decide how far back they should trace their grievances. Finally, they decided to consider only those events that had happened since 1763 so as to focus resentment on the reign of George III.

Delegates also had to decide whether to base their assertion of colonial rights on natural law, on their rights as Englishmen, on their charters, or on all or some of these. They also had to agree on what if any powers they would admit that Parliament could exercise over them. Most believed that the colonies were bound by general English laws in force before emigration began, but there the consensus ended. Ten years earlier, they might have said that Parliament could legislate for—but not tax—the colonies. Now, however, they generally agreed that Parliament had no authority either to tax the colonies or to legislate for them on matters of "internal polity" and that it had clearly overstepped its bounds by passing the Coercive Acts. The more radical delegates insisted that the very broad base of natural rights would give the colonies their strongest and best defense against parliamentary usurpations. Those with more modest long term objectives preferred to rest their case on written laws and charters.

Once it agreed on its grievances, Congress had to decide how to pursue redress. John Adams made himself a list of possibilities. Low-intensity options included petitions to the king, nonimportation, nonexportation, nonconsumption, and establishment of societies to foster American arts and manufactures. Then there were preparations for war—activating the militia in every colony, raising £50,000 for an army of 20,000 men and £200,000 for a navy. Finally there was Joseph Galloway's pet project, establishment of an American legislature co-equal with Parliament under the authority of the king, a plan which borrowed heavily from the one developed by the Albany Congress.

Galloway's Plan. Galloway was determined to provide an alternative to some of the more militant actions on Adams's list. He was as strongly opposed to Parliament's attempts to tax and legislate for the colonies as his more radical counterparts but he firmly believed the colonies needed British protection and owed her allegiance in return. Where the Albany Plan had been primarily designed to unite the colonies, to make them capable of responding to emergencies, and to rationalize their relations with the Indians, Galloway's main objective was to preserve both the union between Britain and her colonies and the colonies' rights to self government. One of the major arguments Galloway advanced in favor of his plan was that the colonies would need some central authority to regulate trade in the event that they chose to deny Parliament that right. Events would prove how correct he was, but he failed to persuade a sufficient number of delegates to his viewpoint.

Galloway's Plan provided for a crown-appointed president-general and a real American legislature (Grand Council). Each colony would retain its present constitution and powers over its internal affairs. Either Commons or the Grand Council, Galloway proposed, could initiate "general regulations" for the colonies, but they would have to be approved by the other legislature. Galloway's discussion of the revenue question was somewhat circumspect. He did not discuss how the government he proposed would be financed. "In time of war," he specified, the Grand Council could "prepare" bills to grant aids to the crown. If approved by the President General, the bills would become law without the approval of the British Parliament and, presumably, without the approval of the thirteen colonial legislatures. (*See Doc. No. 7.*)

In this way, Galloway hoped to bridge the chasm between colonies who believed themselves oppressed by Parliament and a British government determined to assert its prerogatives. He did not succeed. The central government he described had powers on both the imperial and intercolonial levels that went far beyond those claimed by the intercolonial conference body that the present Congress was, and far beyond what the delegates and the colonies they represented were prepared to allow. Congress's attention was directed to finding a remedy for injuries that resulted from the British government's determination to extend its powers beyond limits Americans would accept. The delegates tabled Galloway's plan and eventually decided not to reconsider it.

The Committee on Trade. While the committee of twenty-four was discussing colonial grievances, the committee of twelve had been concurrently reviewing British statutes governing colonial trade and manufacturing and trying to decide whether Parliament could justly claim authority to regulate them. Since any decision the delegates reached might have very dissimilar effects on the different economies they represented, there was no easy road to consensus. Debate continued for well over a year and forecast sectional divisions that endured long after the question of independence had been decided. Delegates positioned themselves on one side or another for reasons as much related to the economic aspirations and frustrations of their colonies as to principle.

Many of the more radical representatives from the plantation colonies, whose freedom to export rice and tobacco was restrained by the Navigation Acts, argued that Britain had no more right to regulate trade than she had to legislate on any other matter. Those who represented the mercantile and seafaring interests in the New England colonies or the grain-producing middle colonies whose opportunities were not unduly restricted saw things differently. They argued that all the colonies, even those established before Parliament had passed the first navigation act in 1651, had accepted its right to regulate commerce. Furthermore, they asserted, the system brought benefits that compensated for the restraints it imposed. They claimed that it was only fair to concede Parliament the right to regulate trade even if Britain benefitted disproportionately because she paid for the navy that protected the empire's commerce. Others feared that, if the colonies challenged the constitutionality of trade regulations, Britain would be unwilling to reach an accommodation with them. Trade, they said, was what made the colonies valuable to her and she would fight to retain her control of it. Delegates inclined to favor Galloway's plan reminded their colleagues that, unless the colonies could agree on a union that had the power to levy uniform duties, they had no alternative but to allow Britain to continue to regulate their trade.

Southern delegates were not convinced by these arguments. They replied that Americans had long overcompensated Britain for her protection. Virginians Richard Bland, Thomas Jefferson, and Patrick Henry, and Christopher Gadsden of South Carolina argued strongly against admitting that Britain had any power to regulate trade and called for having it "open with all the World."[2] Tensions raised by this question spilled over into consideration of whether to use nonexportation as a response to the Coercive Acts. Some southerners, especially South Carolinians, believed that delegates from colonies that did not export staples to Britain favored the tactic not on its merits but because their economies would be much less effected by it. Discussion of an export ban was so divisive that it brought deliberations in Congress to a virtual halt for several days.

The first attempt (October 13) to resolve trade issues found the colonies evenly divided: five of the twelve were willing to accept continued British regulation of their trade on one ground or another, five opposed it unconditionally. The records do not indicate which colonies voted for and against, but evidence from earlier deliberations suggests that the southern colonies stood for free trade while the middle and some of the New England colonies were willing to accept the status quo. If so, it was the first major split along sectional lines. Massachusetts and Rhode Island could not be counted in either column because their delegates di-

---

[2] See Paul H. Smith, Gerard W. Gawalt, Ronald M. Gephart, et al., eds. *Letters of Delegates to Congress: 1774–1789*. 25 vols. (Washington: Library of Congress, 1976–1998; hereafter, *LDC*), 1: 111.

vided among themselves. The next day, a delegate in one of the two states changed his vote. Congress then approved a motion which accepted parliamentary regulation of external trade so long as its purpose was to benefit the commerce of Britain and the other members of the empire. The resolve specifically excluded "every idea of taxation, internal or external, for raising a revenue on the subjects in America, without their consent."[3]

The Declaration and Resolves. This cleared the way for Congress to pass a comprehensive "Declaration and Resolves" which brought together the work of the two committees. This lawyerly document summarized the colonies' major complaints against the British government—its claims to be able to legislate for the colonies in all cases whatever, its attempts to disguise unconstitutional taxation as trade regulation, and its attacks on the colonists' civil and political rights. Congress then asked that the colonies be restored to "that state in which both countries found happiness and prosperity"—a state in which they had run their internal affairs with little interference from Britain.

The Continental Association. To put force behind their petition, the delegates threatened that, if their grievances were not redressed, the colonies would subscribe to a Continental Association that would bind them to stop importing British goods and slaves and exporting American produce to Britain, Ireland, and the West Indies. The Association asked Americans not to consume tea and to boycott British manufactures and other luxuries. The key to effectiveness, of course, would be unanimous ratification and uniform enforcement. Congress asked each county, city, and town to elect a committee to monitor observance and to publish the names of those who refused to conform so that they could be "universally contemned as the enemies of American liberty." It also recommended regulating the price of domestic manufactures to prevent speculators from profiteering. The Association's provisions were to remain in effect until Parliament repealed its revenue acts. Congress would later have reason to rethink its encouragement of price controls and local initiatives in law enforcement.

Sectional and local interests came to the fore during this debate as

[3] See Worthington C. Ford, et al., eds., *Journals of the Continental Congress, 1774–1789*, 34 vols. (Washington, DC: Government Printing Office, 1904–1937; hereafter, *JCC*) 1: 63, 68–69.

well. Virginia insisted that the ban on exports should not be imposed until the year's tobacco crop had been shipped. South Carolina delegates walked out to protest a ban on the export of rice and indigo and were only persuaded to return when rice was taken off the list. This concession saved the day in Philadelphia, but later it was "illy received by the other colonies" and by back country representatives from South Carolina districts where no rice was grown.[4] A majority in favor of the Association was finally obtained on October 18. Two days later it was signed in a manner carefully designed to create an image of unanimity: Congress simply ordered the delegates to set their "respective names [to it] accordingly"—without implying that they agreed as individuals.[5]

Final Tasks before Adjournment. In their final days of work the delegates approved three position papers: a petition John Dickinson drafted asking the king to protect his loyal American colonies against ministerial oppression; an explanation to the Canadians as to why the colonies opposed the Quebec Act, also prepared by Dickinson; and John Jay's draft of an address to the inhabitants of Britain, which emphatically stated that Americans would never accept a subservient position within the empire. Their final tasks completed, the delegates left Philadelphia with the understanding that, if necessary, they would reconvene again on May 10, 1775.

The Colonies Ratify Congress's Decisions. Once home, the delegates worked to win their constituents' approval of the decisions they had taken. Despite some controversy, they were generally successful. Of the twelve colonies represented in Philadelphia, only the New York Assembly refused to ratify the Association. Undeterred, New Yorkers who supported Congress chose a Committee of Sixty, including John Jay, to enforce its provisions. Throughout the colonies, local enforcement committees forced members of their communities to take sides. They humiliated and in some instances seriously menaced the personal safety of those who were lukewarm or hostile to the boycotts. More and more citizens engaged in a wide range of police activities and military drills that began the transition from colonial status to independence as they waited for Britain's reaction to Congress's initiatives.

---

[4] See *LDC*, 1: 293-295.
[5] See *LDC*, 1: 222.

War and trade had stimulated the development of nation-states in Europe in the fifteenth and sixteenth centuries. In eighteenth-century North America, Britain's wars, debts, and imperial interests led Parliament to adopt administrative reforms that the colonies perceived as violations of their political rights and threats to their economic interests. Each side flexed its muscles, unaware or indifferent to how much the exercise diminished the opportunity for reconciliation. Controversy over the tea tax destroyed the fragile tranquility which followed Britain's strategic retreat from full implementation of its new mode of administration and revenue gathering and started the colonies down a slope which led to bloody confrontation between Americans and British soldiers. Britain's decision to punish Massachusetts for destroying the tea by closing Boston to trade and revoking parts of its charter created all the momentum needed to spur the colonies to develop or improve structures capable of coordinating responses to challenges and assuming governmental functions when the occasion arose. By sending delegates to Congress, the colonies intended only to create a mechanism that could more effectively articulate a common response to common grievances and thereby better defend them against a central government they perceived to be abusing its powers. Despite its caution and reluctance, however, Congress found itself called upon to take positions on controversial issues and to act in ways which were appropriate to a central government.

CHAPTER 4

"NEITHER DEPENDENT NOR INDEPENDENT": 1774–1776[1]

Hopes for Reconciliation Fade. The First Continental Congress was neither ready nor eager to declare independence when it finished its work on October 26, 1774, but it would find itself moving inexorably in that direction. Most of the delegates and their constituents hoped that the British government would admit that the issues raised in the "Declaration and Resolves" were valid and would find a way to compromise their differences. Before Congress's proceedings were even published, however, copies of the Suffolk Resolves reached Britain. The king saw them as evidence of "a most daring spirit of resistance and disobedience to the laws" that his other colonies "countenanced and encouraged." On November 30, 1774, he informed Parliament that the government could not possibly ignore what amounted to open rebellion. Large majorities in both houses of Parliament supported the king's determination to compel the colonies to accept Britain's concept of empire. Only a few disagreed. One member of Commons pointed out that the Coercive Acts had *not* humbled the colonies into respectful submission as the ministry had predicted they would. A handful of Lords warned that more force might precipitate a civil war. Their appeal for patience and restraint was overwhelmed by a tide rushing rapidly in the opposite direction.

Parliament Decides on Force. The "Declaration and Resolves" arrived after Parliament had already shut the door on conciliation and just before its winter holiday. It changed few if any opinions about how Britain should respond. By January 19, when Parliament was again ready to devote time to American affairs, it had received a bevy of letters and reports from General Gage and other royal officials in the colonies. They claimed that a rebellion was inevitable and ought to be suppressed sooner rather than later. Parliament pushed aside petitions from British merchants and manufacturing towns, pleas from colonial agents, and a plan of reconciliation proposed by Pitt. It also rejected the pleas of West Indian planters who feared that conflict would deprive

[1] *LDC*, 1: 649

them of supplies from the colonies on which their prosperity depended. On February 9, hard liners put through a formal declaration that Massachusetts was in rebellion and asked the king to take measures to enforce Parliament's laws and authority. Even delegates who were friendly toward America were unwilling to make concessions unless the colonies submitted fully to British authority.

North's Plan for Conciliation. With momentum building toward confrontation, on February 20, 1775, Lord North suggested making the colonies a final offer that might serve as a basis of conciliation. Britain, he proposed, would not lay "internal" taxes on any colony that agreed to tax itself to raise its share of the sums the ministry considered necessary to support the common defense, the civil government and the administration of justice. North anticipated that most of the colonies would reject it, but hoped that one or several might take the bait and fracture the unity Congress had so far managed to maintain. Parliament approved North's plan on February 27, and forwarded it, not to Congress whose legitimacy as a collective bargaining unit it refused to recognize, but to the colonial governors. A few days later, it adopted a punitive "Restraining Act" which forbade New England to trade with any country outside the Empire and closed the North Atlantic fisheries to New England vessels. The trade restraints were later extended to include all the colonies except New York, Delaware, North Carolina and Georgia.

Edmund Burke, one of the few British leaders still willing to speak for the colonists, continued to appeal for concessions that stood a real chance of restoring imperial harmony. The government, he said in a speech delivered on March 22, 1775, should not feel that the colonists were denying imperial authority when they sought to preserve the "local privileges and immunities" they had so long enjoyed. Parliament, he recommended, should admit the colonies "*into an interest in the constitution*" to assure them that the privileges they held, either as a matter of favor or of right, would not be snatched away from them in the future. Parliament did not heed Burke's plea for conciliation.

Gage Recommends a Course of Action. General Gage had been reporting throughout the fall and winter of 1774 that the spirit of defiance had spread throughout New England. He had predicted that the southern colonies would never support New England with anything more than words because they were menaced by "their numerous slaves in the bowells of their country, and the Indians at their backs." By early spring, however, he advised Lord Barrington that Massachusetts had convinced sympathizers in every other colony "to be as violent in their defense as themselves." Gage knew that soldiers in Boston could do little to check the spread of rebellion or to challenge hot spots of resistance outside the city. He argued for enough troops to "terrify" and convince those who were wavering or uncommitted to side with Britain. Anything less than overwhelming force, he suggested, would only encourage more defiance. Barrington believed that a land campaign would be bloody, slow and ruinously expensive. He preferred to use the navy, not the army, to convince the colonies to submit.[2] Neither Barrington nor Gage persuaded the ministry to adopt their points of view, however. The government seriously underestimated how widespread the resistance to its authority was and how difficult it would be for the army to contain rebellion. Well before it sent any meaningful reinforcements to America, it ordered Gage to go into the surrounding countryside to arrest the leaders of the insurrection and seize the arms that Massachusetts towns had been collecting.

Lexington and Concord. On April 18, 1775, Gage ordered a detachment of troops to march out of Boston under cover of night for nearby Concord, where he expected to find and destroy a cache of military stores. Americans were watching British movements closely. They detected the march immediately, and sent Paul Revere and William Dawes to alert the towns of Concord and Lexington. By the time the British reached Lexington on April 19 about a hundred militia had assembled on the town green. The British commander ordered the Americans to lay down their arms and disperse. Outnumbered four to one, they began to walk away but held onto their guns. A single shot was fired, by whom it is not clear. British troops immediately answered it with a volley of gunfire that left eight dead and ten wounded. Then they marched off to Concord unopposed. They found few arms there, but met heavy resistance during their search. By noon they were ready to begin what became a disastrous sixteen mile return to Boston. The militia attacked them constantly as they marched and killed or wounded several hundred more British soldiers before they reached the safety of

---

[2] Gage-Barrington Correspondence, 117–120, 121–123.

the city. The Americans, a British lieutenant reported, exulted in their victory over "the Parliament Troops," and continued to consider themselves "the King's loyal & faithful subjects."[3]

The foray into the Massachusetts countryside cost the British more than the casualties and humiliation they suffered. American propagandists used this encounter as they had used the Boston Massacre—as an example of an unprovoked, brutal overreaction to an insignificant provocation. The British had barely marched out of Lexington when express riders carried the news in every direction that the British had killed and wounded American soldiers on the village green. New England towns immediately sent militia units to Boston. Joseph Plumb Martin, a young lad from New Haven, Connecticut, remembered how he had heard bells tolling and three shots repeatedly fired in rapid succession to call men to enlist. On April 22 Gage reported that the surrounding country had mobilized with amazing speed and that several thousand were now threatening to attack Boston and assembling artillery. A month later he informed the minister at war that the rebels had cut off supplies for his forces, published inflamatory reports of the events at Lexington and Concord, and suppressed any accounts which contradicted them.

Ticonderoga. Three weeks later, on May 10, troops led by Ethan Allen and Benedict Arnold seized Fort Ticonderoga on Lake Champlain in New York. The easy victory gave the Americans control of a strategic post situated on the route that British forces would use if they invaded the Hudson River Valley from Canada. Even more important were the arms, ammunition, and artillery captured there and at Crown Point, a nearby fortress which fell the next day.

The attack on Ticonderoga was significant for more than military reasons. It was an unprovoked, free lance assault on a handful of sleeping British soldiers by Americans who recognized the strategic value of the fort and saw a chance to acquire some badly needed weapons. It was an irregular operation in just about every way. Allen was more a warrior against whatever he considered to be "arbitrary power" than a principled opponent of British policies. Even though he demanded that the British commander surrender in the name of the Great Jehovah and

---

[3] Marion Balderston and David Syrett, eds., *The Lost War: Letters from British Officers during the American Revolution*, (New York: Horizon Press, 1975, hereafter, Balderston/Syrett, *Lost War*), 29–30.

Congress neither they nor the government of New York had authorized him to attack. Connecticut businessmen had raised funds to support his expedition. Allen and most of the troops he led came from territory disputed by New York and New Hampshire that eventually became Vermont. Allen's men followed him out of personal loyalty, not because they were enlisted under the auspices of any government. Arnold, a citizen of Connecticut, had a commission to command an expedition against the New York fort from the Massachusetts Committee of Safety. He had not had time to raise any soldiers, however, and Allen refused to recognize his right to command.

Lexington, Concord, and Ticonderoga made it appear that victory over Britain would be easy. The Second Continental Congress, which convened on May 10, recognized, however, that they made the chance for reconciliation more remote. Against the will of many of the delegates, it was swept into increasingly assertive responses by the military activity in the north and by British attempts to suppress challenges to imperial authority. Many people believed that military operations against Britain were treason. Many others, including most delegates to Congress, did not think the colonies were sufficiently prepared for the challenge of independence. Some worried that the victory would cost them friends in Britain because the forts had clearly been won by an act of aggression. To offset any damage to the image of wronged innocence it was struggling to maintain, Congress attempted to portray the action as legitimate self-defense against a "cruel invasion" from Quebec that it alleged the British ministry was plotting. It also ordered the local committees of safety to move the captured weapons south and inventory them so that they could all be returned to British authorities after their differences had been resolved. In December 1775, John Jay cited this decision as the first of a number of proofs that Congress was not "aiming" at Independence. Once the snow fell, however, Americans dragged Ticonderoga's big guns to Boston, and mounted them on Dorchester Heights which overlooked the city. There, they menaced the British until they evacuated Boston on March 17, 1776.

Ticonderoga illustrated the need for duly constituted central government well before most Americans realized they needed it. Some conservatives, like Joseph Galloway, recognized the need for colonial confederation. Others foresaw that the colonies would resist it because they wanted only the minimal supervision they had been accustomed to before the French and Indian War—a government that could neither tax their developing economy and nor interfere unduly in their lives. Radical delegates who were moving closer and closer to favoring outright independence would prove as suspicious as men from any other political persuasion of a central government that could impose its will on them.

The Need for New Governments. Congress also had to confront a growing tendency in individual colonies to assume governmental powers with or without its blessing. The Massachusetts Provincial Congress sent formal notice that it had decided to raise an army of 13,600 men and to borrow £100,000 to finance military operations. Early in June, Massachusetts wrote another letter that described how difficult it was to raise an army when it had no duly constituted government. After a week's deliberation, Congress decided that the colony was not obliged to obey any governor or council member who subverted its charter. For the present, it said, Massachusetts should consider these posts vacant and elect an executive council to act in their stead—until a governor appointed by the *king* would agree to govern the colony according to its charter of 1691! By the end of June, the colony had chosen a new council.

Next, New York asked how it should respond if the British attempted to reinforce their garrison there. Congress instructed it to train and arm a militia of 3,000 men to prevent the British from taking possession of the city and to establish defensive posts in the Bronx and along the Hudson River. By the end of summer patriot activities had driven the governors of Virginia and North and South Carolina out of their colonies and onto warships off shore. Provincial congresses and committees of safety in other colonies were also active in organizing defenses and assuming control of more functions of government even though they had no constitutional authority to do so. Planter aristocrats like the Laurenses worried that the "lowest Mechanics" played too large a role in public affairs and looked for wise men to "guide these Upstart Patriots" as South Carolina took civil and military initiatives without waiting for authorization from Philadelphia.[4]

Congress Establishes the Continental Army. Although many delegates still hoped that harmony would be restored by peaceful

---

[4] Philip M. Hamer, David R. Chesnutt, James C. Taylor, et al., eds. *The Papers of Henry Laurens.* 14 vols. to date, (Columbia: University of South Carolina Press, 1968-), 10: 76, 167, 169, 170, 185.

means, Congress realized that it had to prepare to defend American liberties by force of arms. First, it ordered all colonies to make a sustained effort to manufacture gunpowder. In June, it decided to raise troops for Boston in colonies as far south as Virginia, and found itself establishing the "Continental" army. This meant asking each colony to recruit a certain number of men, deciding how regiments were to be organized and officered, specifying a pay scale, prescribing a form of enlistment and drafting army rules and regulations.

Charles Thomson's sparse official journal did not mention the controversy these matters generated. Egalitarian New Englanders criticized the salaries Congress granted commissioned officers as extravagant and argued for higher pay for the enlisted men, but they did not prevail. Congress adopted and "Continentalized" the troops who were holding the British at bay in Boston and garrisoning the forts in New York. Fears that a victorious New England general and the army at his command might attempt to "give law" to the southern and western provinces led it to select a Virginian, George Washington, as commander-in-chief—a wise choice as time would prove. Major and brigadier generals were also appointed with sectional concerns in mind. Delegates eagerly reported their efforts to corner key appointments for office-hungry constituents back home.

Paying the Cost of War: Continental Currency. None of the colonies or regions were eager to hitch their wagons to horses they did not control. They firmly believed, however, that the liberties of all Britain's colonies were as much in jeopardy as those of Massachusetts and this helped to forge agreement on measures they needed to take together. Congress decided that the "Continent" should pay and supply the troops it had asked the various colonies to raise. This could only be done by falling back on a familiar expedient—printing paper money. The delegates voted to issue "bills of credit" to a value of not more than two million Spanish milled dollars, backed only by its promise to redeem them somehow later.

Congress approved the first issue of Continental currency on June 22, and a second for another million dollars on July 25. It was not until July 29, however, that it passed a plan for redeeming the currency, that is, handling the debt that it represented—a plan that was unlikely to succeed. Because it had no authority to levy taxes itself, it held each colony responsible for withdrawing its share of the currency by receiving it in taxes or by whatever other means it chose. There were no penalties against colonies that did not turn in their shares of withdrawn currency on schedule. If a colony collected less than its quota of Continental currency, it was supposed to pay the difference to Congress in gold and silver, which soon became scarcer than ever. The process of withdrawing the three million dollars from circulation was to begin in November 1779 and be completed in 1782. Congress did not imagine in 1775 that it would issue $226,200,000 before the first installment from the states was due, thereby rendering arrangements to bring in the first three million meaningless. The more money Congress printed, the quicker its value was destroyed.

The requisition mechanism which Congress adopted resembled the revenue proposition that George Grenville had rejected as an alternative to the Stamp Act and the proposal that Lord North had offered only a few months before. Both realized that the colonies would not commit themselves to pay whatever sums the British government required of them. Americans soon proved to be no more willing or able to raise the funds requested by the governments they hesitantly began to create.

The colonies' attempt to wage war against Britain without a fully empowered government gave their enemies weapons to use against them. Printing presses in pro-British hands turned out counterfeit Continental currency that speeded the devaluation of genuine Continental dollars. Loyalists refused to accept them; patriots who did suffered as their value fell faster and faster as time went on. Since Congress had no revenue powers of its own, there was little else it could have done. Once patterns were established, it was difficult to change them. The people's willingness to deal in Continental currency during the early days of the struggle and the first easy successes on the battlefield against the British hid the dimensions of future problems from their eyes. Congress did not foresee how long the war might last and how disastrously it would disrupt the American economy.

Bunker Hill. While Congress was struggling to deal with a range of issues that would have baffled a fully established government, Gage officially proclaimed Massachusetts to be in a state of rebellion. Less than a week later he and the three major generals (William Howe, Henry Clinton, and John Burgoyne), who had been sent to spur him to action, decided that the British needed more "elbow room" around Boston. They first moved to gain control of the heights that overlooked the city. Americans had advance warning of British intentions and began to entrench themselves on Breed's Hill and Bunker Hill. Surprisingly, the British did nothing to prevent this. By the time some of their most experienced infantry challenged the American positions on the afternoon of June 17, the New Englanders were ready to defend themselves. They had no battle experience, few supplies, and little ammunition or equipment, but they were officered by leaders they respected, some of whom had served with British regulars during the French and Indian War. They fought with enthusiasm and determination and followed orders well enough to withstand two British charges. They gave way before a third only because they were virtually out of ammunition but they managed an orderly retreat.

The British command could hardly savor its victory. A number of officers and over 1,000 soldiers, half the redcoats involved in the battle, were killed or wounded—several times the number of casualties Americans suffered—and they could not be so easily replaced. They had not succeeded in opening Boston to the surrounding countryside. Patriot forces closed all access routes to the city so tightly that supplies of fresh meat, vegetables, and firewood were virtually cut off and the local population and British soldiers began to suffer from scurvy. The militia's impressive performance won the respect of the British generals. It also wrongly convinced many Americans, who were opposed in principle to "standing armies," that there was little or no reason to enlist soldiers for more than a few months or to train a regular army.

Ambivalence. In the two months between April 18 and June 17, 1775, Americans had engaged the British army three times and inflicted significant losses on it in each instance. All the while a majority in Congress and in the population at large still professed loyalty to the king even as they held Parliament responsible for violating their charters and their rights as citizens of the British Empire. On June 23, the day after Congress received news of the battle of Bunker Hill, it appointed a committee to explain its apparently contradictory position. Thomas Jefferson, who had just taken up his seat as a Virginia delegate, and John Dickinson, the "Pennsylvania Farmer," were jointly responsible for the final draft of the document which became known as the Declaration of the Causes and Necessity for Taking up Arms. It charged the ministry and Parliament with ignoring colonial charters, claiming the right to make laws to bind the colonies "IN ALL CASES WHATSO-

EVER," disregarding their petitions, and using force to coerce them to submit. It argued that the colonists had taken up arms to defend their constitutional rights, but suggested that, if their grievances were not redressed, they might ultimately be forced to seek independence. Dickinson did not want this firm and potentially provocative posture to close the door on reconciliation. He prepared a second document, called the Olive Branch Petition, which assured the king that the colonies were still loyal to him and to Britain and appealed for his personal intervention to bring about a "permanent reconciliation." Congress approved both documents in the short space of two days.

Although the British ministry had not sent North's "conciliatory resolution" of February 20 to Congress, it had received copies from several of the colonies. Shortly before it adjourned, Congress appointed Benjamin Franklin, John Adams, Richard Henry Lee, and Thomas Jefferson to prepare a response to North's proposal. Jefferson drafted the reply. Once again he absolutely denied Parliament's right to raise revenue from the colonies. He insisted that Americans had the right to know whether or not their money was being used to finance subversion of their own civil rights or to support armies that had been raised to take away their peace and freedom. He described North's proposal as insidious, divisive, and insulting. He criticized Parliament for trying to intimidate the colonies into granting a permanent revenue. He argued that Britain's revenue demands were all the more unjust and burdensome because it continued to monopolize their trade. He denied that Parliament had any right to meddle with the colonies' governments and noted that North had not promised to stop doing so even if the colonies agreed to grant the revenues. He pointed out that, at the very time the ministry was suggesting reconciliation, it had placed new restraints on colonial trade and denied New England access to its customary fisheries. On these grounds, he said, Congress could only understand the North plan as a device to buy time for the British army to prepare to reduce the colonies to submission.

These three documents, all approved within the last three weeks of July, vividly illustrate the internal conflict Congress was struggling to resolve. Dickinson had convincingly denounced the ominous tendencies of the Townshend Acts in 1767. Now he was straining to preserve the familial ties between the colonies and their king and to prevent any course of action likely to end in what he saw as senseless civil discord. He spoke for many who were comfortable with the imperial structure as it had functioned before the great war for empire began in mid-century. Dickinson and those he spoke for saw Britain and her colonies sliding into a calamitous abyss that promised to swallow up the commerce and prosperity of both. His plea for a peaceful resolution was heartfelt and emotional, but it ignored the momentum that was moving quickly toward a vortex of conflict.

Jefferson spoke for planters who believed the navigation acts deprived them of their fair share of the profits on their crops, and for northerners whose specie-short economies had born the strains of imperial war-making to the point where they would not tolerate any interference with their governments or agree to grant revenues on Parliament's terms. He and they read Britain's willingness to use force as evidence that the last hope of reconciliation had been cut off. The vote to approve his response to the North proposal showed that a growing number in Congress, especially from New England and the south, were moving imperceptibly but surely along the path toward independence. Their vote to approve Dickinson's Olive Branch Petition showed they were willing to be patient a while longer.

Congress and the Indians. The delegates had explanations to make to other powers besides the British. At the end of May 1775, Arnold reported that he expected a British expedition to recapture Ticonderoga and Crown Point. Congress decided to defend the forts. It also received reports from Indian chiefs visiting Philadelphia and the Albany Committee of Safety that Guy Carleton, the British commander in Canada, was inciting the Caughnawaga Indians to raid settlements in northern New York. Gage, who believed that the British could not afford to be "tender of using Indians" had, in fact, instructed Carleton to employ them against the Americans. After some discussion, Congress authorized Philip Schuyler, a New York delegate from the Albany region, to invade Canada to secure the Hudson and Mohawk Valleys against attack by Britain and her Indian allies.

Samuel Kirkland, a missionary to the Oneida Indians in New York, appeared early in July to urge Congress to make a serious effort to secure the friendship or at least the neutrality of the Indians. To do this, it had to be able to provide them with the clothing, arms, and ammunition on which their survival depended. If Congress or the individual colonies could not supply them, the Indians would be driven into the arms of the British, however receptive they might otherwise have been to the colonists' overtures. Arms and ammunition were in very short supply for the struggle against Britain; finding more for the Indians was a virtually insurmountable challenge.

Congress did the best it could, however. It established northern, middle, and southern Indian departments, appointed commissioners to negotiate with the Indian nations associated with each, provided them with a modest budget in Continental currency to purchase whatever goods they could buy with it, and instructed them to find out whether British agents were actively inciting Indians to attack them. Kirkland also suggested sending a formal explanation of the colonies' quarrel with Great Britain to the Iroquois. His recommendation was accepted and he advised the committee that prepared it. (*See Doc. No. 8.*) Congress also arranged for the preparation of wampum belts, used to certify the official character and truthfulness of what was said, to be presented to the Indians.

Southerners did not wait for Congress to develop an Indian policy. Virginian Arthur Lee, who was serving as agent for Massachusetts in London, sent word that the British intended to incite both Indians and slaves against the colonists. The South Carolina Provincial Congress began immediately to raise troops to defend the colony against domestic insurrections instigated by the British as well as against the British themselves. It also voted funds to bring fifty Catawba Indians into its service. It accused the British Superintendent of Indian affairs and his assistant of preparing the Creeks and Cherokees to attack if the king's service required it. To counter their influence, it appointed its own commissioners to these Indian nations. By the end of September, Indian commissioners from the three southern colonies were adapting Congress's address to their local circumstances.

Indians were not the only concern. As planters protested that Americans would never submit to slavery, South Carolina authorities attempted to head off the prospect of a slave insurrection by bringing to trial any slaves suspected of a tendency to rebel. They ordered several to be flogged and banished and persuaded an individual who had been secretly preaching salvation to Negroes to move out of the colony. The dilemma of human bondage in a land moving toward independence because its imperial master refused to respect the natural rights it claimed for all men would not be resolved for generations to come.

Congress Again Considers Establishing a Continental Government. Congress was by now well practiced in articulating the range of grievances that explained its increasingly intransigent posture toward the British ministry and Parliament. It had struggled to maintain the appearance of unity and it had voted to raise an army under Continental command. Even though they had jointly committed their colonies to pay the bills for this military buildup out of a common treasury, however, the delegates were not yet ready to take meaningful steps toward a more substantial "Continental" unity. Once again a Pennsylvanian, this time Benjamin Franklin, a proven patriot, proposed articles of confederation that would establish a "League of Friendship" to provide for the common defense and promote the general welfare.

Franklin's experience with the Albany Plan led him to list provisions designed to protect the colonies' individuality and independence up front, before he mentioned the powers the new congress might exercise. He did not have to be told how wary the colonies were of governments with powers capable of overruling or dictating to their assemblies. Each colony, Franklin provided, would retain "as much as it may think fit of its own present Laws, Customs, Rights, and Privileges." Each would annually elect delegates to a congress that would meet in a different colony each year. The congress would concern itself only with issues related to war, peace, diplomacy and with matters affecting the common welfare, such as "general" commerce and currency, a post office, and administration of the army. Even though the Continental Congress was already operating in a manner that was somewhat consistent with Franklin's plan, the delegates were not yet ready to institutionalize the arrangement and they tabled the proposal.

Congress Considers Commercial Independence. Franklin also reported for a committee that had been considering ways to preserve the colonies' trade. An act of Parliament that banned the export of colonial produce to ports outside the British Empire went into effect on July 20. To counter it, the committee recommended opening colonial ports for at least two years to the trade of any European nation that was willing to admit and protect American commerce. Franklin's committee hoped to give colonial producers and merchants opportunities to earn some credit abroad that would be needed to pay for military supplies and other necessities that would have to be imported in the event of war with Britain. The policy it recommended was as risky as inaction would be. Opening the ports would amount to a declaration of commercial independence, a step most of the delegates were not yet willing to take. Since Congress was preparing to adjourn, it deferred action on the committee's report. It reminded the colonies that the second (nonexportation) phase of the Continental Association was scheduled to go into effect on September 10, 1775. The new regulations prohibited trade with Britain's European dominions and with both British and foreign West Indian colonies from Georgia to the equator. Congress thus cooperated with Parliament to shackle the American economy to the narrow confines of domestic trade. For the next nine months, the colonies had to prepare their defenses with only those resources that were available locally.

Congress reconvened on September 13, 1775. Its first official act was to accept the credentials of three delegates from Georgia, the last of the thirteen colonies to send representatives. Soon after, it appointed a secret committee to arrange to import arms and ammunition. During October it resumed debate on whether the colonies should trade, could trade, and if so with whom. Some delegates opposed relaxing American restrictions because they hoped against all odds that economic pressures would persuade the British to back down even if their political arguments did not. Others were convinced that, if Americans attempted to trade, their ships would be captured and confiscated by the British navy. Others argued that European nations would not risk angering Britain by trading with her rebellious colonies. The issues raised by the discussion were valid. Delegates confronted the perils of their present situation and what they saw paralyzed the decision-making process. The colonies were neither dependent nor independent: they suffered the disabilities of both conditions simultaneously. Independence, when it came, did not significantly expand the options open to them.

Congress Establishes a Navy. Discussions about resuming trade served as a prelude to discussions about what Congress should do to protect it. Soon after he took command of the American army at Boston, Washington commissioned American vessels to attack British ships carrying ammunition and supplies to the royal army. They succeeded in taking a number of unarmed transports before the British began to convoy their supply ships. The destructive potential of the British navy began to be felt in October when a squadron of vessels under the command of Admiral Samuel Graves burned the town of Falmouth (now Portland, Maine) in retaliation for its attack on an British naval vessel. Graves let it be known that he had orders to destroy every seaport between there and Boston.

This led Congress to consider whether it could afford the enormous expense of establishing a Continental Navy. Rhode Island began commissioning vessels to protect its commerce against British vessels patrolling Narragansett Bay. Most of the other colonies followed its lead by the end of 1775. Rhode Island also instructed its delegates to prompt Congress to establish an "American" fleet. Samuel Chase of Maryland considered this the "maddest idea in the world," but other delegates argued that Congress had to make some plan for naval defense even if was not on the scale proposed by Rhode Island. By the end of November, Congress had enlisted Marines and established a Navy. It quickly acquired a handful of merchant vessels and armed them for naval combat. In December it approved an extremely ambitious program for building thirteen frigates.

The Specter of Race War. On November 7, 1775, Lord John Murray Dunmore, Virginia's royal governor, carried out a threat he had made six months earlier: he declared martial law in the colony and announced he would free all indentured servants and slaves who enlisted in the royal army. Virginia delegates received reports that slaves had been "seduced" into the royal service and that Indians had been forced to join as well. David Ramsay recalled when he wrote his history of the Revolution that Dunmore's decree had filled the colonists with horror and detestation for a government that would loosen the bands of society and destroy domestic security.

The King Rejects Reconciliation. As 1775 drew to its close, it became more and more obvious that both crown and Parliament were determined to force the colonies to submit. Early in November, Congress learned that the king had proclaimed "divers Parts" of the colonies in rebellion and enjoined all his loyal subjects to cooperate with measures to suppress it. Word arrived later that the king had refused to receive, much less to consider, the Olive Branch Petition. He had opened Parliament in October with a speech that charged the colonies' leaders with leading his subjects into insubordination and usurping the powers of government. (*See Doc. No. 9.*) There was, thus, little reason to hope that he would either dismiss the ministers responsible for the breach with the colonies or lead the way to reconciliation.

Common Sense. The first copy of king's speech appeared in Philadelphia in early January at about the same time *Common Sense* was published. (*See Doc. No. 10.*) This coincidence gave Thomas Paine's famous pamphlet a special timeliness, because many of its arguments were directed, not against Parliament, which most Americans had long considered to the source of their difficulties, but against the monarch. Paine, a mercurial Englishman with a talent for writing persuasively, had settled in Philadelphia in November 1774, absorbed the critiques of British policy developed since 1763, and attentively studied what was being said in Congress and in the taverns and coffee houses where delegates gathered when their daily deliberations were over. At the suggestion of Benjamin Rush, a Philadelphia physician and advocate of independence, he began to distill their legal arguments into a logic and language everyone could understand. While Rush, Franklin, Samuel Adams and several others offered information and suggestions, it was Paine who infused them with energy and urgency and presented a case that was direct, simple, and readily comprehensible. Anonymity enabled Paine to advocate independence more effectively and in a way neither Congress nor delegates already committed to separation from Britain could because many of their colleagues were still not prepared to take such a decisive step. Furthermore, some colonies (Pennsylvania, Delaware, New Jersey and Maryland), had specifically ordered their delegates not to consent to independence until they had specific instructions to do so.

As English opponents of divine right monarchy had a hundred years earlier, Paine denied that any form of government was divinely ordained and argued instead that government was created by compacts men entered into to protect themselves against their own evil tendencies. Men were, thus, free to establish whatever form of government secured their property and freedom with the least expense. Where Englishmen and Americans had commonly boasted that the British constitution was the best in the world, Paine described it as nothing more than a blend of two forms of tyranny (monarchy and aristocracy), embellished with a few republican trappings. Paine argued that neither king nor commons deserved the people's confidence. Their excesses, he said, could not be restrained by the checks and balances provided by the constitution, but only by the vigilance of the people. Paine's suspicion of government would soon be incorporated into the constitution Pennsylvanians would adopt in September, 1776. Furthermore, Paine said, there was no biblical justification for monarchy—scripture ranked it "as one of the sins of the Jews." Hereditary succession was an added evil: the first king in every line was probably nothing better than "the principal ruffian of some restless gang;" and his successors might well be minors or miscreants.

Paine urged Americans to "put *on*" not "put *off,* the true character of a man" by acting boldly and responsibly. They must, he insisted, think continentally, and recognize that the contest would shape both their own and their children's future. Faced with a choice of independence or reconciliation, Paine said, America must choose independence or find herself vulnerable to the interference of a "treacherous capricious court." The time had come for America to cut her ties with Britain, he argued, and the "present time," was "preferable to all others." If Americans failed to act now, they might risk falling into a state in which "neither *reconciliation* nor *independence* will be practicable."

The first edition of *Common Sense* quickly sold out. Within a month, Paine produced a second edition which included a reply to the king's speech, and then a third. Josiah Bartlett, a New Hampshire delegate, told John Langdon, a New Hampshire compatriot, that it was "greedily bought up and read by all ranks of people," and urged him to "lend round" the copy he was sending to him. Samuel Adams sent his wife a copy and reported to a friend that when the pamphlet appeared in Philadelphia it had "fretted some folks here more than a little."[5] Presses throughout the colonies produced reprints.

Britain Chooses Compulsion. Parliament, meanwhile, took further actions that demonstrated that it intended to subdue the colonies by force. On December 22, 1775, it passed the Prohibitory Act, which authorized the British navy to capture American vessels wherever they might be found. On New Year's Eve, Lord Dunmore attacked and burned Norfolk, Virginia. In January, after Russia declined to provide mercenaries, the British government made arrangements with several German principalities to hire 20,000 soldiers. When reports of these measures reached the colonies in February and March, they ended any chance that Congress would support a plan for reconciliation that Thomas Lundin, Lord Drummond, a Scottish free-lancer who owned land in New Jersey, was discussing unofficially with a handful of delegates from the middle colonies. Congress indefinitely tabled an attempt by John Dickinson and James Wilson of Pennsylvania to make it a matter of record that the colonies were *not* interested in independence. More

[5] *LDC*, 3: 87, 88.

and more delegates were convinced that they must open trade with other European nations and seek military assistance from them. Efforts to manufacture and import military stores took on a greater sense of urgency.

New Governments. Proponents of independence could not rest satisfied that support for it was growing. The colonies could hardly expect to win a war against Europe's foremost power without duly constituted governments to coordinate their own military effort. Discussions about a confederation continued. Samuel Adams would not let the subject die, and, if all the colonies could not be persuaded to join, he was ready to try to confederate the New England colonies. At the same time, the flight of royal governors and defense preparations led Congress and some of the colonies to act as though they were already independent of British authority. In November 1775 Congress overcame its hesitation and authorized New Hampshire, South Carolina, and Virginia, whose governors had fled, to institute whatever form of government would best promote the happiness of their people. Comprehensive instructions to revise colonial governments would wait until a later date.

Trade and Independence. The need to acquire arms, ammunition, medicines, and goods for the Indians from abroad finally forced Congress to recognize that it would have to find foreign suppliers and either go to them or entice them to come to American ports. It had taken the first step in this direction by establishing the Secret Committee of Trade in September 1775. In December 1775, Julian-Alexandre Achard de Bonvouloir, an unofficial emissary of French Foreign Minister Charles Gravier, Comte de Vergennes, informed Congress's Committee of Secret Correspondence that France did not intend to try to recover Canada and that it would admit American ships to French ports. A month later, the Secret Committee of Trade received overtures from two foreigners, J. Pierre Penet and Emmanuel de Pliarne, who were interested in supplying arms to the Continental army. This encouraged the delegates to hope that the colonies would indeed find people willing to do business with them. Although Congress appointed a committee to work out the regulations under which trade with foreign nations would be conducted, debate on trade policy continued well past March 1, the date it had set for opening American ports to foreign trade. Opening the ports also argued for an explicit declaration of independence because, as some delegates repeatedly pointed out, France would hardly be eager to take on the colonies as trading partners while they still considered themselves British subjects.

The "Inhuman Pirating Act." Congress learned early in March that Parliament had passed the Prohibitory Act. It forbade all trade with the colonies, made American ships or goods on the high seas subject to capture and confiscation, and held their officers, crews, and passengers subject to impressment into the British navy. On March 23, 1776, Congress retaliated by issuing commissions to private citizens to outfit armed vessels, called privateers, to cruise against British shipping. Ships they captured and their cargoes were sold for the benefit of the privateers' owners and crews. Congress justified this decision on grounds that Britain had burnt their towns, encouraged Indians and Negroes to wage war on them, and that it had proclaimed the colonies to be in open rebellion. Ship owners whose merchant vessels had been idled by American and British trade restrictions rapidly converted them into privateers. Raids on British shipping began immediately and inflicted significant losses until the Royal Navy began to convoy merchant vessels and blockade the coast. Britain retaliated by commissioning its own privateers to operate against American vessels in European and American waters. Finally, on April 6, 1776, Congress took the step it had been so long postponing. It inched closer to full independence by opening American ports to foreign trade.

Parliament's Prohibitory Act had one feature that allowed Americans reluctant to part ways with Britain a ray of hope. It provided for the appointment of commissioners who could inquire into colonial grievances and determine whether any colony had returned to "that state of obedience, which might entitle it to be received within the king's peace and protection." Some delegates held out the possibility that this offered a last chance for reconciliation. John Adams, however, disagreed. He considered the act as Parliament's way of declaring independence for the colonies. Why they would not declare it for themselves he could explain only by accusing the south and proprietary interests of the middle colonies of being reluctant to accept republican government. Intercolonial conflicts over land claims, he believed, might also be a factor.

Southern Support for Independence. There was still a wide range of opinions on independence. Carter Braxton of Virginia, was willing to declare it if it could be done with "Safety and Honor." He felt, however, that the proper time to do so would not come until the colonies had seen what the British commissioners had to offer *and* had an alliance with a foreign naval power capable of protecting American trade and an effective intercolonial confederation in place. Braxton voiced the sentiments of a minority that was rapidly growing smaller. On April 12, North Carolina authorized its delegates to vote for independence if other colonies did so. An impatient letter of May 12, 1776, from Richard Henry Lee reminded Edmund Pendleton, a member of the Virginia Assembly, that American trade had to be opened. That could not happen until it could be protected and some foreign power induced to trade with the colonies. "About this no time is to be lost," Lee said. He asked Pendleton to see to it that the Virginia delegation got positive instructions to move a declaration of independence and to authorize Congress to form foreign alliances and establish a confederation. Pendleton did his job. On May 15, the Virginia Assembly instructed its delegates to propose independence. On May 27, Virginia's motion and North Carolina's instructions authorizing its delegates to vote for independence were presented in Congress.

The Formation of New Governments. Meanwhile, Congress had taken another major step toward independence on May 10. It approved a resolution proposed by John Adams which advised the colonies that the time had come to create new governments. Because it wished to avoid dictating how much democracy each colony should embrace, Congress decided against providing the colonies with a model constitution. Five days later, however, it adopted a controversial preamble to the act of May 10 that unequivocally declared that the time had come to remove all traces of British authority from colonial governments. There were immediate repercussions in Pennsylvania, which had recently elected a number of moderate delegates to new seats in its assembly. Radicals used the resolutions to rally popular support for a constitutional convention which undermined the colonial assembly, approved independence in June, and produced the most democratic of all the state constitutions in September.

Independence. The tide had, thus, already turned by June 7, when Richard Henry Lee moved for independence in Congress. Assuming that the motion would be approved, Congress postponed action on it until July 1. The delay was intended to give time for delegates who were not yet authorized to vote for independence to receive the necessary instructions from their assemblies. On June 11, Congress appointed a committee of five, Thomas Jefferson, John Adams, Benjamin Franklin, Roger Sherman and Robert R. Livingston, to prepare a draft declaration. The next day it appointed a grand committee (one delegate from every state), chaired by John Dickinson, to draft articles of confederation that would define the purposes and limits of the colonies' union.

One by one, assemblies in Delaware, New Jersey, and Maryland authorized their delegates to vote for independence. When the resolution came up for a final vote on July 2, there were twelve votes in favor. New York, whose delegation had been instructed not to take a stand on the issue, abstained. Congress debated the all-important resolution vigorously until, on July 4, it agreed on and adopted the final version of its statement to the world. (*See Doc. No. 11.*) Five days later, Washington ordered the Declaration read publicly to his troops in New York City as the New York Provincial Congress convened at White Plains. There, it received a copy of the Declaration from its congressional delegation and voted to approve it.

In two short years, the British government's determination to assert its authority over its colonies collided repeatedly with the colonies' determination to preserve a premodern imperial arrangement that guaranteed them a large measure of independence. Burke, their advocate, had asked Parliament to recognize Britain's "ancient constitutional policy" on representation, and to admit the justice of "taxation of America by *grant*, and not by *imposition*." It refused to do so. The war of wills led not only to petitions, explanations, and rebuffs, but to towns in flames and armed encounters. A conference of delegates called to articulate the colonies' grievances presided over steps that led, unintentionally but irrevocably, to a declaration of their independence from the most powerful nation in western Europe. They and the states they represented voted to approve the document and signed it with a flourish, but with only the vaguest anticipation of the struggles over governmental authority and taxation that lie ahead.

CHAPTER 5

INDEPENDENCE, ALLIANCE, AND THE EXPERIENCE OF WAR: 1776–1780

The decision the thirteen colonies, now states, reached on July 2, 1776 was truly momentous. There was, however, little time for celebration. The new nation was held together only by a decision, passionately advocated by some and strongly opposed by others, to preserve cherished political values and strive for a prosperous future outside the confines of the British empire. Independence would have to be defended. Americans, who had rebelled because of the stresses created by Britain's previous war debt, would now have to assume all of the responsibility for waging and paying for their own war and distributing the costs equitably among a population that did not uniformly support it. Congress, which was not yet a government, would have to try to become one. It would have to enlist allies to support its cause, but it would have to do so cautiously to ensure that it was not trading one foreign master for another. The road from colonial dependency to nationhood was uncharted and treacherous. Survival was by no means guaranteed.

War. War had already begun on several fronts. The volunteer army which Congress had authorized to invade Canada in June 1775 captured Montreal late in the year but failed to take Quebec. Enlistments expired as a hard Canadian winter brought hunger, disease, and death that further emasculated the force. In the spring, Pennsylvania troops under General John Sullivan arrived on the scene to reinforce the survivors. Early in June 1776 Sullivan ordered an attack on a British garrison at Three Rivers, whose strength he underestimated. American losses were significant and convinced Sullivan to order his army to retreat to Fort Ticonderoga. There, under the direction of Generals Horatio Gates and Benedict Arnold, American forces prevented a counterinvading British army commanded by Guy Carleton from advancing beyond the fort.

Americans managed a few more victories elsewhere before the British army was at full strength. North Carolina patriots had defeated 1,500 loyalists at Moore's Creek in February 1776. General Henry Clinton took a force of 2,000 British and Hessian solders to the Carolinas on nine British men of war commanded by Commodore Peter Parker. They attacked Sullivan's Island in Charleston Harbor on June 28. Continental soldiers and militia from North and South Carolina led by General Charles Lee and Colonel William Moultrie successfully defended the city and forced the British to withdraw. Cherokee Indians reported to have been stirred up by British agents simultaneously attacked settlements on South Carolina's western frontier. Continental soldiers and militia from North and South Carolina and Virginia waged a three months' campaign against the Cherokee and destroyed many of their towns and crops.

British troops from Halifax landed on Staten Island on July 2, the day Congress voted for independence. Reinforcements from Europe, including 9,000 Hessians arrived soon afterwards. All told, General William Howe had over 25,000 soldiers under his command—a number roughly equivalent to the population of New York City at the time. They were supported by a fleet under his brother, Admiral Richard Howe, and by remnants of the squadron from Charleston. By the end of August, British naval forces at New York totaled more than 10,000 sailors, seventy warships and double the number of transports. It was a formidable force. The British intended, as Washington had anticipated, to capture New York City and then, with loyalist support from the middle colonies, to isolate New England from centers of rebellion farther south.

Washington had already rushed his soldiers from Massachusetts to defend New York. He commanded 17,000 men but they were hardly a well-supplied and disciplined fighting army. At the end of August they suffered heavy casualties when Howe attacked their positions in Brooklyn. Those who survived barely managed to escape to Manhattan. Several weeks later they were driven north from New York City, and narrowly avoided being cut off before they could cross the Hudson River to New Jersey. Thereafter, Howe divided his attention between pursuing Washington's retreating troops and expanding British control over northern New Jersey where there were many loyalists. The Americans suffered yet another humiliation when General Charles Lee, victor at Charleston, spent a night outside American lines at a lightly guarded New Jersey tavern. A tory advised a British patrol of his whereabouts. The next morning he was captured and held prisoner for over a year.

Holiday Victories. At year's end, the American army, which had already lost many men through casualties and capture, was reduced even further as enlistments expired and soldiers took the weapons they had been issued and went home. The campaign would have ended on a very discouraging note if Washington and about 3,000 men had not ruined British holiday celebrations by capturing a Hessian garrison at Trenton on December 26 and defeating British forces at Princeton on January 3, 1777. These were the first victories since the Declaration of Independence and they restored some of the morale destroyed by the loss of New York City. Washington had avoided total defeat and reduced the portion of New Jersey under British control. This was a respectable, if not a glorious measure of success. It taught those who had expected a complete and easy victory over professional British soldiers and their mercenaries that it would take more than patriot militia to win the war and establish independence. Men who joined the Continental army in 1777 were enlisted for three years or the duration of the war.

Confederation. While Washington was struggling against all odds to keep some semblance of an army together and to insure that the British did not swallow it up, Congress was occupied with major political and diplomatic projects. Its most important challenge was developing a framework for a central government capable of enlisting domestic and foreign support. Declaring independence from Britain carried no message about what kind of nation, if any, would come to be in its place. The states had few mutual bonds of interest or affection on which to build. Their rejections of previous proposals for confederation showed clearly that they felt no compelling need for structural unity even in the face of pressing military need. A long decade of struggle against Parliament's encroachments had taught many Americans who were committed to independence to fear that an effective central government was only one small step away from tyranny, even when the government was in their own hands.

Despite this dilemma, most delegates recognized that they must make some move toward a "grand Continental League" with "a superintending Power also," a "coalition formed sufficient to withstand the power of Britain."[1] Otherwise, states would not contribute to the common cause. All would be mired in embittering attempts to measure the resources, contributions and sufferings of other states against their own. It would be impossible to develop a coherent military strategy and to keep a credible army in the field. Foreign governments would be un-

[1] *LDC*, 3: 523.

likely to trade or supply arms unless there was some recognized authority that could guarantee compliance with the terms of any agreements made. The committee Congress appointed to prepare articles of confederation in June 1776 presented it with a draft based on Franklin's earlier proposal. Congress debated it and ordered a revised version to be printed but then it turned its attention to more pressing concerns. It was not until November 1777 that it adopted a final version of articles of confederation and sent it to the states for their approval.

Anxieties about a central government capable of threatening the interests of individual states focused on how to allocate voting power in Congress as they had when the First Continental Congress first met. Once again, large, populous, and wealthy states demanded proportionally greater weight in the decision-making process. Smaller states feared that they would be overwhelmed by powerful neighbors and insisted that their efforts to contribute should be recognized by allowing them equal voting strength. A majority of the delegates again acknowledged that, under present circumstances, it was impossible to count population or measure wealth accurately enough to base representation on either. The final draft preserved the one state/one vote system. There was also disagreement about how much control Congress should exercise over Indian affairs and whether western lands claimed by individual states should be considered common property of the confederation so that proceeds from their sale could be used to satisfy the common debt.

Is a "League" a Nation? The Articles created a defensive "league of friendship" among the thirteen states, whose individual sovereignty it guaranteed and to whom it reserved all powers not specifically granted to the Confederation Congress. They described a government with substantial control over war, peace, and foreign, Indian, and interstate relations, but they withheld some very critical powers from it. Although every free inhabitant was to have all the "privileges and immunities of free citizens in the several States," the Confederation government could not act directly on its citizens. Neither could it determine the qualifications for delegates to Congress or how they were to be chosen. Instead, it was pledged to accept those who were annually appointed "in such manner as the legislature of each State shall direct."

The delegates struggled to find a formula that would fairly distribute the expenses of the common defense among the states. Although they agreed that the war debt should be paid out of a common treasury, they did not dream of suggesting that Congress should have the authority to levy taxes. Instead they preserved the cherished system of requisitions. Congress would estimate the amount of men and supplies that would be needed, apportion the totals among the states on the basis of their estimated land values and count on them to pay—it had no authority to deal with states that defaulted. It had exclusive power to regulate weights, measures and the coinage issued under its authority, but it could not regulate commerce.

The conflicts with British government that had led to independence explain why the Articles assigned only limited powers to Congress and left the "league" a virtual hostage to any one of the individual states. All thirteen had to ratify the Articles before they would become effective and approve any subsequent amendments. Most states ratified the Articles soon after Congress transmitted them. Not so Maryland, which stood aloof until Virginia ceded her claims to lands north of the Ohio River to Congress. Somehow, the war against Britain was carried on for five years without a duly established government—the Articles did not go into effect until March 1, 1781. (*See Doc. No. 12.*) By that time, Congress had already suggested an amendment that would give it the power to levy and collect a 5 per cent duty on imports.

The Articles described how power was to be distributed between the states and the central government. They did not take the further step of dividing the powers of the central government into the three branches with which we are familiar. The "United States in Congress assembled" *was* the central government. It chose a president annually from among its own members. He received diplomats and was given a small budget to cover his expenses. Communications to and from Congress were issued in his name. The office conferred a certain dignity but none of the power that George Washington and his successors would exercise under the United States Constitution. Congress was very hesitant about making executive establishments. In October 1777, it created boards of war, admiralty, and treasury, some of whose members were not members of Congress. Prior to that time, despite the fact that it was never at full strength, it had dealt with all matters that came before it, from the most mundane to the most important, by assigning them to committees of delegates for a report. Its inability to manage the war, to administer the Confederation's finances and diplomacy, and to conduct the ordinary business of government was increasingly apparent.

During this period, either by holding constitutional conventions or by legislative enactments, the states provided themselves with new constitutions. Some of them were hastily composed and would be revised at a later time. A few, like Pennsylvania's, had distinctly democratic tendencies, such as wide suffrage, strong legislatures, and weak executives. Others, like Maryland's, were markedly conservative and designed to ensure domination by the local elite. Massachusetts chose to emphasize that a charter of government had a higher status than ordinary legislation by calling a special convention distinct from the state legislature to write its constitution. The document it produced was then approved by referendum on March 20, 1780. The precedent it established would be followed by other states thereafter and by the nation as a whole in the process by which the Articles were replaced.

A Model Treaty. Congress undertook a second major endeavor in June 1776. It appointed a five-man committee to prepare a plan or model for treaties with foreign powers. Previous discussions had already established, as Paine had reported in *Common Sense*, that the new nation intended to base its foreign policy on commerce, not on alliances that required political and military commitments and that would involve America in European quarrels.

John Adams, who was generally recognized as a careful student of foreign relations, drafted the committee's report. The "model treaty" opened with a revolutionary proposal: trade should be free of mercantilist restrictions. Commerce between the treaty partners should be conducted according to the same rules that the draft Articles of Confederation prescribed for commerce among the thirteen states. Each nation would impose no duties on trade with its partner beyond those that its own citizens paid. Each would also protect the trade of its partner from enemy attacks. The United States promised that it would not side with Britain against any nation on which Britain declared war because it had signed a treaty with the United States. Anticipating future European wars, the plan broadly defined the rights of neutral nations that traded with belligerents.

If only France signed a treaty based on the model, she would, to the extent that her economy complemented the American economy, replace Britain in a newly formed quasi-mercantilist arrangement. French and American merchants would have unique advantages in each other's markets and be bound to one other by mutual self-interest. The committee expected, however, that if one European nation abandoned its restrictive regulations, other nations would do the same to gain equal advantages in the rapidly growing American market. This would amount to a commercial revolution against prevailing mercantilist doctrine and it would open markets and provide advantages and opportunities previously denied to American planters and traders. The plan was reported out on July 18, but Congress did not consider it for another month. Adams's handiwork so well represented the thinking of Congress, however, that his draft was easily approved. (*See Doc No. 13.*)

Secret Committee Operations. In March 1776, two congressional committees had sent Silas Deane, formerly a Connecticut delegate, to France. They instructed him to present himself as a private merchant interested in buying goods for the Indian trade, for which he held contracts from the Secret Committee of Trade. He was also assigned by the Committee of Secret Correspondence to purchase much needed military supplies and to determine whether Vergennes, the French Foreign Minister, would enter into either a commercial or military alliance with the Americans.

France could not openly allow official agents of Britain's rebel colonies to buy munitions without provoking Britain to declare war against her. Therefore, Deane and other Secret Committee agents disguised their procurement operations as private transactions. Agents were not salaried. They earned commissions on business they transacted for the public, but since years might elapse before they could collect them, they supported themselves by seizing whatever opportunities for private trade came their way. Furthermore, Congress was rarely in a position to pay for what it ordered. It often had to depend on its agents to use their own private resources or credit to cover purchases. Agents became personally liable for debts they incurred for the public. In turn, they borrowed from government funds at their disposal when they felt the need and had the opportunity. While such practices were open to abuse, they were common in the eighteenth century.

Because they were engaged in covert operations, agents blended public and private transactions in their books. Subsequent protracted efforts to settle their accounts left significant ethical and fiscal ambiguities unresolved. Many who worked with the Secret Committee were suspected of profiteering, fraud, corruption, and cheating the government. Some profited from their activities and some did not. Among the most prominent were Deane and Robert Morris, a Pennsylvania delegate who chaired the committee and conducted many of its operations through his private business firm. Deane was summoned home from Europe in 1778 to answer charges made by his ever-suspicious colleague, Arthur Lee, that he had misused public funds entrusted to him. The affair polarized Congress, which never succeeded in conclusively establishing either Deane's guilt or his innocence. His accounts still unsettled, Deane returned embittered and unpaid to Europe. There he began to publicly question the wisdom of America's decision to seek independence from Britain.

Robert Morris, who believed that men could simultaneously pursue private gain and the public good, became one of the wealthiest men in the United States. His Secret Committee operations may have played some role in his prosperity, but it did not principally depend on them. In 1781, Congress chose Morris to rescue it from the desperate financial crisis brought on by the depreciation of the Continental currency. In 1795 a public auditor concluded that Morris and his partners owed the government $93,000 for Secret Committee operations. Morris disagreed with the ruling but acknowledged the obligation. He assigned assets to cover what he owed, but soon went bankrupt. William Bingham, agent at Martinique, profited handsomely from his operations there and lived an affluent life thereafter. Another agent, Oliver Pollock spent time in a Havana jail because neither the United States nor Virginia paid debts he had contracted on their behalf. Doing the business of the Revolution sometimes paved the way to wealth and power, but it involved a high degree of risk.

Diplomatic Overtures to France. As soon as Congress approved the treaty plan in September, 1776, it named Deane, Franklin, and Arthur Lee its official commissioners to the French court. It directed them to conclude a treaty modeled as closely as possible on the plan and specified which points were negotiable and which were not. Congress was clear about its priorities. If France would not admit Americans to trade in France on the same terms as French citizens did, the commissioners should try to obtain commercial reciprocity and most favored nation status. Under such terms, the signatories would give each other the best conditions that they offered to any other foreign nation. If the French would not agree to this either, the commissioners were to "insist" on protection for American ships in French waters.

Congress offered France little in the way of compensation if Britain declared war on her for signing a treaty with the United States. There was to be no "entangling" alliance. The United States would promise only that it would not assist Britain in a war against France, that it would never acknowledge allegiance to Britain, and that it would not grant her more trade privileges than it gave to France! Congress hoped that France's desire to diminish Britain's power and her eagerness to expand her trade with the United States would entice her to support the American cause and perhaps carry her into the war. It did not intend to purchase French belligerency at the price of political dependence. Neither did it intend to promise that it would not resume trade with Great Britain at the end of the war.

The French were definitely interested in exploiting the possibilities of a rupture between Great Britain and her colonies and were willing to provide covert military aid through a fictitious firm, Roderigue Hortalez and Company, managed by the French playwright Pierre Augustin Caron de Beaumarchais. The French foreign minister did not, however, leap at the offer of a formal alliance, political or commercial, with an unproven partner. Not until American forces defeated and captured a British army under General John Burgoyne at Saratoga in October 1777 did Vergennes begin serious negotiations for an alliance with Franklin.

The Campaign of 1777. Although the British were unable to settle on a strategy that would give them a decisive victory, they hoped to win the war in 1777. General John Burgoyne planned a three-pronged northern campaign. An army under his command including British regulars, loyalists, and Indians, would invade New York State from Canada. He would fight his way south until he joined forces with General William Howe, who, he anticipated, would have subdued resistance in the lower Hudson region. An auxiliary force under Colonel Barry St. Leger, mostly loyalists and Indians, would clear the Mohawk Valley to the west of Albany. Success would give the British control of major interior waterways and a major center of the Indian trade (Albany). It would also separate New England from the other rebel colonies.

Howe and his brother the admiral, however, decided to attack Philadelphia. Most of the British forces stationed in New York City boarded ships there at the end of July, landed in Maryland, and began to march toward Philadelphia. Washington's army met them at Brandywine Creek to the west of the city on September 11, took double the number of casualties that it inflicted on the British, and lost the battle. Congress fled to Lancaster, Pennsylvania, before the British entered Philadelphia on September 26. In early October, Washington suffered heavy casualties in another major encounter with the British at Germantown, Pennsylvania. Nevertheless, these engagements kept Howe from reassigning any units to the campaign in New York. Washington then settled what was left of his half-starved and poorly clothed army at Valley Forge where it endured the first of several hard winters to come. (*See Doc. No. 14.*)

The American Victory at Saratoga. While Howe was moving on Philadelphia, Burgoyne was marching his army farther and farther from its supply bases in Canada and deeper and deeper into New York. He easily recaptured Fort Ticonderoga in early July, but then took his army southward into a forested wilderness. St. Leger, operating in the Mohawk Valley, retreated to Canada after Benedict Arnold deceived him into thinking that he was confronting a much stronger American contingent than was the case. The force moving northward from New York City under General Henry Clinton had turned back for reinforcements.

Burgoyne's problems became increasingly serious. His recruitment of Indians had alarmed frontiersmen for miles around. Large numbers of militia and volunteers rushed to support the Continental army, commanded by General Horatio Gates. Americans felled trees in Burgoyne's path and otherwise slowed his forward progress. His Indian allies began to desert. He was alarmingly short of supplies. Arnold defeated him in several encounters and isolated him from any possibility of relief or retreat. Realizing he had no other option, Burgoyne surrendered his entire army to Gates at Saratoga on October 17. The American victory marked the end of major military engagements in New York and New England. It erased some of the disgrace and despair patriots felt when Congress was driven out of Philadelphia. Finally, it convinced the French Foreign Minister, Vergennes, that Americans might indeed win the war with French support, and he hurried to negotiate an alliance with them before the British offered a peace proposal they might be tempted to accept.

Alliance with France. Vergennes's strategy was to make American independence the "work of France," thereby preventing Britain from regaining supremacy over her former colonies or from making an ally of them. The two treaties that effected the alliance in February 1778 were drawn to French, not American specifications. France's best offer in the treaty of commerce was "most-favored nation" status and generous rights for neutral trade in the event of future war. The French did not give Americans any of the special trade privileges they hoped to obtain, nor did they lower duties or remove restrictions on American trade with the French West Indies. The treaty of alliance bound each party not to end the war against Britain until the other agreed to do so. Although they fell far short of the optimum terms the "plan of treaties" described, Congress gratefully ratified both on May 4, 1778.

Vergennes believed that Spanish cooperation was important to ensure victory against Britain and, after a year's diplomacy, he persuaded Spain to join the conflict by meeting her conditions. The two nations recorded their agreement in a convention signed at Aranjuez in April 1779. Under its terms, Spain declared war on Britain as an ally of France but not of the United States. France agreed to attempt a joint invasion of Britain and promised that she would not make peace until Spain had recovered Gibraltar. This entangled the United States in Spanish war objectives because it indirectly pledged the United States to remain at war with Britain until Spain made peace with her—if all three parties kept their commitments to each other.

Americans were elated that France had recognized their independence and confident that her support would enable them to win the war against Britain. Nevertheless, French involvement in the struggle against Britain caused controversy on both sides of the Atlantic even before the alliance was concluded. The colonists had long despised Britain's traditional enemy as a corrupt, Catholic, and autocratic power. Their about-face caused a British officer to mock the "Presbyterian fanatic Clergy of New England" for praying "publickly for their great Ally the french King, as the great protector of Civil and Religious Liberty."[2] Americans correctly realized that France would pursue her own interests before those of her new ally and would exact a high price for her support. American diplomats found themselves engaged in a continual struggle to prevent French objectives from prevailing over American interests as they begged and cajoled for the troops, ships, and loans needed to keep the American army in the field. Dependent as they were on French good will, the Americans operated from a position of weak-

---

[2] Balderston/Syrett, *Lost War*, 167.

ness as they sought to obtain entrée into European diplomatic and financial circles.

Vergennes had begun preparing for war with Britain long before he concluded treaty negotiations with the American commissioners in February 1778. A naval squadron of twelve ships of the line under the Comte d'Estaing left for America in April carrying 12,000 soldiers and Conrad Alexandre Gérard, the first French minister to the United States. French involvement forced Britain to change the way it waged war in North America. Henry Clinton was ordered to evacuate Philadelphia as soon as the British learned d'Estaing's destination. The government now had to defend the British Isles against possible invasion and secure its possessions in the West Indies and India. There would now be sharp limits on the number of men and ships it could commit to North America. British strategists recognized that they had made little headway against the rebellion in the north and middle colonies during the first two years of the war by capturing, holding, and then evacuating Boston and Philadelphia. Despite their defeats in the Carolinas in 1776, however, they once again decided on a southern campaign. Loyalist support, they hoped, would enable them to take and hold Charleston and Savannah and then extend their control to the entire south.

The British Offer Peace without Independence. Burgoyne's surrender at Saratoga also shocked the British government into reevaluating its political strategy. It decided to rush a peace commission headed by the Earl of Carlisle to America in hopes that it could persuade Congress to accept reconciliation without independence before it ratified the alliance with France. Congress, now at York, Pennsylvania, informed Carlisle that it would only discuss recognition of American independence and the withdrawal of British forces. The British did not give up easily. Before he left Philadelphia, George Johnstone, one of the commissioners, offered Congressmen Joseph Reed, Robert Morris, and Francis Dana hefty bribes if they would agree to be "instrumental" in bringing about a restoration of harmony with Britain. Publication of Johnstone's letters totally discredited the commission and ended any prospect for its success. In a last, desperate attempt to achieve its mission the commission published a manifesto that threatened relentless war if Americans chose to "mortgage" themselves and their resources to Britain's enemies. This won no converts to their cause and prompted

Congress to announce that it would retaliate if Britain engaged in acts of brutality.

Military Operations in 1778. Victory looked much closer when Congress celebrated Independence Day in Philadelphia in 1778. D'Estaing's fleet arrived in the Delaware days after British forces completed their withdrawal. D'Estaing left Gérard in Philadelphia and then sailed for New York. Seeing its well-defended harbor, he decided not to attack the city. Instead, the new allies hurriedly planned a land-sea attack on British forces based at Newport, Rhode Island. General John Sullivan, American commander in Rhode Island, received orders to call out the militia. Washington rushed several Continental army brigades under the Marquis de Lafayette, a French volunteer, to join them.

D'Estaing's fleet arrived off Newport at the end of July and a British fleet commanded by Richard Howe arrived to do battle. A severe storm, however, damaged both squadrons and put an end to hopes that the allies could deliver a quick knockout blow against the British. The French sailed to Boston for repairs. Sullivan, who had to improvise a withdrawal from Newport to avoid being stranded on the island, criticized d'Estaing for abandoning him. However justified, his comments threatened to jeopardize good working relations between the new allies. Congress and Washington struggled to control the diplomatic damage as best they could.

Looking Ahead to Peace. Peace terms were an issue from the moment Congress ratified the treaty of alliance with France. Congress and Vergennes agreed that recognition of independence and withdrawal of British armed forces were necessary conditions of peace. The French foreign minister, however, wanted a peace that gave the new nation little beyond this, and he was determined to prevent the Americans from holding out for more. Vergennes instructed Gérard to moderate American peace demands. Since the Treaty of Aranjuez had not yet been concluded, the French were particularly concerned to prevent Congress from seeking a settlement that threatened Spanish interests in America. Gérard raised doubts about the motives of delegates who opposed French objectives and hired writers to publish essays that supported positions he advanced.

Gérard also involved himself in a contentious congressional debate over peace objectives and the appointment of American ministers—and he achieved outcomes largely acceptable to France. Franklin, a French favorite, remained minister to France; John Jay, not Arthur Lee (a Franklin critic), was sent to Spain; Henry Laurens was named to the Netherlands. John Adams, who would become a thorn in the French side, was named minister plenipotentiary to negotiate treaties of peace and commerce with Britain. Neither the fisheries nor navigation of the Mississippi River would be necessary conditions for peace, although American negotiators would be free to press for them.

Americans did, in fact, have aspirations which made France and Spain uncomfortable. States with extensive western land claims, land speculators, and frontiersmen already settled west of the Appalachians hoped for boundaries that extended to the Mississippi River and the right to navigate it. Some southerners wanted the Floridas. Spain anticipated these aspirations with alarm. New Englanders wanted Canada and the right to fish in the territorial waters off British North America they had enjoyed before the war. France, however, hoped to use the war to expel the British from the fisheries and had pledged in the Treaty of Aranjuez to open them to Spain if she succeeded. Peace was very much in the future, however.

War in the South. While major military campaigns had been concentrated in the north during the first three years of the war, loyalist and patriot militia had waged vicious partisan warfare in Georgia and the Carolinas. Georgia had also been prey to cross-border raids from British East Florida. There had been little cooperation between the state government, its militia, and Continental units stationed there. This made it easy for British forces to capture Savannah in December 1778. Continental troops from South Carolina attempted to retake Savannah in the fall of 1779 with support from d'Estaing's fleet, but the British withstood their poorly coordinated efforts and refused to surrender. Success in Georgia encouraged British forces under Generals Henry Clinton and Charles Cornwallis to attack Charleston in the spring of 1780. The American commander, General Benjamin Lincoln, was determined to defend the city. The British cut off all lines of retreat and forced him to surrender 5,400 soldiers and a large supply of military stores.

The loss of Charleston was as significant a blow to the Americans as the surrender of Burgoyne at Saratoga had been to the British. Its effect was compounded several months later when Cornwallis defeated Continental forces under General Horatio Gates at Camden, South Carolina. These two important victories, however, did not give the British the uncontested domination of the south they had hoped to achieve. Retreating Continental forces under Generals Daniel Morgan and Nathanael Greene drew the British into the interior and defeated them there in separate battles early in 1781. Their presence, however, intensified the brutal civil war that had been raging in the back country between loyalists and patriots.

The Experience of War. Once the theater of military action moved away from Massachusetts, more and more people experienced the turmoil, privation, social and economic disruption it spread, even if they were not directly involved in the fighting. Not all Americans supported the war against Great Britain. Some were steadfastly loyal to the king or owed their livelihood and status to the British government. Others considered it better to accept the imperfections of a legitimate government than to overturn it in hopes that a more perfect one would emerge. Some were willing to declare their convictions only if the appropriate army was nearby. Others did not want to take sides at all. While ethnic and racial factors shaped decisions to enlist on either side of the conflict, loyalists and patriots did not divide according to class lines. Prominent loyalists sometimes had their property confiscated or were driven into exile. (*See Doc. No. 15.*) A few paid for their convictions with their lives. Some loyalists organized regiments or supported British military operations by destroying crops, raiding towns, and terrorizing, kidnaping, or murdering patriots. Patriots reciprocated in kind.

The Declaration of Independence divided friends, neighbors, family members, and coreligionists against one another. It forced Quakers to try to negotiate between the pacifism to which their religion pledged them and the civic duties prescribed by the newly established governments. For some Friends, these choices were complicated or facilitated by sympathy for the British cause. Members of pietist groups found themselves compromised by their reluctance to swear oaths of allegiance or to pay the taxes the new governments imposed. Frontiersmen fought against governments that seemed to favor the interests of settled coastal regions over those of scattered inland communities. Some used the opportunity to settle other scores. Honest men were sued, lost property, or were imprisoned for debt because the government could not pay them for their goods or services. Unscrupulous men advanced their interests unhindered by religious or moral principle. Occasionally, trusted comrades were discovered to be traitors or enemy spies. Benedict Arnold, one of the better generals in the Continental army, supplied intelligence to the British and conspired to hand over the American army's headquarters at West Point in return for a large sum of money. The Continental army was rarely up to strength and desertions were not uncommon. The response to militia call-ups was less and less enthusiastic as the war dragged on.

Americans might have expected that they would be able to field and feed a large army easily but they could not. Enlisting agricultural workers in military service caused labor shortages at critical planting and harvest times. Since hostile armies were frequently situated in the same general area, they competed for supplies. The one best supplied with specie, never the Continental army, was able to buy locally while the other was forced to scrape by with leftovers, run the risks and pay the extra cost of transporting food from a distance, or starve. Armies were unreliable customers. They might arrive or leave an area unpredictably, thus making it impossible for farmers to know how much to plant or to anticipate whether their farms would be targets for destruction by hostile forces. Farmers and traders sold to whomever would pay the best price, often the British, regardless of the impact on the war effort.

For long intervals of time the British navy was extremely successful at capturing American merchant vessels engaged in overseas trade. Farmers came to fear that they could neither sell their crops for money that would hold its value nor purchase supplies they needed. They were, thus, unwilling to invest their time and labor to produce crops that might rot before they found a market or be seized by military impressment brigades. In some areas, the economy retrogressed to the barter and subsistence level. In others, producers held crops from market until they could get a better price. Wages did not rise in tandem with prices. Poor folk in the city suffered especially.

Governments Confront the Chaos of a Wartime Economy. To a certain degree, Congress and the American people had no one but themselves to blame for some of the economic crises that intensified between 1778 and 1781. They had struck the first blow against their own economy by shutting down their own trade in hopes that this would compel Parliament to rescind its offensive measures. Congress had issued a currency that would retain its value only if the amount it printed was proportioned to the needs of trade and could be withdrawn by means of taxation before it depreciated. It was not able to hold itself within these limits, however, and the purchasing power of Continental dollars dropped precipitously. An occasional piece of good news, a major victory like Saratoga or France's decision to enter the war against Great Britain, might arrest its slide and let people hope that the war might soon be over. It was not, and the currency continued to loose value. By the end of 1779, Congress had issued $226,200,000 Continental dollars, far more than the economy could absorb. Other forms of government IOUs circulated at the same time. Paper money of all sorts competed on unequal terms against specie injected into the economy by British and French military spending.

Economic distress touched most people of all classes, although they experienced its effects in different ways. These differences exacerbated social tensions. The burdens of military service fell disproportionately on the lower classes. Those higher on the socioeconomic ladder were able to hire others to serve in their place. A soldier's pay, if and when he received it, was barely enough to satisfy his own needs. If married, his wife was left with full responsibility for caring for the children and the elderly and providing for the family's support. In some cases, wives' only option was to follow their husbands into the army where they could hope to collect rations for themselves and their children in return for cooking or doing laundry for the soldiers.

The economic policies of the early years of the war appeared to favor the lower classes. In reality, however, they created as many economic problems for all levels of society as they pretended to solve. Depreciating currency and (tender) laws which required creditors to accept paper money at face value made it easier for renters and debtors to satisfy their obligations. When and where they could be enforced, tender laws eroded creditors' assets and upper class standards of living declined as a result. Cutbacks in production meant that everything but paper money was in short supply. Food shortages and price increases prompted state legislatures to set maximum prices at which basic foodstuffs could be sold. To insure that there would be enough to supply local populations and the army, they passed embargoes that forbad traders to export wheat and flour beyond state lines. Popular committees enforced the regulations. They could not, however, prevent farmers from producing less, holding their surpluses from market, or contriving to sell them to agents purchasing supplies for foreign armies. Businessmen came to feel that their opportunity to make a profit was cut off at every pass. Merchants and other members of the upper classes appeared to prosper unduly from the high prices soldiers and their families struggled to pay.

Lower classes saw wealth as evidence of both greed and Tory sympathies and condemned the rich. Political, social, and economic tensions erupted in bloody confrontation in Philadelphia in October 1779. Radical activists, many of them members of Philadelphia militia units, answered a call, weapons in hand, to "drive off from the city" all "disaffected persons." They attacked the home of James Wilson, a former and future member of Congress and one of the city's leading attorneys, who had represented clients accused of violating price controls. Both sides suffered casualties before a troop of upper-class horsemen arrived to disperse the attackers. Congress could not ignore the conflict that was acted out beneath its eyes, but neither it nor the state government had any ready solutions for the panoply of problems which ignited it. (*See Doc. No. 16.*)

By the end of 1779, it was clear that there was no point in issuing any more Continentals. In March 1780, Congress cobbled together a plan for exchanging them for a "new emission" to be issued by the states. It was hoped that the new money would hold its value but it did not. Debates about monetary policy occupied Congress and filled the newspapers. Some people argued that, if United States agreed to pay the debt represented by the currency at face value as it had promised to do, their children's children would still be laboring under a crushing burden of taxation. They believed that depreciation was the most effective and equal tax that could be designed to finance the war, and they were relatively indifferent to the claims of those who held debt certificates.

Others, mostly spokesmen for the upper classes, argued that Congress was honor bound to take measures to see that the currency was gradually restored to face value. This could be done and justice upheld, they believed, by taxation. They were confident that the American economy would expand so dynamically once the war was over that the public debt could easily be repaid. Corrupt monarchies, they said, routinely did grave injustice to their creditors, but it was both dangerous and morally indefensible for a republic, especially an infant one, to imitate them. Restoring the currency's value, of course, stood to benefit not only original holders of debt certificates but also speculators who gambled that the government would one day pay its debts and bought them up for much less than their face value. It was not easy to devise a solution that would satisfy the needs of lower class working people in the cities, farmers whose harvests were appropriated by military impressment details, soldiers who starved and shivered in the cold of winter, businessmen who had long-standing claims against the government, and foreigners who had invested in American debt certificates. (*See Doc. No. 17.*)

Privation and Mutiny in the Army. Washington spent much more of the seven war years keeping the Continental army in existence and training it for battle than he did fighting the British. The army incurred many more losses from hunger and disease than it did in actual combat. Under the best of circumstances, it would have been difficult to provision two or three armies (American, French, and British) in geographic proximity to one another. The military supply system that Congress cobbled together at the beginning of the war depended on the willingness and the ability of the states to assemble and deliver the supplies that Congress indicated were necessary. When the British threatened a given area, states became more willing to contribute, but were generally less able to do so. Many states collected their revenues in whatever commodities their citizens produced. It was not always easy to convert tobacco into bread and meat to feed the army when and where it was needed. Waste, inefficiency, and a measure of corruption made for a system that failed more often than it succeeded.

Not even military discipline was enough to restrain the anger unpaid soldiers felt at the continual privation they suffered. After a hard winter in which they had had little to eat but corn meal, two Connecticut regiments stationed in New Jersey mutinied in May 1780. (*See Doc. No. 18.*) In June, Esther DeBerdt Reed, wife of the president of Pennsylvania, formed an association of women who cut back spending on their clothing and personal appearance and donated the money they saved to make soldiers' lives more "pleasant." Women from several states and all walks of life contributed over $350,000 Continental dollars. Wealthy citizens of Pennsylvania subscribed substantial amounts of money to purchase supplies for the army.

These voluntary measures were far from enough to meet the army's needs, however. Pennsylvania troops enlisted for "three years or the end of the war" had received little or no pay for the military service they had already rendered. This made them deeply resent the generous specie bounties their state offered to new recruits to persuade them to enlist. Furthermore, they were convinced that they were obliged to serve no more than three years. When they were told they would not be discharged until the war was over, eleven Pennsylvania regiments stationed in New Jersey mutinied on January 1, 1781 and began to march toward Philadelphia. Congress and the state government established a joint committee and sent Joseph Reed, President of Pennsylvania, to negotiate with the soldiers at Princeton. The troops submitted after Reed promised that the state would deal with pay and supply issues. He also authorized discharges for those who had served three years and did not want to remain in the army. Congress and Pennsylvania authorities were pleased that the soldiers had rejected an offer made by two British agents, who promised that General Henry Clinton would protect them and pay them all that Congress owed them if they would desert a cause that had brought them only misery and suffering. American authorities did not, however, presume that the British offer would fall on deaf ears. They made a concerted but not entirely successful effort to answer their complaints. Days later, mutiny erupted in the New Jersey line. Several months later, some of the Pennsylvania units, angry that the promises made to them in January had not been kept, mutinied once again.

These troubles were symptomatic of much wider problems. Several years of military training and discipline had made the Continental army a respectable fighting force, but it was undermanned and so poorly fed, clothed, supplied, and paid that some doubted whether it could or would take the field against the British. Few questioned the commitment of the veteran soldiers who had served and fought shirtless, shoeless, and half starved for months on end, but mutinies provided stark evidence that there was a limit to the army's patience. The patriotism that angry troops displayed in the midst of their confrontations with authority had to be carefully pointed out to America's new allies to insure that their protests were taken as evidence that more support was needed and not that it should be withdrawn or denied.

The Articles, even when ratified, gave Congress no power either to tax or to regulate commerce. Americans had not yet reached a consensus about what kind of a revolution they wanted or needed, and the price of their indecision became more and more apparent. Congress and the states wrestled with problems that had no easy solutions. At both the confederation and the state levels, Americans were forced to confront the implications of independence and the limitations of the governmental structures they had chosen to replace the British imperial administration.

War with Britain had brought with it internal divisions that at times reached the proportions of an undeclared war among Americans. High prices and hunger did not generate either patriotism or optimism that the Revolution would succeed. Support for independence was tested by economic hardship that partisans of all persuasions experienced in varying degrees. Alliance with France would eventually ensure victory but it did not do so immediately, and it did not come without cost. Frontier conflicts, civilian riots, and mutinies provided the most painful but not the only illustrations of how difficult it was to function as a nation at war without a duly constituted government.

CHAPTER 6

EXPERIMENTING WITH CONFEDERATION: 1781–1783

A Turning Point. As 1780 drew to a close, Americans had reason to wonder whether they had made any progress toward winning their independence. "The public Complexion," wrote Rhode Island Congressman James M. Varnum in January 1781, "is such At present that there is Reason to apprehend every Evil but that of Conquest."[1] British forces held New York and Charleston, two of the most important port cities. Loyalist raids and frontier violence reached new levels of intensity in interior parts of the country. Benedict Arnold, until recently an American hero, had defected to the British. His treason suggested that it was futile to continue the struggle against British military might. French forces had arrived but had not yet turned the tide toward victory in any military engagement.

While the war seemed to be going nowhere, public finances were going downhill at an ever accelerating pace. Congress had publicly acknowledged that it was bankrupt by devaluing the Continental currency and asking the states to issue new currency and to pay the regiments they had raised for the Continental army. The people, however, would not exchange the old Continental dollars for the new state money at the stipulated rate of 40 to 1 because, as Connecticut Congressman Jesse Root said in January 1781, it was "neither equal to Silver nor to itself." "Is not this a wonderfull paradox," Root continued, "that there is in the States, for its so in this State, Such a plenty of money that it is worth nothing—at the Same time a vast plenty of provisions & goods & yet no money to purchase them—& the people Complaining they Cant pay their rates [taxes]."[2]

Developments on the political front were slightly more positive. The acrimonious investigation into Silas Deane's operations had come to an end. It had been the most important but not the only partisan dispute that had divided Congress, absorbed its flagging energies, and prevented it from giving attention to more critical matters. The initial round of state constitution-making was finally completed. Maryland had used

[1] *LDC*, 16; 644.
[2] *LDC*, 16: 640–641.

Virginia's reluctance to renounce her claims to western lands as a reason not to ratify the Articles of Confederation. Virginia finally ceded her lands on terms acceptable to Congress. Official notice of Maryland's ratification reached Congress in February 1781. The "firm league of friendship" was finally and fully established on March 1.

Congress and the Public Business. Americans could not seem to shake their deep fear that, if they gave power to the central government, it would become corrupt and tax them oppressively. Some members of Congress considered themselves the guardians of the Revolution's political principles. They were deeply committed to preventing any concentration of power from developing and slow to acknowledge that success in waging war against Britain might require an executive capable of energizing all available forces. As a result, Congress was often better at preserving a democratic mode of operations than it was at operating efficiently. Delegates served no more than three consecutive one-year terms. Many failed to appear on time or to remain for the duration of the session; some did not attend at all. This meant that, on occasion, questions were decided as much by who was absent as by who was present for a vote. If not enough states were represented, they could not be decided at all. Experience and continuity of leadership were easily lost.

In the beginning Congress functioned as a conference. It made all its decisions, large and small, either by considering issues as a committee of the whole or by assigning them to committees to report on. When the volume of business made this unworkable, it created boards of war, admiralty, and treasury, and a committee on foreign affairs. They were composed of both members and nonmembers of Congress and managed their operations subject to Congress's approval. The boards, however, proved no more able to keep up with the work load than Congress had. There were other disadvantages. Theoretically the board system allowed members to develop expertise and prevented power from being centered in the hands of any one person. In practice, however, nonattendance of some meant that a single active member could control operations. At the same time, boards diffused responsibility and therefore compromised efficiency and accountability.

Necessity forced Congress to appoint personnel to take on the numerous tasks for which it was responsible, but it strove to keep the bureaucracy or "civil list" to a bare minimum. Salaries were low and paid in Continental currency, which made it difficult to attract and retain qualified and honest employees. Supervision was a problem and daily business was not always well taken care of. In the balance, despite earnest effort, it was obvious that Congress had failed to develop a system of government that preserved revolutionary ideals *and* provided the means to achieve the Revolution's ultimate objective—American independence.

The Revolution Reversed or Betrayed? Increasingly desperate circumstances forced Congress to consider two critical and sensitive reforms. By the fall of 1780, many delegates were convinced that Congress could not carry on the war unless it had sources of revenue more reliable than a requisition system that left it to the states' honor to contribute their assessed share of the common expenses. Congressional committees considered a range of measures for dealing with the crisis. Because paper money had failed so completely they concentrated their efforts on measures that would produce specie (gold and silver). Some delegates proposed asking Americans to loan their cash to Congress. Others wanted to "call it in" by taxation. One delegate suggested selling "all the Continental naval vessels of war *and* all the Publick Stables & the Barracks at Cambridge & all Naval Stores"—for specie. There was a long discussion about establishing a bank. If people could be convinced to purchase stock shares with specie, a bank could then expand the money supply by issuing notes backed by the capital its stockholders had paid for their shares. Congress could ask the states for authority to raise revenue by levying a specie tax on trade—to give it the very power the British government had tried to exercise. It could make a concerted attempt to borrow substantial amounts of money abroad. Delegates even considered whether Congress had the power to coerce the states to comply with its requisitions.[3]

On February 3, a month before the Articles were ratified, Congress asked the states to authorize *it* to levy an impost, a 5 percent tax on imports. (*See Doc. No. 19.*) Article VIII described a revenue system whereby the states levied taxes on their own citizens, collected them with state and local agents, and then, at Congress's request and according to quotas it established, sent some of the proceeds to the United States Treasury. All thirteen states would have to approve the recom-

---

[3] *LDC*, 16: 305–314.

mendation to grant the "central government" the power to impose a tax under its own authority. Their consent would not be easy to obtain. Congress hoped, however, that it would be forthcoming and that it would convince prospective foreign lenders that there was a realistic chance that any monies they loaned to support the war effort would be repaid.

Many delegates also recognized that there would be no progress in the war effort unless and until the public's business was more energetically and efficiently managed. Americans, however, had not forgotten their years of struggle against the British ministry, so creating a fully empowered executive branch of the government was out of the question. While various writers tried to educate the public about the need for a more effective government, congressional leaders put together the votes needed to replace the existing boards with executive departments of foreign affairs, war, marine, and the treasury. Their heads, styled secretary, agent, and superintendent—not minister—would report to Congress. Critics of the executive system believed that men entrusted with power would inevitably be corrupted by it. Those who advocated establishing the executive departments argued that qualified men could be found who were patriotic enough to serve the public interest. (*See Doc. No. 20.*) They prevailed, but Congress found it difficult to agree on nominees. Furthermore, even though the salaries provided were respectable, candidates were not always eager to accept the responsibilities and restrictions established by Congress and Congress was not always willing to agree to the conditions they demanded.

A Superintendent of Finance. The only nominee seriously considered for the powerful and critical position of Superintendent of Finance was Robert Morris. He was the first to be appointed (February 20, 1781) and the first to accept, although he did not do so immediately. His credentials, wide-ranging experience in international business and finance and personal credit far better than the government's, gave reason to hope that he could put the government's house in order, supply the army, and win the confidence of foreign lenders. They also led people to fear that he would be just the type of power-hungry, corrupt minister that republican ideology abhorred—an executive Congress would be unable to control, who would be likely to use his office to enrich himself and his partners. The delegates' concerns were further fed by unanswered questions about Morris's Secret Committee accounts and by his refusal to accept the office unless Congress allowed him to retain his business interests and gave him the power to appoint and remove any official who was entrusted with public property.

Congress twisted in anguish over his terms for a while, but knew that it had to choose between him and utter bankruptcy. After a few weeks' deliberation it accepted his conditions. In turn, Morris gambled that the states would pay their shares of the specie requisitions Congress passed and would approve the impost amendment. Both would be necessary to enable him to pay off the obligations he contracted in the public's name in real money. This and this alone would establish that Congress was now credit-worthy. If he ever failed to fulfill an engagement, he told George Washington, he would quit his Office "as useless from that Moment."[4]

Foreign Loans. While Morris was endeavoring to put American finances in order at home, others were struggling to raise funds in Europe to support the war. Once France had recognized American independence, Congress appointed Benjamin Franklin its minister to Paris. It also named John Jay to Madrid in hopes that the Spanish would receive him and enter into an alliance with the United States. One of the principal responsibilities American diplomats shouldered was obtaining gifts, loans, or subsidies to support the war. Early in 1781, a faction in Congress that lacked confidence in Franklin sent John Laurens of South Carolina as an "envoy extraordinary" to solicit a substantial loan and naval aid from France. Before he arrived, however, Franklin succeeded in obtaining a loan of 4,000,000 and a gift of 6,000,000 livres from France. Not to be outdone, Laurens persuaded the French court to guarantee repayment of a 10,000,000 livre loan that was then being marketed to Dutch investors and to advance the entire amount of it immediately. Much of the money raised was applied to satisfy outstanding obligations in Europe. In previous years, Congress had simply drawn bills—assigned outstanding debts—to be paid by its commissioners there whether or not they had raised the money to cover them. Some of what remained was used to buy military supplies in Europe. Laurens returned from France on August 25, 1781, with clothing, arms, and $463,000 in specie. Inconveniently for Washington's army, which was

---

[4] E. James Ferguson, et al., eds. *The Papers of Robert Morris*, 9 vols. (Pittsburgh: University of Pittsburgh Press, 1973-1999, hereafter *PRM*), 1: 94.

already marching toward Yorktown, Virginia, the French frigate that carried Laurens, the specie, and the goods he had purchased put in at Boston, too far away to be applied directly to cover the expenses of the campaign in the Chesapeake.

The Bank of North America. Morris sprang into action soon after he agreed to serve as Financier. His first priority was the currency crisis. By May 1781, he presented Congress with a plan to establish the Bank of North America. He hoped to raise its capital, the modest sum of $400,000 by selling $400 shares payable in gold or silver. Even though the bank promised dividends to its stockholders there were few patriots who had disposable cash and were willing to invest it in this way. Washington informed Morris that, much as he would have liked to become a stockholder, his income was so far behind his expenses that he had had to sell some of his lands to pay his taxes. Other army officers let subscription agents know that going without their salaries was the best and only support they were able to offer.

Finally, Morris was compelled to use $254,000 of the specie John Laurens had brought to purchase shares for the government. The silver was repacked in strong iron-strapped oak chests and then transported under guard by oxcart over the safest possible route from Boston to Philadelphia. Although the bank was a private, not a public institution, the government's purchase of shares made the public its largest stockholder. It would soon become the bank's major borrower as well. After the bank was capitalized, both Congress and Pennsylvania granted it charters of incorporation. At the first meeting of its stockholders, Morris's business partner, Thomas Willing, was elected president. Once established, the bank issued notes backed by its specie deposits that provided businessmen with a currency that circulated at or near face value. It also stimulated economic activity by making short-term commercial loans.

Military Contracts. The army desperately needed food and clothing so that it could take the field. Morris cajoled business acquaintances to advance their own funds or credit to buy flour for the troops stationed in New York. This was only an interim measure, however. He also immediately developed plans for privatizing the procurement system. Previously the Quartermaster and Commissary Departments had been responsible for obtaining the flour, meat, and other supplies issued to the army. Sometimes they obtained them from the states. Sometimes they purchased what they needed, but frequently they impressed goods and issued certificates which indicated the value of what they had taken. In the end, the certificates totaled many millions of Continental dollars. Morris hoped to end such impressments. He believed that the government could save money and feed the army better if he negotiated yearlong, fixed-price deals with businessmen to procure and transport army rations. The contract system, however, would only work in states which collected money—not just beef, flour or tobacco—in taxes *and* paid their specie quotas into the Continental treasury. It was not easy to find entrepreneurs who were willing and able to make contracts with the Continental government. Bidders had to have extensive supply networks and enough capital to buy and deliver large quantities of merchandise. They also had to trust that the government would make contract payments on schedule and in specie. By year's end, Morris had concluded several contracts to supply army posts. While both he and the contractors ran into problems when the states failed to raise their tax quotas, the army was much more reliably supplied than previously and at significantly less cost.

The Southern Campaign. While Congress and its ministers were tackling financial and administrative problems, American generals were preparing for the 1781 campaigns. The fighting season began early in the south. Charles Cornwallis, commander of British forces based in Charleston, South Carolina, marched inland and then headed through North Carolina to Virginia. His passage set off a series of brutal loyalist-patriot encounters in the back country. Continental troops and militia under the command of Nathanael Greene and Daniel Morgan harassed and defeated him several times along his way. Nevertheless, he reached Virginia in May and joined forces with a detachment commanded by the traitor, Benedict Arnold. Together they raided and terrorized the countryside and freed hundreds of slaves. In early August, under orders from Henry Clinton, Cornwallis settled on the Yorktown peninsula and began to fortify it.

During the spring and early summer, Washington had been conferring about a joint attack on New York with the Comtes de Rochambeau and de Barras, commanders of the French troops stationed in Rhode Island and a naval detachment based at Newport. By July, the French and American forces had converged and begun to probe British defenses north of the city. In mid-August, however, they received definitive word that a naval force under the Admiral de Grasse was headed for the Chesapeake. This created the possibility that, if Washington and Rochambeau rushed their armies to Virginia, they could, in cooperation with de Grasse, trap Cornwallis's 10,000-man force on the Yorktown peninsula and compel him to surrender.

Yorktown. On August 19, Washington's and Rochambeau's troops began a long, rapid march from New York through New Jersey and Pennsylvania to Maryland. There, some were put on boats for Virginia while the remainder continued on foot. Supplies for the soldiers had to be gathered along the way. As many transport vessels as possible had to be assembled to speed the armies' journey. Washington was concerned about taking his men south because most of them were northerners who feared the fevers that were prevalent there in late summer and early autumn. More important, his soldiers had not been paid in recent memory and they were angry because of it. Washington begged Morris to provide them with a month's pay in specie. Only a specie loan from the French army made it possible for him to fulfill Washington's request. New York Congressmen James Duane and Ezra L'Hommedieu reported that they had "suffered the greatest Anxiety 'till this Object was accomplished, for the Discontent of the Corps was great and just as well among the Officers as Soldiers."[5] One month's pay jingling in their pockets, Washington's men left Philadelphia for Yorktown.

By mid September, de Grasse and de Barras had gained control of the Chesapeake. American and French troops blocked Cornwallis's escape by land, but they had to find a way to force his surrender before de Grasse's scheduled return to the West Indies on November 1. After that, there would be nothing to prevent the British navy from relieving Cornwallis by sea. The allied armies, about 16,000 men, hurriedly dug trenches, set up gun emplacements for the siege artillery de Barras had brought, and then gradually advanced and penetrated British fortifications. Outnumbered, convinced he could not be relieved, and ever shorter on supplies, Cornwallis surrendered on October 19.

The War Continues. The last major battle of the war was over, but the war itself was by no means at an end. After their defeat at York-

[5] *LDC*, 18: 29.

town, Britain curtailed offensive operations on land but stepped up its war on American commerce. When the trading season opened in the spring of 1782, British Rear Admiral Robert Digby threw every ship he commanded into an intensive blockade of the American coast from Massachusetts to the Carolinas. Few American vessels made it through. Most of those that tried were captured, brought to ports under British control, and then sold or commissioned into the British navy. American merchants suffered immense losses as a result. With legal trade a virtual impossibility, American farmers near British lines earned what income they could by selling their crops to the enemy. Merchants in British-occupied territories smuggled manufactures across the lines and sold them for cash to American purchasers starved for imported goods. There was little Congress could do either to save American commerce from destruction or to prevent the clandestine trade and the specie drain that was its inevitable corollary. The Continental navy had only two frigates fit for service, the *Alliance* and the *Deane*. Neither they nor the remnants of state navies could offer protection against British naval power.

The British blockade brought another wave of economic and fiscal disaster in its train. Legal trade was the major source of the silver Congress hoped to draw into the Continental treasury through the impost and the states' requisition payments. Without it, everything Morris was working to set on a sound footing—the Bank, the contract system, a reliable, productive revenue system, and restoration of public credit by promptly paying obligations he had pledged his country's and his own honor to meet—would be reduced to naught. The desperate situation led him to suggest that Congress once again ask the French to provide greater protection for American commerce. Hopes that the French would agree were dashed before the request was formally made. In April 1782, a short five months after the victory at Yorktown, de Grasse lost five ships, including his own, to a British fleet under Admiral George Rodney in the Battle of the Saintes off the island of Guadaloupe. De Grasse himself was taken prisoner and sent to England. When convenient, French naval squadrons convoyed American vessels to or from Europe, but they did not promote French-American trade by providing it with systematic protection.

Shortly after news of Yorktown reached Britain the North government fell and was replaced by a government under the Marquis of Rockingham and the Earl of Shelburne, both of whom were committed to bring the war to an end. Peace talks began soon afterwards but there were no treaties for well over a year. The prospect that peace would be negotiated and the uncertainty about when also disrupted American economic activity. Farmers could not predict how much demand there would be for their crops. They could not tell whether the British and French armies, their valued customers, would soon be withdrawn, or whether West Indian and European markets closed to them by the blockade would suddenly be reopened by a cessation of hostilities. Merchants willing to run the blockade had to risk ordering consumer goods at high wartime prices and paying stiff insurance premiums. They could sell their cargoes at substantial profits if the war continued and the goods arrived while they were still in high demand. Peace would put an end to shipping risks, but it would flood American markets with goods that would then sell below cost.

France and the Diplomacy of Peace. Peace negotiations brought diplomatic complications as well. The Chevalier de la Luzerne, who had replaced Gérard as minister to the United States, was even more adept at dispensing money and favors and employing pressure to advance French interests than his predecessor had been. By 1781, Congress was increasingly dependent on France for loans and military support and this disposed various congressmen to be receptive to La Luzerne's point of view. In Europe, John Adams was suspicious of French motives and the French were increasingly uncomfortable with him. His determination to secure New England fishing rights was well known. Adams was also critical of the genial relations Franklin maintained with the French and suspected that he might be less than zealous in defending American interests.

On instructions from Foreign Minister Vergennes, La Luzerne complained to Congress about Adams and suggested that it would be wise to restrict his role and to grant France more control over peace negotiations. Some delegates considered that it would be "an act of too great obsequiousness" to oblige Vergennes. Others, including General John Sullivan, now a congressmen and a recipient of French largesse, used his position as a member of the committee that conferred with La Luzerne to advocate compliance under the guise of "attachment to the alliance." Congress eventually diluted Adams's authority by appointing a five man peace commission: Franklin, Adams, Jay (who suspected French motives as much as Adams did), Jefferson, who did not accept appointment to the commission, and Henry Laurens, by then a British prisoner. It then drafted new instructions which gave the French great influence over the negotiations. Virginia delegates argued that American dependence on French benevolence made it necessary to agree to these conditions. Over the protests of delegates who considered the terms "Abject and Humiliating," the instructions were approved.[6] (*See Doc. No. 21.*) With American compliance in his pocket, Vergennes then informed the British that France would not support any American demands beyond recognition of independence.

The Articles of Confederation Revisited. Many accounts of the American Revolution move swiftly from the victory at Yorktown to the successful if intrigue-filled diplomacy that ended when Britain recognized the independence of its former colonies and granted them fishing rights and boundaries generous enough to disquiet France and Spain. They overlook the critical internal struggle that contending political factions were waging over what revolutionary principles should define the new nation while the American commissioners were forging an acceptable peace. The Articles of Confederation provided a minimal structure of government, but it satisfied neither those who wanted nothing more than a loose "league" and a central government that was small and weak nor those who wanted a union capable of dealing effectively with domestic problems, advancing American interests, and of standing up to foreign powers.

The central government's impotence under the Articles was especially obvious with regard to the pressing questions of taxation, finance, and the public debt. Had the depreciating currency equitably distributed the cost of the war among all citizens? Would Congress be able to raise enough funds through taxation and foreign borrowing to keep the army in the field and government employees in their offices until the war was over? How long could the government postpone paying those who had contributed most to the war effort? Should Congress be given the power to tax so that Continental army troops could be paid their wages? So that wealthier American and foreigner creditors whose support had contributed to the victory could be paid? Who would reap the benefit when Congress paid its debts—those to whom they were originally owed, or speculators who had bought debt certificates from poor

[6] *LDC*, 17: 307, 311, 325–326.

people who could not wait for the government to pay? Should public creditors be satisfied that the war had been won and forget that Congress owed them money? Should the demands of justice and gratitude be listened to or ignored? How could they be satisfied? How much power should a central government be allowed to exercise over individual and regional prosperity? If Congress had the power to tax would future generations be saddled with a heavy burden of debt that might impoverish them for years to come?

These questions were not academic. Funds from foreign loans and state payments on requisitions were swallowed up almost instantaneously. Most of them were earmarked for current expenses and could not be used to pay past debts. The British had not gone home after Yorktown. They held Savannah and Charleston until July and December 1782 and New York City until November 1783. While Americans might hope that the war was over, no one knew what the new British government would do. Washington had to be ready for any eventuality. Most American soldiers were better fed in 1782 than previously but they were not adequately clothed. The states contributed only a pittance toward their quotas. This meant that paying the army was well beyond Congress's capabilities even though Washington reminded it on more than one occasion that mutinous rumblings were once again growing more insistent.

Shall Congress Have the Power to Levy a Tax? Much of the tension these questions generated focused on ratification of the impost amendment Congress had approved and sent to the states in February, 1781. At the time, the sense of crisis was acutely felt. The Pennsylvania line had just mutinied and discontent festered in other regiments as well. Yorktown was months in the future. As far as Congress and the states knew, no loans or subsidies had been obtained in Europe. These circumstances induced some states to approve the impost amendment quickly, even if they made their ratifications subject to various conditions. British control prevented the legislatures of South Carolina and Georgia from voting, but it was assumed that they would ratify as soon as they were free to assemble. By the end of the summer of 1781, of the eleven remaining states only Massachusetts, Rhode Island, Maryland and Delaware had not signified their approval. Massachusetts had postponed consideration until its legislature's next session. Governor John Hancock correctly anticipated that it would go "heavily thro."[7] It was not until May 1782 that Massachusetts approved the impost. Delaware and Maryland sent in ratifications in July of that year. Rhode Island was the outstanding holdout.

Rhode Island and the Impost. Governor William Greene had informed Morris in November 1781 that Rhode Island could not decide whether the impost measure was useful or not. He suggested that the amount of revenue "this Little State" could be expected to raise "would not be worth collecting." Therefore, he said, Rhode Island would withhold its approval until all other states had adopted the tax. Then, it would cheerfully agree to do "whatever is for the advantage of the Union."[8] By the time the Maryland and Delaware ratifications were received, a majority of Rhode Island's political leaders had reached a consensus that the impost would *not* be to the "advantage" of the Union but they had not yet made their decision official and public. Believing they still had time to influence the state, Congress and Morris attempted to identify and resolve the specific issues which stood in the way of ratification. Their correspondence with Rhode Island's delegates, governor, and legislature, and a lively debate in Rhode Island's newspapers revealed both economic and political objections to the tax.

Rhode Island's most outspoken opponent of the impost was David Howell, a congressman who was closely connected to some of the state's leading merchants. At the end of July, Howell offered a series of economic reasons why the state opposed the impost. Where those who favored ratification argued that the tax would be productive and fair, he insisted that it would disproportionately burden either Rhode Islands merchants or its consumers. This, he argued, would lead to attempts to evade it. "Profanations of oaths and corruption in various forms" would, he foresaw, inevitably follow. Howell also objected to Congress's plan to appoint its own officers to collect the impost. Federal agents, he insisted, would be another useless layer of bureaucracy that would have to be supported at an "enormous additional charge."[9] Proponents of the measure had argued that foreign loans could be obtained only if the states ratified the impost. Howell and his allies pointed out, however, that the French and more recently the Dutch had agreed to lend without

---

[7] *PRM*, 3: 267.
[8] *PRM*, 3: 138.
[9] *PRM*, 6: 114.

it. They did not, however, speculate about when or how the loans would be repaid.

Just before the Rhode Island legislature was scheduled to vote the impost up or down, Howell and his fellow delegate, Jonathan Arnold, presented the political case against the impost in a letter to Rhode Island Governor William Greene. They voiced a fear of centralized power that overwhelmed any concern about governmental impotence or the success of the common cause. They cast Rhode Island as the principal defender of the principles of a revolution that had begun as a protest against taxes imposed by a central government. Ratification, they claimed, would be a virtual repudiation of revolutionary ideals. (*See Doc. No. 22.*) In November 1782, the legislature refused by a huge majority to approve the amendment, and this prevented the impost from taking effect. The Virginia legislature, no longer menaced by the British army, made the rejection even more resounding by repealing its ratification a month later.

Financial Crisis. Rhode Island and Virginia ignored mounting evidence that the requisition system had not met present needs for revenue and could not be expected to do so in the future. Although Howell and Arnold pretended that the states paid the entire amount they had been assessed, treasury accounts showed that none of them had come at all close to meeting their quotas. The contract to supply Washington's army had collapsed because Morris could not pay on time and in cash. He was compelled to negotiate a new one with a different firm that offered longer credit but at a significantly higher price. Proceeds from the foreign loans were nowhere near enough to cover all the demands on the Continental treasury. At year's end, Morris received dispatches from Europe that informed him that he had overdrawn his account in France. Soon after the war, principal and interest on foreign debts would begin to fall due and some congressmen expressed fears that, if they were not paid on schedule, European powers might attempt to collect the debts by force. The early national history of several Latin American countries shows that these fears were not without foundation.

Army Pay. By the end of 1782, many Continental officers and soldiers were owed up to six years' back pay. With peace in sight, they became more and more fearful that they would be sent home before Congress had made a firm commitment to pay them. They visualized having to beg to support themselves on their way home and feared returning to their families penniless, without even a certificate that stated the amount of money the government owed them. This was especially important to those who had gone into debt to support themselves and their families during the war, since they were liable to be sued and imprisoned for defaulting as soon as they returned to civilian life. Soldiers were not the only ones victimized by the debt predicament. Many bureaucrats and ordinary civilians also faced the danger of losing their property or their liberty to an unrelenting creditor because the government could not pay for services they had rendered or goods contracted for in its name.

Officers in the Main Army headquartered at Newburgh decided that the time had come to determine whether or not Congress intended to keep its commitments to them. Late in December 1782, shortly after Rhode Island rejected the impost amendment, they sent a delegation to Philadelphia to ask for settlement of their accounts, some pay immediately, and a firm commitment for the rest of what was owed to them. Congress could not deny that the army's demands were reasonable and just. It asked Morris if he could issue the army some pay in cash immediately. The Financier replied in no uncertain terms that he could only do so if France agreed to loan more funds in 1783. *One* month's pay for the officers and men totaled $253,232, far more money than Morris had on hand or had any immediate prospect for obtaining. Furthermore, he had to pay government workers and the contractors who supplied army rations large amounts of money. If he did not, the army would go hungry—a further incitement for it to mutiny.

The Financier Resigns. Desperate, Congress authorized Morris to gamble that France would grant more funds and he agreed to issue the army one month's pay in cash on this basis. Several days later, however, the French minister refused to allow the Financier to take measures based on this assumption. This brought Morris to the point he had told Washington in 1781 that he must avoid: he had made engagements that could not be fulfilled. He did what he had told Washington then he would have to do—quit his office "as useless from that Moment." In a letter of January 24, 1783, he informed Congress that he would resign at the end of May if public finances had not been put on a sound footing by that time. (*See Doc. No. 23.*) Congress considered Morris's resignation conditional, and voted to keep his letter a secret.

Rhode Island's refusal to ratify the impost had raised serious questions about the viability of the nation whose independence was soon to be recognized. After several months' struggle to find the cash for the army's one month's pay, relatively little had been raised. Meanwhile, influential delegates had informed Morris there was virtually no chance the states would approve a comprehensive revenue plan like the one he had submitted to Congress the previous July. Therefore, they told him, Congress would send out only a new impost proposal, and it would be tailored to meet the objections the states had raised to the first one. The tariff was to be in force for twenty-five years and no longer, whether or not the debt had been paid by that time. The states, not Congress, would appoint the collectors. Even though the federal government was bankrupt, Congress was asking for less, not more. This convinced Morris that his condition for remaining in office—effective measures to provide for the entire public debt—would not be met and so he asked Congress to allow him to make his resignation public. It agreed, and Morris's letter of resignation was published in a number of newspapers. It reached army headquarters at Newburgh along with a report from General McDougall on Congress's response to army's demands.

The Newburgh Affair. The news from Philadelphia led some officers to conclude that there was little reason to think that Congress was about to discover a way to pay its debt to the army. On March 10, 1783, several aides to General Horatio Gates circulated an anonymous invitation to their fellow officers to meet to discuss options. They suggested that the army should send another, more forceful petition to Congress and hinted that if the response was not satisfactory, the army should take stronger action. The Newburgh addresses strongly suggested a prospect that responsible leaders had long feared: that the army would end its tradition of subordination to civilian government and launch a coup d'état to gain its objectives. Washington's critical and timely intervention in the officers' meeting, his explanation of the difficulties Congress experienced in raising the necessary revenues, and his pledge to champion the army's cause prevented the protest from developing into a more serious challenge to its authority.

Peace. While the movement toward fiscal responsibility was grinding to a halt in America, American commissioners in Europe had been making significant progress on several fronts. Franklin, Adams, and Jay had defied their instructions and negotiated very favorable peace terms in Paris with British negotiator Richard Oswald. The United States obtained unqualified recognition of its independence, the fishing rights it demanded, and reasonable northeastern and generous western boundaries. Although Franklin had originally suggested that Britain cede "every part of Canada," the three commissioners agreed to accept a boundary line that followed the Great Lakes to the Mississippi River. They signed a preliminary treaty on November 30, 1782—without the French Foreign Minister's prior approval, and before Britain concluded a treaty with either France or Spain. While Vergennes was angry that he had not been consulted about the treaty, Franklin adroitly reminded him that friction between France and America would encourage the British to hope they had damaged the Alliance. He not only carried the point, but managed to persuade the financially strapped French government to grant a new loan of 6,000,000 livres. He also arranged for an initial payout of 600,000 livres to be shipped to the United States on the *General Washington*, the very vessel that carried the provisional treaty and a British passport to ensure its safe passage.

Lieutenant Joshua Barney did not bring the *General Washington* into port at Philadelphia until March 12, 1783, two days after the discontent that had been roiling under the surface at Newburgh broke out into the open. Congress could not celebrate the peace treaty with unrestrained joy. The notes Madison made on its deliberations on March 17 aptly summarized how anxieties about the army, the manner in which the peace had been achieved, and Morris's resignation overwhelmed any elation Congress felt at the war's end. (*See Doc. No. 24.*)

"Lucius." A week before news of the peace or the events at Newburgh reached Philadelphia, an anonymous critic using the pseudonym "Lucius" launched a "republican" assault on the Financier and on the publication of his letter of resignation. In the first of five vitriolic essays "Lucius" charged that Morris had implied "that injustice is the principle of the supreme council of these United States—and . . . that as a nation we merit neither confidence nor credit." The "worst foe to our cause," he continued, could not have contributed more to its ruin. A second, even more scathing essay (*See Doc. No. 25.*), appeared on the very day Congress received the momentous news from France that the *General Washington* brought. After information about the Newburgh affair reached Philadelphia, "Lucius" also accused Morris of having driven the army to the verge of "the most desperate and dangerous commotions." Although his charges were never proven, they helped shape historians' interpretation of the Newburgh affair, the controversy over taxation and the public debt, and of the experiment with executive power. (*See Doc. No. 26 and Doc. No. 27*)

The crises confronting Congress were sufficient to enable it to approve a funding plan and send it to the states for their ratification. The plan contained a newly designed impost, still under congressional authority but with other offensive features of the impost of 1781 removed. Congress also asked the states to pass supplementary taxes of their own choosing to raise the remainder of their quotas for funding the national debt. The sense of urgency was not, however, acute enough to win the unanimous consent required to ratify it. As had the impost of 1781, the new funding plan died a slow death when it was submitted to the states. Most eventually ratified the impost, but they did not impose the supplementary taxes the revenue plan called for. Rhode Island stalled until 1786, and then voted to approve it. At that point, one hold-out remained —New York—which had ratified the impost but on terms Congress could not accept. There would be no congressionally imposed taxation under the Articles of Confederation.

With peace came the problem of disbandment. After difficult negotiations, Congress had agreed to provide the army with a bit more pay before it was sent home. It had also assured the army that every effort was being made to settle its complicated accounts so that the full amount owed to each soldier could be determined. The best Morris could do when furloughs began to be implemented in June 1783, however, was to issue another three months pay, not in cash, but in tax-anticipation notes that would not put money in the soldiers's pockets until six months after the date of issue. Few of them could afford to wait that long. Most sold their pay notes to the army contractors or other speculators who gave far less than face value in return. The army did not quietly resign itself to going home in poverty. Angry units made their displeasure known by visiting state legislatures to insist that their representatives take measures to provide them with pay. In the course of one such mutinous demonstration, the Pennsylvania line unintentionally induced Congress to flee Philadelphia and to resettle in cramped quarters in Princeton, New Jersey. As "republicans" feared it would, the army's harsh experience with the ideologically correct requisition system helped build its support for constitutional revision that would lead to a central government with power to levy taxes and collect its own revenues.

Reversals. The crises that came to a head in 1780 had allowed Congress to set aside several sacred tenets of republican ideology and to take measures designed to improve governmental effectiveness and national solvency and to meet the needs of the army. Delegates committed to reform mustered sufficient votes to allow embryonic executive power to emerge and to lay claim to a power that had hitherto been sacred to the states—taxation. In the midst of the new and very real crises of 1783, dissident delegates and states that saw themselves as defenders of republican principles began to challenge the course Congress had marked out in 1781. With the threat from the common enemy removed, they returned to policies which set state and regional priorities above national concerns, emasculated the executive departments, and frustrated the attempt to establish taxation levied and collected by the central government. With their increasing ascendancy, the struggle for the control of the Revolution entered a new phase.

CHAPTER 7

EXPERIMENTING WITH REPUBLICAN IDEOLOGY IN THE POSTWAR PERIOD: 1784–1787

The years immediately following the peace offered a time, although certainly not an ideal one, to test how effectively a nation could operate under republican principles. Even though Britain had recognized American independence, those most dedicated to revolutionary ideals did not assume that they had triumphed. For them, the fate of the Revolution still hung in the balance, a prey to the machinations of corrupt men who set their personal desires for wealth and power above the well-being of the commonwealth.

The Society of the Cincinnati. Army officers who demanded that Congress approve a plan to provide the back pay and pensions it had promised them during the war were high on the list of those republicans came to suspect of counterrevolutionary tendencies. Fears born during the Newburgh crisis intensified when the army officers established the Society of the Cincinnati, a national fraternal organization with chapters in each state, in June 1783. Members had badges and ribbons similar to decorations worn by European nobility and their constitution specified that they could pass on their membership to their eldest sons or other designated male heirs.

The Society was named for a Roman statesman who had been entrusted with dictatorial power when the Roman Republic was in crisis—power that he had ceded back as soon as he had rescued the state from danger—but this did not relieve anxiety about it. Pensions, decorations, and a "hereditary peerage," some charged, amounted to an American military aristocracy, a blatant violation of the Articles of Confederation, which expressly forbad titles of nobility. The Society was further faulted for opening a branch for French officers, many of them nobles, who had fought for American independence. Certain American and French civilians who had served the cause were also admitted as honorary members. Among them were the past and present French ministers to the United States, whose influence republicans had long feared, and Robert Morris, who was equally unpopular in republican circles. Washington agreed to serve as the national society's president and persuaded it to drop the provision for inheritable membership but this did not satisfy critics, especially since some of the state societies failed to adopt the change. The Society, republican keepers of the Revolution were convinced, was well enough organized to elect many of its members to Congress and to state legislatures. Thus, it could well serve as the entering wedge by which the forces of aristocracy and despotism would come to dominate and alter the central government and destroy the liberties the Revolution had been fought to preserve. (*See Doc. No. 28.*)

Congress and the Executive in the Postwar Period. Congress's undignified flight from Pennsylvania soldiers who had fought loyally under its banner called attention to the increasing impotence of the central government. Congress itself began to disintegrate. Attendance was so poor that serious issues were left unattended. It was unable to muster a quorum in time to ratify the definitive peace treaty and return it to Britain on schedule. Those delegates who had been most dedicated to enlarging its powers left, either because they had wearied of the struggle or because they had served three consecutive years and were not eligible for reelection. Delegates who were committed to republican ideology dominated the decision-making process.

Most symbolic of Congress's feeble authority and loss of prestige and effectiveness was its decision not to return to Philadelphia after the mutiny came to an end. Pennsylvania's leading citizens appealed for its return, but the delegates chose instead to remain in cramped, uncomfortable quarters in Princeton throughout the summer heat. When they reconvened, it would be in Annapolis. Then, to spread the benefits of serving as seat of government more equally, Congress moved itself to Trenton, New Jersey, and finally, to New York City, where it remained until it was superceded by the first Congress elected under the United States Constitution.

Philadelphia had become a symbol of the evils that might destroy the noblest achievements of the Revolution. It was large, expensive, and worldly, the home of the Bank of North America and the temple of the commercial ethic. This made it convenient, republicans charged, for self-interested men to manipulate the power of the central government to maximize their own gain at public expense. They argued that Congress should permanently remove itself from urban corruption and the influence of the Financier and the French minister. It should, they suggested, either seat itself inland or keep itself on the move. A "perambulatory Congress," David Howell asserted, favored republicanism while a "permanent" one tended to "inveterate power—Aristocracy—and Monarchy."[1] Substantial inconveniences attended adherence to these principles. The moves suggested instability, led to increased absence by delegates, and further impeded the conduct of official business. Most of the public records remained in Philadelphia. Communication between Congress and those government officers still exercising their functions was plagued by distance and delay. Representatives of foreign powers grumbled about having to travel from Philadelphia or move their residences if they wanted to communicate with Congress directly. One of them warned that foreign aid might not follow Congress if it moved too far away from commercial centers.

The embryonic executive also evaporated. There was a long interregnum with no credible regent in charge. The executive heads of both the foreign affairs and war department had resigned by December 1783. Underlings carried on department business as best they could during the months before they were replaced. The Financier remained in office in caretaker capacity to raise the funds to cover the army's pay notes and other debts contracted during his administration. He submitted his final resignation on November 1, 1784. Although Congress was to have begun its session the previous day, only seven delegates had appeared. A month passed before it took formal action on his letter. Those delegates who had most strongly opposed his administration were determined to prevent any single individual from exercising the authority Congress had conferred on him. They agreed on a familiar alternative—a treasury board—but it took them more than a year to reorganize the treasury department and longer to make appointments.

The regulations Congress finally approved significantly limited the discretionary powers of the three commissioners who constituted the new treasury board. The republican architects of the new system wanted men whose only concern was public service and intended to discourage those who saw appointment as a path to wealth and power. To this end, they provided the commissioners with only modest salaries and required them to post high performance bonds. Few public-spirited men were eager to take on treasury duties under these terms, and it was not until July 1785 that all three positions were filled.

[1] *LDC*, 21: 225.

Morris's most strident critics had argued that the states would gladly comply with Congress's requisitions once he no longer headed the treasury department. They soon learned that the states were no more willing or able to pay their quotas under the new treasury administration than they had been previously. The postwar economic depression made it difficult for them to satisfy their obligations to Congress, but many lacked the will to try. Finally, in February 1786, New Jersey announced outright that it would not comply with a requisition Congress had approved the previous September. Its blatant refusal was one of the factors which prompted Congress to consider amending the Articles.

Revenue from the sale of western lands was far below the expectations of those who had believed it would easily pay the war debt. Since some states had not approved the revenue plan Congress had submitted to them in the spring of 1783, Congress was left without any reliable source of income. Inevitably, it defaulted on its debt to France. More and more states began to pay off the public debt owed to their own citizens, not in specie but in one form or another of paper money whose value never remained at par. There was widespread indifference to the just claims of "foreign" creditors the states' plans ignored. By paying off their own citizens the states lessened the need for a central government and eroded one of the bonds that kept them united. Eventually more and more delegates of all political persuasions reached the same conclusions the British ministries and American advocates of the impost had drawn—that a revenue system based on suggested levels of contribution and voluntary compliance would not generate enough income to hold a nation together and support the operations it had to undertake. Men who had been most reluctant to concede any meaningful powers to a central government now confronted the prospect that the American "league" would disintegrate unless they moved to strengthen it.

Loyalists and British Creditors. There were diplomatic difficulties to be confronted as well. At the start of the peace negotiations Britain had insisted that properties confiscated from loyalists should be restored. It had also attempted to obtain broad immunity for them from prosecution for whatever "part" they had taken in the war. When the American commissioners resisted these high demands, Britain settled for a clause which pledged Congress to urge the states to provide for the restitution of all loyalist estates, rights and properties. Congress fulfilled this obligation when it proclaimed its ratification of the definitive peace treaty on January 14, 1784. State governments, however, were finding it difficult to pay debts to their own citizens. They had no funds to compensate those who had recently been enemies in their midst and there was no public support for doing so. Antiloyalist passions raged in some locations. Even those British sympathizers who had *not* been actively belligerent feared criminal prosecution and loss of their civil rights and property—with good reason. The total value of holdings expropriated from loyalists *after* the war ran high. Some found ways to remain in the country, salvage assets and reintegrate themselves into American life. Many, perhaps 80,000 persons, chose exile, fully realizing that the treaty which promised to safeguard them against "future loss or damage" offered no substantial protection at all because Congress had no power to enforce its recommendation on the states.

The treaty also stipulated that creditors on either side should meet with "no lawful impediment to the recovery of the full value of bona fide prewar debts in sterling money." The ink on it was barely dry before Virginia began to discuss suspending executions on judgments for debts contracted before the war. Many planters owed large sums to British merchants. They had not yet recovered from the economic devastation wrought by the British army and been robbed by it of many of their slaves. Thus, they argued, they were not in a position to pay debts to anyone, let alone their recent oppressors, and they complained vociferously that the treaty had not taken their plight into account. Congress was powerless to prevent states from passing laws that delayed or impeded debt collections. It could do nothing when Britain used American treatment of loyalists and creditors as a pretext for refusing to evacuate strategic forts in the northwest and return slaves to their masters.

Congress and the West. Soon after it ratified the peace treaty, Congress put its shoulder to the task of developing a system for the orderly settlement of western lands and the establishment of republican governments there. On March 1, 1784, three years to the day after the Articles of Confederation had gone into effect, Thomas Jefferson presented a committee proposal for administering the western territories democratically—not as colonies but as future states. (*See Doc. No. 29.*) Congress approved Jefferson's Ordinance with few revisions but never put it into effect. In 1787, it approved the Northwest Ordinance, which superceded Jefferson's plan but incorporated some of its provisions. The new ordinance gave Congress significantly more control over the governments that administered territories before they were admitted to statehood than Jefferson's had. It did not, however, alter the policy of allowing new territories to emerge from colonial status to statehood. The rejection of colonialism ranks among the most significant and praiseworthy decisions made by Congress in the postwar period.

Indians. Neither the British nor the Americans did themselves honor by the way they treated those who had occupied the conflict's no man's lands: Indians and slaves. Britain did not insist that its Indian allies had to be represented in the peace negotiations and did not protect them in the peace treaty. Americans had begun the war by trying to convince the Iroquois and other Indian nations that their interests would be best served by staying out of their family quarrel. While this may have been true in some respects, in others it was not. One of the first postwar projects Congress undertook was to negotiate cessions from Indian nations that claimed lands on the frontiers of white settlement. It lacked the funds to maintain a credible military force there, however, and could not move quickly enough to keep settlers off Indian lands until it had concluded treaties that "extinguished" their claims. Sporadic, vicious warfare was the result. Since Indian populations were on the decline, victories against the dynamically expanding European settlers came at a cost they could not afford.

Americans' indifference to Indian claims was born both of land hunger and of republican principles. Those who had been ruined by the war, many of them veterans who had been given land bounties, hoped to build better futures for themselves in the west. Speculators were eager for the profits the new territory promised. Foes of the congressional funding plan expected that revenues from land sales would pay the war debt, thereby reducing or eliminating the need for taxation by the central government. Jefferson's Plan of Government of 1784, which so carefully prescribed a democratic form of government for white settlers, gave no consideration to the rights of Indians. The Northwest Ordinance of 1787 stated that neither lands nor property should ever be taken from the Indians "without their consent," and that they should "never be invaded or disturbed," unless Congress authorized "just and lawful wars" against them. "Just" wars were a common pretext throughout the Americas for depriving Indians of their lives, liberty, and property. The new nation availed itself of war or negotiation as the case required.

The American Revolution and Social Change. The acknowledged concerns which formed the original substance of the independence movement were largely political and economic, not social. The principal beneficiaries of the victory against Great Britain were white males who found new political and economic opportunities opened to them. Nevertheless, because they had embedded the discussion of their grievances in a rhetoric of liberty and natural rights, Americans had to confront the broader implications of the ideology which sustained their struggle. Eventually, groups which in one way or another constituted disadvantaged minorities—nonestablished churches, slaves, and women—found their status improved.

Freedom of Religion. Many of the thirteen colonies had initially been strongly identified with one denomination or other, usually either Anglican or Congregational Protestantism. During the eighteenth century, however, immigration and reform movements that challenged the traditional churches produced both a remarkable diversity of religious belief and a high level of religious indifference. Nevertheless, one or another Protestant denomination was "established"—given state support and protection—in many of the thirteen colonies. Nonbelievers and religious minorities, Catholics, Jews, and members of Protestant evangelical sects, suffered under various civil disabilities. They might be taxed to support churches of which they were not members, or be prevented from holding office or exercising other civil rights by law or because they would not take oaths which violated their consciences. Their failure to join established churches left them open to suspicion that they did not share the community's values. Even Pennsylvania, whose bill of rights (1776), protected freedom of conscience and worship, required delegates to the assembly to acknowledge that both the Old and New Testament were divinely inspired. Jews would have to wait until Pennsylvania revised its constitution (1790) before they qualified to hold office in the state.

American challenges to Britain's political authority suggested that the logic which gave one church preferred status over all others should also be questioned. Once independence was declared, the Anglican church, whose titular head was the British monarch and a majority of whose clergy was loyalist, was soon disestablished. Consensus began to build in favor of equal treatment for all Protestants and of greater toleration for Catholics and Jews. After the war was over, Thomas Jefferson and James Madison led a trailblazing debate in Virginia about the proper relationship between church and state. Their campaign to end public support for any religion in Virginia evolved, with ratification of the Bill of Rights in 1791, into national acceptance of complete separation of church and state.

Slavery. The war had brought more suffering than benefit to slaves who had attempted to secure their freedom by seeking protection from or joining the British army. Lord Dunmore eventually abandoned many of the slaves he had recruited in Virginia in 1775. Others were sold back into bondage in the Caribbean. While the British formed some of their black recruits into fighting units, most served more in slave than in soldierly capacity by performing the heavy manual labor of building fortifications or by doing menial chores. Many of the slaves Cornwallis liberated in the course of his march through the Carolinas to Virginia were left to die of starvation as the siege of British positions at Yorktown intensified. The most fortunate were the approximately 5,000 persons whom the British evacuated from New York to Nova Scotia at the war's end in violation of the peace treaty, which required British forces to withdraw "without . . . carrying away any negroes or other property of the American inhabitants." Their removal led to a string of appeals from prominent patriots for assistance in recovering their "property." Slaves also served in the Continental army. Many of the northern states enlisted free blacks and slaves into both integrated and segregated units. Their masters received bounties in compensation. Southern states were more reluctant to put guns in the hands of slaves, and planters were more likely to attempt to renege on the promises of freedom offered as an inducement to enlist.

Both slaves and patriot leaders recognized that slavery could not be reconciled with the ideal of liberty. Henry Laurens, whose substantial fortune depended both on the slave trade and slave labor, blamed Parliament for establishing it, and Englishmen for enslaving the men and women he held. Yet, in a letter of August 14, 1776, he could tell his son that he abhorred slavery and intended to move cautiously to bring it to an end. James Madison found himself faced with the same dilemma as he prepared to return to Virginia at the end of his term as delegate to Congress. The manservant who had accompanied him to Philadelphia, he feared, could not be reintegrated into Virginia's slave system, and so he arranged to leave him in Pennsylvania. (*See Doc. No. 30.*)

Revolutionary principles were not powerful enough to raise slaves to the status of citizen even if they had borne arms against the British. Slavery was most easily abolished in those areas where it was least important to the structure of the local economy. Court challenges ended it in Massachusetts and New Hampshire. In other northern and middle Atlantic states, abolition was gradually achieved by allowing masters to hold those slaves they presently owned but denying them the right to their slaves' progeny and by forbidding them to purchase others. The Northwest Ordinance of 1787 reinstated the ban on slavery Congress had deleted from the Ordinance of 1784 except as punishment for crimes. It opened the door to future conflict, however, by allowing fugitive slaves to be apprehended there and reclaimed by their owners.

Most leaders in the Chesapeake and southern colonies believed it would be impossible to restore plantations to productivity and repair the economic devastation of the war without slave labor. Abolitionist impulses were further restrained in the south by fear of slave insurrections and by the endemic debts which limited owners' ability to liquidate their assets by manumission. Guilt induced by these dilemmas was somewhat lessened by a belief that the demise of slavery was, if not immediate, eventually inevitable. Finally, slavery's divisive potential was clearly recognized as threatening to the union. Given the choice between preserving its existence and liberating slaves, most leaders of the Revolution unhesitatingly chose a course that favored the union.

Women. Few patriots, women or men, expected the Revolution to improve the legal or civil status of women. One of those who came closest was Abigail Adams, who, in 1776, asked her husband, John, to "Remember the Ladies" as he helped write a code of laws for the nation whose independence was soon to be declared. Abigail was most interested in revising laws which gave husbands virtually unlimited power over their wives, not in enlarging their political spheres. Nevertheless, she suggested that, if women were ignored, they would not hold themselves "bound by any Laws" in which they had no "voice, or Representation." John made light of what he termed her "extraordinary" proposal and claimed that male dominance was more fictional than real.[2]

Abigail's request, however, seems to have influenced a broader discus-

---

[2] L. H. Butterfield, et al., eds. *Adams Family Correspondence*, 6 vols. (Cambridge, MA: Belknap Press of Harvard University Press, 1963–1993), 1: 370, 382.

sion on citizenship and voter qualifications John had soon afterwards with a friend, James Sullivan. (*See Doc. No. 31.*) Both men agreed that the only moral foundation of government was the consent of the governed. Adams, however, argued that a line had to be drawn between those who were and were not capable of voting responsibly. Among the latter he listed women. Hindsight might have forced him to acknowledge that the war had given "the Ladies" the opportunity to demonstrate many of the qualifications he considered essential: experience in the business of life, and in military and civic affairs. In the prewar period, women had advanced the patriot cause by demonstrating against British authority and supporting boycotts. Their efforts to craft domestic replacements for goods no longer being imported was vital to the economy. Once the fighting began, women managed family farms and businesses in the absence of their husbands. They formed voluntary organizations to raise funds for soldiers. Women hired to sew clothing for the army suffered from the government's inability to pay them. Some were forced by poverty to serve as camp followers. Others were more closely associated with military operations as couriers and spies.

Women had also become more and more acquainted with public affairs and more inclined to debate them. After the war, Mercy Otis Warren, an accomplished author and friend of the Adamses, drew on her own knowledge and experience of the Revolution and her contacts with some of its leading participants to publish an intensely political account of the great struggle for independence. In the end, however, state legislatures chose not to consider women's qualifications. As had John Adams, they acted as though any attempt to alter the traditional composition of the electorate would open a dangerous Pandora's box. Three states, New York, Pennsylvania, and North Carolina, permitted free black males to vote. New Jersey alone allowed women to do so, but disenfranchised them in 1807.

Women who could afford to relax after struggling to keep their families and family enterprises functioning during the war apparently welcomed the opportunity to concentrate on the domestic sphere once it was over. Most did not contend generally or vigorously for the right to contribute directly to the formulation of public policy. At a time when the churches' ability to serve as spokesmen for civic responsibility was lessened by disestablishment and religious indifference, women appreciated themselves and were valued by their husbands and sons for their ability to inculcate and sustain the ideals of "republican virtue." This role gave them a stronger claim on an education that prepared them for this serious responsibility.

Regulation of Commerce. As soon as hostilities were over, the new nation was inundated with imports. Congress was unable either to control the flood because it had no power to regulate trade or to derive any revenue from it because the states had not yet acted on the impost (tariff), proposal it had only recently submitted to them. The American market was so overstocked with foreign goods that prices fell below their original cost, bankrupting merchants on both sides of the Atlantic. Because the war had disrupted production, Americans had little to sell abroad and few ships of their own to take it there. They paid for what they could in cash, leaving the economy as much strapped for specie as it had been during the war.

The Treaty of Paris had given the Americans all they could have reasonably hoped for in terms of boundaries and fishing rights. One critical area of concern remained to be resolved: commerce. Independence deprived the United States of its privileged trading position within the British Empire and neither France nor Spain offered any significant concessions to fill the void. British and American peace commissioners had agreed to deal with commercial issues in a separate treaty. Lord Shelburne, the effective head of the British government, hoped to regain the new nation's affection and weaken its ties to France by pursuing a policy of reconciliation. He appeared to be prepared to grant a generous commercial treaty that left Americans with most of the privileges they had enjoyed as members of the Empire. His government did not, however, survive the British public's disgust at the concessions he had already made in the Treaty of Paris and prospects for a commercial treaty fell with it.

The driving force of the American economy was foreign trade—with the British Isles, the West Indies, southern Europe, and Spanish and Portuguese islands off the west coast of Africa. Independence altered the conditions on which the first two would be conducted. The prized objective American negotiators sought was the right to ship American goods on American vessels to the British West Indies on the same terms that they had enjoyed before the war. This, however, was far more than Britain's new coalition government was willing to grant. The United States's ability to bargain was weakened considerably when individual states threw open their ports to trade with Britain soon after the end of hostilities was proclaimed and before any concessions had been obtained.

A powerful pamphlet written in 1783 by John Baker Holroyd, Lord Sheffield, argued persuasively that Britain should pursue a restrictive trade policy. The United States, Sheffield asserted, had sought and won independence and should now be treated like any other foreign nation under British mercantile law. Its products should not have their former privileged status in British markets nor should they have unhindered access to the British West Indies. France, he observed, had refused to open her West Indian colonies to the United States in the Treaty of Commerce of 1779, and it would be foolish for Britain to do so now. (*See Doc. No. 32.*)

Sheffield argued that Britain should carefully preserve her Navigation Act, which required goods imported from foreign markets to be carried on British vessels. The Act had, he said, been responsible for the development of Britain's naval power, her greatest strength. Sheffield believed that there was no need for Britain to fear American retaliation because the Articles of Confederation gave Congress no authority to regulate trade. He correctly predicted that the individual states would not be able to agree on a common response, and that Americans would be unable to develop manufacturing rapidly enough to produce alternatives to British products in the near future. The former colonists, he was sure, would still buy British goods because they were the best and cheapest available and because only British merchants could provide the extensive credit American merchants needed. Therefore, he concluded, it would not be necessary to make concessions with regard to the "carrying trade" to win back American consumers.

Sheffield's arguments generally prevailed. A liberal trade bill went down to defeat and the king and his council assumed responsibility for regulating commerce with the United States. On July 2, 1783, they issued an order which enumerated (and therefore limited), the American products that could be imported to the British West Indies and the products of the British West Indies that could be imported to the United States. Furthermore, the trade had to be carried on vessels built and owned by British citizens; American ships were allowed to carry unmanufactured American produce only to ports in the British Isles.

The Order in Council was a severe blow to American aspirations for a sweeping change in the terms on which the commerce with European colonies in the Americas was conducted. Free trade, as described by the model treaty plan of 1776, would, they hoped, help them avoid a morass of debt and economic dependence. The United States had a negative balance of trade with Europe. Without the profits earned through the carrying trade and the specie the West Indies trade produced, Americans would continue to suffer the crippling currency and balance of payments problems that had crimped economic activity before and during the war. With the most important avenues of legal trade closed to them, the development of American commercial and maritime enterprise would be sharply limited.

During the war, France and Spain had relaxed bans on trade between the United States and their possessions in the Caribbean to ensure that military forces stationed there could be adequately supplied. Monopoly interests in both nations were, however, eager to reclaim their privileges. Soon after peace was declared, French and Spanish colonial governors were ordered to shut their ports to American trade. The best endeavors of American policy makers and negotiators failed to persuade any of the three major powers to lift restrictions on American trade with their Caribbean colonies. Americans were, thus, forced to continue to do after the war what they had become expert at doing before it: they smuggled until the wars generated by the French Revolution prompted European governments to lift restrictions once again on trade with the West Indies.

Amending the Articles. Certain American policy makers, however, believed that European trade restrictions would do exactly what Sheffield claimed they could not—convince the states to give Congress the power to regulate trade. Postwar experience persuaded many Americans that Congress had to be given that power. Various states informed their delegates that they were willing to see the Articles amended so that the United States could pass uniform regulations to retaliate against foreign commercial restrictions. Some had enacted their own retaliatory duties, only to see their trade move to the ports of states which did not have them. Congress was encouraged by what seemed to be growing sentiment in favor of a centralized response. In April 1784 it sent the states two proposed amendments to the Articles of Confederation. If approved, they would have given Congress the power to retaliate against foreign nations that had not concluded commercial treaties with the United States by preventing their merchants from "carrying" goods to her on their own vessels. Eventually, all states granted Congress some power to regulate trade, but, as in the case of the revenue amendments, the variations in their acts could not be reconciled. Progress toward ratification was troubled by sectional rivalries and, once again, by fears that any movement to amend the Articles would open the door to a flood of changes which would eventually remove all protection against arbitrary power and self interest.

Congress was also confronted with a series of troublesome boundary and frontier issues, involving both Britain and Spain. Its lack of authority over the states and its inability to control settlement on the frontier presented diplomatic dilemmas it could not resolve. There was no consensus on how to find a solution to any of the broad range of problems it confronted. By 1786, Congress was concerned enough about its inability to deal with pressing national revenue and commercial problems to appoint a committee to consider remedies. The committee suggested amending the Articles to give Congress power to regulate foreign and interstate commerce and to penalize states that were delinquent in complying with revenue requisitions. It recommended lowering the number of states required to approve revenue amendments from thirteen to eleven. It also proposed creating an embryonic federal court with jurisdiction over federal officials, foreign relations, and commercial and revenue regulations. Congress considered these recommendations and decided there was no chance whatever that the states would approve them, so it did not even send the amendments out for their consideration. (*See Doc. No. 33.*)

Virginia responded to the deadlock by inviting all the states to send delegates to a special convention held at Annapolis in September 1786. Nine agreed to do so, but the twelve delegates in attendance when the conference opened represented only five states. This poor showing fell far short of the unanimous accord required to grant Congress the power to regulate commerce. Instead, the delegates, led by Alexander Hamilton, suggested that Congress should invite all states to send representatives to a convention that would consider broad revisions to the Articles of Confederation.

Shays's Rebellion. Thomas Paine had contemplated the prospects for amending the Articles before the postwar crisis fully unfolded and had judged that "*the country was not yet wrong enough to be put right.*"[3] Other observers had predicted that failure to deal comprehen-

---

[3] Philip S. Foner, ed., *The Complete Writings of Thomas Paine*, 2 vols. (New York: The Citadel Press, 1945), 2: 914.

sively and justly with the debt would erode the moral fabric of the new republic. By the mid-1780s, it was obvious that things were now very wrong on many fronts. The economy staggered under the weight of indebtedness, specie shortage and commercial dislocation. Many states attempted to cope with these problems by issuing some form of paper money. Massachusetts, however, refused to do this. Its legislature imposed heavy taxes in specie. Debtors and tax delinquents were prosecuted, their properties seized, and those whose assets were not sufficient to cover their obligations went to jail. These stresses exacerbated the political cleavage between people who lived by frontier agriculture on the fringes of a specie economy, who bore a disproportionate share of the tax burden, and those more closely tied to the coastal world of transatlantic trade.

In the late summer of 1786, embers of discontent burst into open flame. Fifty towns in Hampshire County (western Massachusetts) protested that their concerns had been ignored by the legislature which had just adjourned in Boston. They met in convention and criticized the structure and functioning of the state government, court, and tax system, and the salaries paid to government officials. They also instructed their representatives to support issuing paper money that their creditors would be legally bound to accept in payment of their debts. (*See Doc. No. 34.*) Bands of armed men closed courts to prevent foreclosure actions. The disturbances spread throughout western Massachusetts. In September, debt-plagued Daniel Shays, who had worked his way up from enlisted man to the rank of captain in the Continental army, led 500 armed rebels to Springfield, where the Massachusetts Supreme Court was in session, and forced it to adjourn. Other court closings followed, and more recruits joined Shays's band. It was not until January 1787 that Massachusetts troops under Benjamin Lincoln, former secretary at war, dispersed the rebels and brought those who were apprehended to trial.

Many of the new nation's outstanding leaders saw the revolution against Great Britain as an opportunity to establish a virtuous nation. In their minds, the most worthy citizens were responsible, hardy, disinterested, God-fearing, self-sufficient men. Those who were concerned primarily with the pursuit of wealth and power, they considered, were inclined to "aristocracy" and thereby given to corruption and influence-peddling. Throughout the years, they had fought to safeguard the nation they were in the process of creating from the sinister designs of such men.

Shays's Rebellion showed them another enemy in their midst, lower on the social echelon and equally if not more to be feared. Many Shaysites were veterans who had been forced by poverty to sell their pay notes for a pittance to speculators and who found themselves deeply entangled in the web of debt and high taxes that the war had saddled them with. Worries about such folk were not limited to Massachusetts; New Hampshire had already had to call out its militia to disperse a mob bent on persuading the legislature to issue paper money. Widespread depression heightened fears that Shays's rebellion would ignite similar disturbances in other states. (*See Doc. No. 35.*) Some republicans who had been alarmed at the prospect that the central government might gain and use the power to tax and raise a standing army to establish tyrannical rule now began to worry that there was no force capable of preventing rebellious debtors from overthrowing the state governments they had so carefully established and replacing them with chaos, anarchy, or popular despotism. When pacified Shaysites followed the advice they had been given and sent more representatives to the Massachusetts legislature, many republicans also began to discover the possibility that a central government might be needed to check the excesses of state legislatures that might favor debtors over creditors by passing "unjust" laws. Some of the most persistent adversaries of a strong central government found reason to reconsider their positions.

Jefferson had written in the Declaration of Independence that, whenever any form of government did not realize the objectives for which it was established it was the right of the people "to alter or to abolish it, and to institute new government, laying its foundation on such principles and organizing its powers in such form, as to them shall seem most likely to effect their safety and happiness." Days before Congress approved these principles, John Adams had defined a less universal, less revolutionary body politic in response to James Sullivan's proposal for revising voter qualifications. Jefferson did not criticize the Shaysites. Mercy Otis Warren, a member of the Adams circle still firmly committed to republican ideology recognized that some of the rebels were innocent victims of the war and the depression—some, but not all. Others, she charged, had impoverished themselves by engaging in speculative adventures or by greedily purchasing imported luxuries. British emissaries, she believed, were everywhere, sowing discord and eroding men's faith in their governments and in one another. In the end, however, she found the ultimate explanation for Shays's rebellion and similar "commotions" in other parts of the country in "discontents artificially wrought up, by men who wished for a more strong and splendid government."[4]

As the postwar political crisis deepened, it was uncertain which interpretation of it would be accepted as valid and which vision of the nation would prevail. Few saw the rebellion as Jefferson did—as the Revolution renewing itself. Some continued to hold, as Warren did, that the nation suffered from the moral weakness of its citizens and the sinister connivings of its domestic and foreign enemies. More agreed with Adams that the most responsible portion of the citizenry had to be made to predominate.

The dissolution of the embryonic executive, the emasculation of Congress, unsolved commercial and diplomatic problems, and the emergence of "aristocratic" and popular forces which threatened the established order made space on the public stage for actors who were determined to establish a nation that was capable of defending its interests against domestic and foreign threats and of improving its condition. These men were about to take the Revolution into their own hands and give it a shape more congenial to their purposes. They looked beyond military and popular unrest and saw it for what it was, a symptom of larger problems. They argued that debts which were unprovided for destroyed the social fabric, that the extreme federalism which left the central government without the powers it needed to collect revenues, pay foreign and domestic debts, enforce treaties, and regulate commerce made nationhood a fiction that could barely be sustained. They persuaded Congress, state legislatures, delegates to the convention called for Philadelphia in the fall of 1787, and thereafter state ratifying conventions and ultimately the American people, to consider whether the radical ideals which had given birth to independence were, in fact, adequate to direct their lives now that they were a nation.

---

[4] Mercy Otis Warren, *History of the Rise, Progress and Termination of the American Revolution*, 2 vols. (Indianapolis: Liberty*Classics*, 1988), 2: 651.

CONCLUSION AND EPILOGUE

On February 21, 1787, three weeks after Shays's Rebellion was brought to an end, Congress approved a resolution calling on the states to send delegates to a convention whose purpose was to revise the Articles of Confederation. Two months later, fifty-five delegates from eleven states (Rhode Island sent none and New Hampshire's delegates did not arrive until July), gathered in Philadelphia. There, they set themselves to the task of achieving a goal first envisioned by Benjamin Franklin in the 1750s. They wished, they said, to "form a more perfect Union, establish Justice, insure domestic Tranquility, provide for the common defence, promote the general Welfare, and secure the Blessings of Liberty" to themselves and their posterity.

At the convention, the delegates continued to grapple with the same fundamental question that had precipitated the conflict with Great Britain—a question to which the Revolution had not forged a satisfactory answer: what functions could properly be entrusted to a government remote from the people? Some delegates—and many Americans—felt comfortable only with a government that was close to them and local in scope. From the very start, they approached idea of a federal union with extreme caution and continued to fear that the liberty they wished above all else to preserve would be overwhelmed or suppressed by a tyrannous, oppressive, and corrupt central government. The Confederation's manifest inability to deal effectively with internal dissent and with matters of trade and diplomacy had, however, caused a number of them to ask whether a "more perfect" union was needed to remedy some of the ills that plagued their existence as a fledgling nation. Yet, they were still extremely concerned about conferring too much power on a small number of men, especially the power to tax.

Other delegates spoke for sectors of American society that were more confident—perhaps because they were better situated. They were more determined to expand their horizons than they were concerned about defending their hearths against the possibility of executive tyranny or insensitivity and oppression by a distant legislature. They believed that establishing a meaningful central government capable of doing "Justice" would enable them to fund the development of their resources, magnify their strengths and their opportunities, and secure a fuller measure of liberty's blessings to themselves and their children. They

CONCLUSION AND EPILOGUE

looked forward to building a nation that could stand as an equal among other nations. Some of them envisioned an American empire.

Early on in the deliberations, key delegates convinced themselves and then their fellows that they had to expand upon the commission they had been given—to amend the Articles of Confederation. They decided that they had to create a government from new cloth. They saw their primary function as endowing government with sufficient power, not as guaranteeing that it could do no harm to its constituents. Nevertheless, they thought very seriously about the issue of power, divided it carefully among three branches—a true and powerful executive; a legislature structured to represent the states as equal entities and in proportion to their demographic strength; and an independent judiciary which, it would be discovered, could overturn the decisions of the other two branches. They abandoned the requisition system and settled the issue of taxation once and for all: the central government they created had the power not only to contract debt, but to raise the revenues necessary to pay it off. It had the capacity to promote the common welfare and to defend national interests. It also, however, left local governance in the hands of the states. This done, they put their faith in the excellence of the constitution they had drafted.

Many of the fifty-five delegates gathered in the State House were men who had played major roles in the struggle against Great Britain from its earliest days and had been schooled by the struggle to govern a nation on republican principles. Two notables were absent: John Adams and Thomas Jefferson were representing American interests at the courts of London and Paris. Their contributions to American political and constitutional thought were, however, widely known and respected. At the very first meeting, Robert Morris rose to nominate George Washington president of the convention. He was easily elected. Benjamin Franklin, James Wilson, Gouverneur Morris, John Dickinson, James Madison, Rufus King, Elbridge Gerry, Alexander Hamilton and other eminent figures whose roles were not detailed above were also in attendance. Gerry, and Virginians Edmund Randolph and George Mason, who held the torch of republican ideology to the last, voted against the constitution that was forged after months of arduous effort and difficult compromises, even though Randolph had proposed the arrangement of powers which was largely adopted by the convention.

The delegates had learned yet another lesson from their experience with government under the Articles: they did not allow Rhode Island or any other recalcitrant state to crumble the edifice they had constructed. The new constitution provided that "The Ratification of the Conventions of nine States, shall be sufficient for the Establishment of this Constitution between the States so ratifying the Same." Ratification did not come easily in many states. "Federalists" and "Anti-Federalists" battled over the issues they had been contesting since the first Congress began to grapple with how to structure representation, distribute power, and preserve the liberties Americans had fought to preserve. People and states would not always be as virtuous as republicans expected they should be: both political conviction and private or local interests dictated how they voted on the constitution.

Finally, all states, even "other-wise minded" Rhode Island, found their way into the new and presumably "more perfect" union. The new constitution remedied the defects of the Articles of Confederation and redefined the nation which emerged independent and republican from its struggle against Great Britain. People debated its "original meaning," and amended it. It represented a temporary triumph for the forces orthodox republicans feared, but there would be no final victory for any of the competing voices and contradictory forces which were at work in revolutionary America. It did not definitively settle the old, familiar questions—about the feasibility and advisability of union, the size, powers, and functions of government.

Many Americans continued to be concerned about the tendency of central government to distribute privileges to favorites, encroach upon the prerogatives of state and local government, to tax and spend, to burden the people with debt and deprive them of their liberty and property—and about the unwillingness or inability of the states to protect minorities against the tyranny of the majority. The new constitution failed to ensure representation for Americans who, some would judge, were not properly qualified for citizenship. It did, however, provide space for the debate to continue. It endowed the majority with sufficient voice, flexibility, and confidence in the fundamental soundness of the formula developed in Philadelphia in 1787 to survive the challenge of secession, war, and the emergence of the American nation as a major industrial and imperial power.

PART II

DOCUMENTS

DOCUMENT NO. 1

BENJAMIN FRANKLIN'S "SHORT HINTS" FOR ESTABLISHING A UNION OF THE COLONIES*

Franklin had already been thinking about a union of the colonies for several years before he jotted down this sketch of a colonial union. It described a central government capable of taking initiatives to solve problems and to promote development whose operations were to be financed by a tax imposed on all the colonies.

γ γ γ

N York June 8, 1754

A Governour General

To be appointed by the King.
To be a Military man
To have a Salary from the Crown
To have a negation on all acts of the Grand Council, and carry into execution what ever is agreed on by him and that Council.

Grand Council

One member to be chosen by the Assembly of each of the smaller Colonies and two or more by each of the larger, in proportion to the Sums they pay Yearly into the General Treasury.

Members Pay

_____ Shillings sterling per Diem deuring their sitting and mileage for Travelling Expences.

Place and Time of meeting

To meet _____ times in every Year, at the Capital of each Colony in Course, unless particular circumstances and emergencies require more frequent meetings and Alteration in the Course, of places. The Governour General to judge of those circumstances &c. and call by his Writts.

---

* Leonard W. Labaree, et al., eds., *The Papers of Benjamin Franklin* (35 vols. to date, New Haven, CT, 1959-), 5: 337–338.

General Treasury

Its Fund, an Excise on Strong Liquors pretty equally drank in the Colonies or Duty on Liquor imported, or ____ shillings on each Licence of Publick House or Excise on Superfluities as Tea &c. &c. all which would pay in some proportion to the present wealth of each Colony, and encrease as that wealth encreases, and prevent disputes about the Inequality of Quotas.

To be Collected in each Colony, and Lodged in their Treasury to be ready for the payment of Orders issuing from the Governour General and Grand Council jointly.

DUTY AND POWER of the Governour General and Grand Council
 To order all Indian Treaties.

 make all Indian purchases not within proprietary Grants

 make and support new settlements by building Forts, raising and paying Soldiers to Garison the Forts, defend the frontiers and annoy the Ennemy.

 equip Grand Vessels to scour the Coasts from Privateers in time of war, and protect the Trade

 and every thing that shall be found necessary for the defence and support of the Colonies in General, and encreasing and extending their settlements &c.

 For the Expence they may draw on the fund in the Treasury of any Colony.

Manner of forming this Union

The scheme being first well considered corrected and improved by the Commissioners at Albany, to be sent home, and an Act of Parliament obtain'd for establishing it.

DOCUMENT NO. 2

THE PETITION OF ANSON COUNTY, NORTH CAROLINA*

Anson County is in south-central North Carolina, then the western frontier of settlement. The passionate tone of the appeal gives some sense of how deeply the petitioners, called Regulators, felt their political and economic grievances. The Regulators were not the first, nor would they be the last "marginalized" Americans to protest their inadequate representation at the centers of established political power and the hardships they suffered as a result. North, south, and west, before, during, and after the war, people on the fringes of a commercial economy continued to ask how much their governments deserved their loyalty and how well they represented them.

γ γ γ

[October 9, 1769]

MR. SPEAKER AND GENTLEMEN OF THE ASSEMBLY:
The Petition of the Inhabitants of Anson County, being part of the Remonstrance of the Province of North Carolina,
HUMBLY SHEWETH: That the Province in general labour under general grievances, and the Western part thereof under particular ones; which we not only see, but very sensibly feel, being crouch'd beneath our sufferings: and notwithstanding our sacred priviledges, have too long yielded ourselves slaves to remorseless oppression.—Permit us to conceive it to be our inviolable right to make known our grievances, and to petition for redress; as appears in the Bill of Rights pass'd in the reign of King Charles the first, as well as the act of Settlement of the Crown of the Revolution. We therefore beg leave to lay before you a specimen thereof that your compassionate endeavours may tend to the relief of your injured Constituents, whose distressed condition calls aloud for aid. . . .   A few of the many grievances are as follows, (viz.)

1. That the poor Inhabitants in general are much oppress'd by reason

---

* William L. Saunders (ed.). *The Colonial Records of North Carolina* (10 vols., 1886–1890). vol. VIII (1769–1771), 75–78.

of disproportionate Taxes, and those of the western Counties in particular; as they are generally in mean circumstances.

2. That no method is prescribed by Law for the payment of the Taxes of the Western Counties in produce (in lieu of a Currency) as is in other Counties within this Province; to the Peoples great oppression.

3. That Lawyers, Clerks, and other petitioners; in place of being obsequious Servants for the Country's use, are become a nuisance, as the business of the people is often transacted without the least degree of fairness, the intention of the law evaded, exorbitant fees extorted, and the sufferers left to mourn under their oppressions.

4. That an Attorney should have it in his power, either for the sake of ease or interest, or to gratify their malevolence and spite, to commence suits to what Courts he pleases, however inconvenient it may be to the Defendant: is a very great oppression.

5. That all unlawful fees taken on Indictment, where the Defendant is acquitted by his Country (however customary it may be) is an oppression.

6. That Lawyers, Clerks, and others, extorting more fees than is intended by law; is also an oppression.

7. That the violation of the King's Instructions to his delegates, their artfulness in concealing the same from him; and the great Injury the People thereby sustains: is a manifest oppression.

And for remedy whereof, we take the freedom to recommend the following mode of redress, not doubting audience and acceptance; which will not only tend to our relief, but command prayers as a duty from your humble Petitioners.

1. That at all elections each suffrage be given by Ticket & Ballot.

2. That the mode of Taxation be altered, and each person to pay in proportion to the profits arising from his Estate.

3. That no future tax be laid in Money, untill a currency is made.

4. That there may be established a Western as well as a Northern and Southern District, and a Treasurer for the same.

5. That when a currency is made it may be let out by a Loan office (on Land security) and not to be call'd in by a Tax.

6. That all debts above 40s. and under £10 be tried and determined without Lawyers, by a jury of six freeholders, impanneled by a Justice, and that their verdict be enter'd by the said Justice, and be a final judgment.

7. That the Chief Justice have no perquisites, but a Sallary only.

8. That Clerks be restricted in respect to fees, costs, and other things within the course of their office.

9. That Lawyers be effectually Barr'd from exacting and extorting fees.

15. That all Taxes in the following Counties be paid as in other Counties in the Province (i e) in the produce of the Country and that ware Houses be erected as follows (Viz.)

In Anson County at Isom Haleys Ferry Landing on PeDee River, Rowan and Orange at Cambleton in Cumberland County,

Mecklenburg at _____ on the Catawba River, and in Tryon County at _____ on _____ River.

16. That every denomination of People may marry according to their respective Mode Ceremony and custom after due publication or Licence.

17. That Doctor Benjamin Franklin or some other known patriot be appointed Agent, to represent the unhappy state of this Province to his Majesty, and to solicit the several Boards in England:—

DOCUMENT NO. 3

ADDRESS OF THE VIRGINIA HOUSE OF BURGESSES TO THE HOUSE OF LORDS*

The Virginia House of Burgesses reacted immediately to Grenville's plan to ask Parliament to impose a stamp tax on the colonies. A committee of the legislature composed addresses to the king, the House of Lords, and Commons that challenged Parliament's right to tax the colonies and argued that the only proper mode of raising a revenue was by the traditional requisition system. The Addresses sounded themes the colonists would repeat over and over: that they enjoyed full rights as Britons, that they were not and could not be represented in Parliament, that they could only be taxed by their own legislatures, and that they had met their obligations to contribute to the expenses of the last war. They also complained about the shortage of specie and the hardships imposed on them by British trade restrictions.

* John Pendleton Kennedy, ed., *Journals of the House of Burgesses of Virginia, 1761–1765.* (Richmond, VA.: The Colonial Press, E. Waddey Co., 1907), 302–304.

γ γ γ

[18 December 1764]

To the Right Honourable the Lords Spiritual and Temporal in Parliament assembled:

The Memorial of the Council and Burgesses of *Virginia*, now met in General Assembly, Humbly represents,

That your Memorialists hope an Application to your Lordships, the fixed and hereditary Guardians of *British* Liberty, will not be thought improper at this Time, when Measures are proposed subversive, as they conceive, of that Freedom which all Men, especially those who derive their Constitution from *Britain*, have a Right to enjoy; and they flatter themselves that your Lordships will not look upon them as Objects so unworthy your Attention as to regard any Impropriety in the Form or Manner of their Application, for your Lordships Protection of their just and undoubted Rights as *Britons*.

It cannot be Presumption in your Memorialists to call themselves by this distinguished Name, since they are descended from *Britons* who left their native Country to extend its Territory and Dominion, and who happily for *Britain*, and as your Memorialists once thought for themselves too, effected this Purpose. As our Ancestors brought with them every Right and Privilege they could with Justice claim in their Mother Kingdom, their Descendents may conclude they cannot be deprived of those Rights without Injustice.

Your Memorialists conceive it to be a fundamental Principle of the *British* Constitution, without which Freedom can no Where exist, that the People are not subject to any Taxes but such as are laid on them by their own Consent, or by those who are legally appointed to represent them: Property must become too precarious for the Genius of a free People which can be taken from them at the Will of others, who cannot know what Taxes such People can bear, or the easiest Mode of raising them; and who are not under that Restraint, which is the greatest Security against a burthensome Taxation, when the Representatives themselves must be affected by every Tax imposed on the People.

Your Memorialists are therefore led into an humble Confidence that your Lordships will not think any Reason sufficient to support such a Power in the *British* Parliament, where the Colonies cannot be represented; a Power never before constitutionally assumed, and which if they have a Right to exercise on any Occasion must necessarily establish this melancholy Truth, that the Inhabitants of the Colonies are the Slaves of *Britons*, from whom they are descended, and from whom they might expect every Indulgence that the Obligations of Interest and Affection can entitle them to.

Your Memorialists have been invested with the Right of taxing their own People from the first Establishment of a regular Government in the Colony, and Requisitions have been constantly made to them by their Sovereigns on all Occasions when the Assistance of the Colony was thought necessary to preserve the *British* Interest in *America;* from whence they must conclude they cannot now be deprived of a Right they have so long enjoyed, and which they have never forfeited.

The Expenses incurred during the last War, in Compliance with the Demands on this Colony by our late and present most gracious Sovereigns, have involved us in a Debt of near Half a Million; a Debt not likely to decrease under the continued Expense we are at in providing for the Security of the People against the Incursions of our savage Neighbours, at a Time when the low state of our Staple Commodity, the total Want of Specie, and the late Restrictions upon the Trade of the Colonies, render the Circumstances of the People extremely distressful, and which, if Taxes are accumulated upon them by the *British* Parliament, will make them truly deplorable.

Your Memorialists cannot suggest to themselves any Reason why they should not still be trusted with the Property of their People, with whose Abilities, and the least burthensome Mode of taxing (with great Deference to the superior Wisdom of Parliament) they must be best acquainted.

Your Memorialists hope they shall not be suspected of being actuated on this Occasion by any Principles but those of the purest Loyalty and Affection as they always endeavoured by their Conduct to demonstrate that they consider their Connexions with *Great Britain,* the Seat of Liberty, as their greatest Happiness.

The Duty they owe to themselves and their Posterity lays your Memorialists under the Necessity of endeavouring to establish their Constitution upon its proper Foundation; and they do most humbly pray your Lordships to take this Subject into your Consideration with the Attention that is due to the Well being of the Colonies, on which the Prosperity of *Great Britain* does in a great Measure depend.

DOCUMENT NO. 4

RESISTANCE TO THE STAMP ACT*

Henry Laurens was a wealthy merchant and planter who had great stature in his community. Although he had strong ties to Britain, he became an important leader in South Carolina's movement toward independence and held many important positions in its government after 1775. In 1777, he was elected to Congress and soon afterwards Congress elected him its president. Common folk who would ordinarily have deferred to a man of his rank did not, however, hesitate to investigate a charge that he had agreed to distribute stamped paper.

γ γ γ

Henry Laurens to Joseph Brown

[Charles Town] 28th October 1765

Dear Sir,

. . . . I had intended to have set out upon my journey on Friday last but an unlucky circumstance that occur'd on Wednesday night the 23d has so affected Mrs. Laurens's bodily health as well as her Spirits that my presence & attention at home are become absolutely necessary. . . .

At Midnight of the said Wednesday I heard a most violent thumping & confus'd Noise at my Western door & Chamber Window, & soon distinguished the sounds of *Liberty, Liberty & Stamp'd Paper, Open your doors & let us Search your House & Cellars*. I open'd the Window, saw a croud of Men chiefly in disguise & heard the Voices & thumpings of many more on the other side, assured them that I had no Stamp'd Paper nor any connexion with stamps. When I found that no fair words would pacify them I accused them with cruelty to a poor Sick Woman far done with Child & produced Mrs. Laurens shrieking & wringing her hands adding that if there was any one Man amongst them who owed me a spite & would turn out I had a brace of Pistols at his service & would settle the dispute immediately but that it was base in such a multitude to attack a single Man. To this they replyed in general that they Loved

---

* George C. Rogers, Jr., David R. Chesnutt, Peggy. J. Clark, et al., eds. *The Papers of Henry Laurens*. 14 vols. to date, (Columbia: University of South Carolina Press, 1968–), 5: 29–31.

RESISTANCE TO THE STAMP ACT

& respected me, would not hurt me nor my property but that they were sent even by some of my seemingly best friends to search for Stamp'd Paper which they were certain was in my Custody advised me to open the door to prevent worse consequences.

Conscious of my innocence, I was pausing whether to refuse every one of their demands or barely to open the door, at which they still continued knocking as if they would have beat down the House, & to let them proceed as their rage & madness should impel them, but Mrs. Laurens's condition & her cries prompted me to open the door which in two minutes more they would have beat thro. A brace of Cutlasses across my breast was the salutation & Lights, Lights, & Search was the Cry. I presently knew several of them under their thickest disguise of Soot, Sailors habits, slouch hats, &Ca. & to their great surprize called no less than nine of them by name & fixed my eye so attentively upon other faces as to discover at least the same number since. They made a very superficial search indeed or rather no search at all in my House, Counting House, Cellar, & Stable. After that farce was over they insisted upon my taking what they called "A Bible Oath" that I knew not where the Stamp'd Paper was which I absolutely refused not failing to confirm my denials with Damns of equal weight with their own, a language which I only had learned from them, they threatned then to carry me away to some unknown place & punish me. I replyed they might if they would, they had strength enough but I would be glad to have it attempted by any Man alone, either among them or of those who they said had sent them. When they found this attempt fruitless a softer Oath, as they thought, was propounded. I must say "May God disinherit me from the Kingdom of Heaven" If I knew where the Stamped Papers were. This I likewise premptorily refused & added that I would not have one word extorted from my Mouth. That I had voluntarily given my word & honour but would not suffer even that to pass my Lips by compulsion, further that If I had once accepted of a trust they might Stamp me to Powder but should not make me betray it, that my sentiments of the Stamp Act was well known. I had openly declared myself an Enemy to it & would give & do a great deal to procure its annihilation but that I could not think they pursued a right method to obtain a repeal, &Ca., &Ca. Some times they applauded, some times cursed me at length one of them holding my Shoulders said they loved me & every Body would Love me if I did not hold way with one Governor Grant. This provoked me not a little as it exhibited to me the Cloven foot of a certain malicious Villain acting behind the Curtain who could be reached only by suspicion. I answer'd that if he meant that I corresponded with Governor Grant & esteem'd him as a Gentleman I acknowledged with pleasure that I did *"hold way"* as he called it with him, that I knew nothing in Governor Grants conduct or principles as a Gentleman that could shame my acquaintance with him, that if Governor Grant had any criminal schemes or projects he was too prudent to trust me with his secrets, but in one word for all Gentlemen I am in your power. You are very strong & may if you please Barbicue me. I can but die, but you shall not by any force or means whatsoever compel me to renounce my friendships or to speak ill of Men that I think well of or to say or do a mean thing. This was their last effort, they praised me highly & insisted upon giving me three Cheers & then retired with God bless your honour, Good night, Colonel, We hope the poor Lady will do well, &Ca., &Ca. A Thousand other things you may believe were said & done in an hour & a quarter (the time of their visit) but the above is a fair abstract of all that is important.

Is it not amazing that such a number of Men many of them heated with Liquor & all armed with Cutlasses & Clubbs did not do one penny damage to my Garden not even to walk over a Bed & not 15/ damage to my Fence, Gate, or House?

DOCUMENT NO. 5

PHILLIS WHEATLEY'S POEM TO LORD DARTMOUTH*

Phillis Wheatley had, as her master said in a letter introducing her volume of poetry, been "brought" from Africa in 1761 as a very young girl. She rapidly learned to speak, read, and write English and then began to study Latin. Her literary achievement was so astounding that her publisher prefaced her book with testimonials stating that she was truly its author. Governor Thomas Hutchinson, Lieutenant Governor Andrew Oliver, and John Hancock were among those who signed.

* Phillis Wheatley: *Poems on Various Subjects, Religious and Moral.* By Phillis Wheatley, Negro Servant to Mr. John Wheatley, of Boston, in New England. London: Archibald Bell, 1773), 73–75.

Slavery was one of the metaphors that Americans frequently used when they charged Parliament with attempting to deprive them of their rights as Englishmen. Phillis's message to Dartmouth throws into sharp relief the disparity between the colonists' sense of their own political plight and their acceptance of her enslavement, which the testimonial described as her "disadvantage." Although she believed that slavery had brought her the benefits of Christianity and education, Phillis refers to it in much less neutral terms than her patrons do. She was freed by her master in 1773. Thereafter, she, visited London, married a black lawyer, and had several children. She died in 1784 at the age of thirty.

γ γ γ

To the Right Honourable WILLIAM, Earl of Dartmouth,
His Majesty's Principal Secretary of State for North America, &c.

[1772]

HAIL, happy day, when, smiling like the morn,
Fair *Freedom* rose *New-England* to adorn:
The northern clime beneath her genial ray,
Dartmouth, congratulates thy blissful sway:
Elate with hope her race no longer mourns,
Each soul expands, each grateful bosom burns,
While in thine hand with pleasure we behold
The silken reins, and *Freedom's* charms unfold.

Long lost to realms beneath the northern skies
She shines supreme, while hated *faction* dies:
Soon as appear'd the *Goddess* long desir'd,
Sick at the view, she languish'd and expir'd;
Thus from the splendors of the morning light
The owl in sadness seeks the caves of night.

No more, *America*, in mournful strain
Of wrongs, and grievance unredress'd complain,
No longer shall thou dread the iron chain,
Which wanton *Tyranny* with lawless hand
Had made, and with it meant t' enslave the land

Should you, my lord, while you peruse my song,
Wonder from whence my love of *Freedom* sprung,
Whence flow these wishes for the common good,
By feeling hearts alone best understood,
I, young in life, by seeming cruel fate

Was snatch'd from *Afric's* fancy'd happy seat:
What pangs excruciating must molest,
What sorrows labour in my parent's breast?
Steel'd was that soul and by no misery mov'd
That from a father seiz'd his babe belov'd;
Such, such my case. And can I then but pray
Others may never feel tyrannic sway?

For favours past, great Sir, our thanks are due,
And thee we ask thy favours to renew,
Since in thy pow'r, as in thy will before,
To sooth the griefs, which thou did'st once deplore.
May heav'nly grace the sacred sanction give
To all thy works, and thou for ever live
Not only on the wings of fleeting *Fame,*
Though praise immortal crowns the patriot's name,
But to conduct to heav'ns refulgent fane,
May fiery coursers sweep th' ethereal plain,
And bear thee upwards to that blest abode,
Where, like the prophet, thou shalt find thy God.

DOCUMENT NO. 6

"NOVANGLUS" ATTACKS CORRUPTION IN GOVERNMENT*

"Novanglus" (New England) was a pen name John Adams used when he replied to essays published by Daniel Leonard, a "tory" lawyer who wrote as "Massachusettensis." Leonard had defended Francis Bernard, Governor of Massachusetts from 1760–1769, for advising the British ministry that a "new regulation of the American governments" was both necessary and desirable. Adams considered Bernard's recommendations outrageous. They had, Adams alleged, been instigated by a "junto," whose most important members were Lieutenant Governor Thomas Hutchinson, and Andrew Oliver, all of whom, Adams believed, were motivated only by self-aggrandizement, greed,

---

* *The Works of John Adams, Second President of the United States: with a Life of the Author, Notes and Illustrations,* by Charles Francis Adams, vol. 4 (Boston: Charles C. Little and James Brown. 1851), 23–25.

corruption, and conspiracy. Republicans maintained vigilance against such tendencies throughout the revolutionary period. (See Doc. No. 25.)

γ γ γ

January 30, 1775

The intention of the junto was, to procure a revenue to be raised in America by act of parliament. Nothing was further from their designs and wishes, than the drawing or sending this revenue into the exchequer in England, to be spent there in discharging the national debt, and lessening the burdens of the poor people there. They were more selfish. They chose to have the fingering of the money themselves. Their design was, that the money should be applied, first in a large salary to the governor. This would gratify Bernard's avarice; and then, it would render him and all other governors, not only independent of the people, but still more absolutely a slave to the will of the minister. They intended likewise a salary for the lieutenant-governor. This would appease in some degree the gnawings of Hutchinson's avidity, in which he was not a whit behind Bernard himself. In the next place, they intended a salary to the judges of the common law, as well as admiralty. And thus, the whole government, executive and judicial, was to be rendered wholly independent of the people, (and their representatives rendered useless, insignificant, and even burthensome) and absolutely dependent upon, and under the direction of the will of the minister of state. They intended, further, to new-model the whole continent of North America; make an entire new division of it into distinct, though more extensive and less numerous colonies; to sweep away all the charters upon the continent with the destroying besom of an act of parliament; and reduce all the governments to the plan of the royal governments, with a nobility in each colony, not hereditary indeed, at first, but for life. They did indeed flatter the ministry and people in England with distant hopes of a revenue from America, at some future period, to be appropriated to national uses there. But this was not to happen, in their minds, for some time. The governments must be new-modelled, new-regulated, reformed, first, and then the governments here would be able and willing to carry into execution any acts of parliament, or measures of the ministry, for fleecing the people here, to pay debts, or support pensioners, on the American establishment, or bribe electors, or members of parliament, or any other purpose that a virtuous ministry could desire.

DOCUMENT NO. 7

JOSEPH GALLOWAY'S PLAN OF UNION*

Galloway, Speaker of the Pennsylvania Assembly, had been an ally of Benjamin Franklin in prerevolutionary Pennsylvania politics. He learned as Franklin had that it was no easy task to persuade Americans to accept colonial union, even if it brought with it an increased amount of self rule. At the end of debate on September 28, by a vote of six states to five, the delegates deferred further consideration of the plan and later voted to expunge it from the minutes, reportedly at a time when some of its supporters were not in attendance.

γ γ γ

[September 28, 1774]

Resolution submitted by Joseph Galloway:

Resolved, That the Congress will apply to his Majesty for a redress of grievances under which his faithful subjects in America labour; and assure him, that the Colonies hold in abhorrence the idea of being considered independent communities on the British government, and most ardently desire the establishment of a Political Union, not only among themselves, but with the Mother State, upon those principles of safety and freedom which are essential in the constitution of all free governments, and particularly that of the British Legislature; and as the Colonies from their local circumstances, cannot be represented in the Parliament of Great-Britain, they will humbly propose to his Majesty and his two Houses of Parliament, the following plan, under which the strength of the whole Empire may be drawn together on any emergency, the interest of both countries advanced, and the rights and liberties of America secured.

A Plan of a proposed Union between Great Britain and the Colonies.

That a British and American legislature, for regulating the administration of the general affairs of America, be proposed and established in

---

* Worthington Chauncey Ford, et al., eds. *Journals of the Continental Congress: 1774–1789.* 34 vols. (Washington, DC: U.S. Government Printing Office, 1904–1937), 1: 49–51.

JOSEPH GALLOWAY'S PLAN OF UNION

America, including all the said Colonies; within, and under which government, each colony shall retain its present constitution and powers of regulating and governing its own internal police, in all Cases what[*so*]ever.

That the said government be administered by a President General, to be appointed by the King and a grand Council, to be chosen by the Representatives of the people of the several colonies, in their respective assemblies, once in every three years.

That the several assemblies shall choose members for the grand council in the following proportions, viz. . . .

Who shall meet at the city of _____ for the first time, being called by the President-General, as soon as conveniently may be after his appointment.

That there shall be a new election of members for the Grand Council every three years; and on the death, removal or resignation of any member, his place shall be supplied by a new choice, at the next sitting of the Assembly of the Colony he represented.

That the Grand Council shall meet once in every year, if they shall think it necessary, and oftener, if occasions shall require, at such time and place as they shall adjourn to, at the last preceding meeting, or as they shall be called to meet at, by the President-General, on any emergency.

That the grand Council shall have power to choose their Speaker, and shall hold and exercise all the like rights, liberties and privileges, as are held and exercised by and in the House of Commons of Great-Britain.

That the President-General shall hold his Office during the pleasure of the King, and his assent shall be requisite to all acts of the Grand Council, and it shall be his office and duty to cause them to be carried into execution.

That the President-General, by and with the advice and consent of the Grand-Council, hold and exercise all the legislative rights, powers, and authorities, necessary for regulating and administering all the general police and affairs of the colonies, in which Great-Britain and the colonies, or any of them, the colonies in general, or more than one colony, are in any manner concerned, as well civil and criminal as commercial.

That the said President-General and the Grand Council, be an inferior and distinct branch of the British legislature, united and incorporated with it, for the aforesaid general purposes; and that any of the said general regulations may originate and be formed and digested, either in the Parliament of Great Britain, or in the said Grand Council, and being prepared, transmitted to the other for their approbation or dissent; and that the assent of both shall be requisite to the validity of all such general acts or statutes.

That in time of war, all bills for granting aids to the crown, prepared by the Grand Council, and approved by the President General shall be valid and passed into a law, without the assent of the British Parliament.

DOCUMENT NO. 8

CONGRESS ADDRESSES THE IROQUOIS*

Both the British and the Americans tried to influence how the Indians viewed the emerging conflict. Guy Johnson, Britain's agent to the Iroquois, informed them that the king had to chastise the colonists for destroying the tea. Congress's elaborate explanation of the tensions with Britain, which was designed to convince the Iroquois to remain neutral, was read to representatives of the Six Nations (Iroquois) at Albany on August 28. After careful consideration, the Indians pledged they would not become involved in the conflict. Eventually, however, their pledge broke down under the stresses of the war.

γ γ γ

July 13, 1775

A Speech to the Six Confederate Nations, Mohawks, Oneidas, Tuscaroras, Onondagas, Cayugas, Senekas, from the Twelve United Colonies, convened in Council at Philadelphia.

BROTHERS, SACHEMS, AND WARRIORS,

We, the Delegates from the Twelve United Provinces, . . . now sitting in general Congress at Philadelphia, send this talk to you our broth-

* Worthington Chauncey Ford, et al., eds. *Journals of the Continental Congress: 1774–1789.* 34 vols. (Washington, DC: U.S. Government Printing Office, 1904–1937), 2: 178–183.

ers. We are sixty-five in number, chosen and appointed by the people throughout all these provinces and colonies, to meet and sit together in one great council, to consult together for the common good of the land, and speak and act for them.

Brothers, in our consultation we have judged it proper and necessary to send you this talk, as we are upon the same island, that you may be informed of the reasons of this great council, the situation of our civil constitution, and our disposition towards you our Indian brothers of the Six Nations and their allies.

(Three Strings, or a small Belt.) [of wampum]. . . .

BROTHERS AND FRIENDS, OPEN A KIND EAR!

We will now tell you of the quarrel betwixt the counsellors of king George and the inhabitants and colonies of America.

Many of his counsellors are proud and wicked men.—They persuade the king to break the covenant chain, and not to send us any more good talks. A considerable number have prevailed upon him to enter into a new covenant against us, and have torn asunder and cast behind their backs the good old covenant which their ancestors and ours entered into, and took strong hold of.

They now tell us they will slip their hand into our pocket without asking, as though it were there own; and at their pleasure they will take from us our charters or written civil constitution, which we love as our lives—also our plantations, our houses and goods whenever they please, without asking our leave.—That our vessels may go to this island in the sea, but to this or that particular island we shall not trade any more.— And in case of our non-compliance with these new orders, they shut up our harbours.

Brothers, this is our present situation—thus have many of the king's counsellors and servants dealt with us.—If we submit, or comply with their demands, you can easily perceive to what state we will be reduced. —If our people labour on the field, they will not know who shall enjoy the crop.—If they hunt in the woods, it will be uncertain who shall taste of the meat or have the skins.—If they build houses, they will not know whether they may sit round the fire, with their wives and children. They cannot be sure whether they shall be permitted to eat, drink, and wear the fruits of their own labour and industry.

BROTHERS AND FRIENDS OF THE SIX NATIONS, ATTEND,

.... Thus stands the matter betwixt old England and America. You Indians know how things are proportioned in a family—between the father and the son—the child carries a little pack—England we regard as the father—this island may be compared to the son.

The father has a numerous family—both at home and upon this island.—He appoints a great number of servants to assist him in the government of his family. In process of time, some of his servants grow proud and ill-natured—they were displeased to see the boy so alert and walk so nimbly with his pack. They tell the father, and advise him to enlarge the child's pack—they prevail—the pack is increased—the child takes it up again—as he thought it might be the father's pleasure—speaks but few words—those very small—for he was loth to offend the father. Those proud and wicked servants finding they had prevailed, laughed to see the boy sweat and stagger under his increased load. By and by, they apply to the father to double the boy's pack, because they heard him complain—and without any reason said they—he is a cross child—correct him if he complains any more.—The boy intreats the father—addresses the great servants in a decent manner, that the pack might be lightened—he could not go any farther—humbly asks, if the old fathers, in any of their records, had described such a pack for the child—after all the tears and entreaties of the child, the pack is redoubled—the child stands a little, while staggering under the weight—ready to fall every moment. However he entreats the father once more, though so faint he could only lisp out his last humble supplication—waits a while—no voice returns. The child concludes the father could not hear—those proud servants had intercepted his supplications, or stopped the ears of the father. He therefore gives one struggle and throws off the pack, and says he cannot take it up again—such a weight would crush him down and kill him—and he can but die if he refuses.

Upon this, those servants are very wroth—and tell the father many false stories respecting the child—they bring a great cudgel to the father, asking him to take it in his hand and strike the child. . . .

BROTHERS AND FRIENDS!

We desire you will hear and receive what we have now told you, and that you will open a good ear and listen to what we are now going to say. This is a family quarrel between us and Old England. You Indians are not concerned in it. We don't wish you to take up the hatchet against the king's troops. We desire you to remain at home, and not join on either side, but keep the hatchet buried deep. In the name and in behalf of all our people, we ask and desire you to love peace and maintain it, and to love and sympathise with us in our troubles; that the path may be kept open with all our people and yours, to pass and repass, without molestation.

Brothers! we live upon the same ground with you. The same island is our common birth-place. We desire to sit down under the same tree of peace with you: let us water its roots and cherish its growth, till the large leaves and flourishing branches shall extend to the setting sun, and reach the skies.

BROTHERS, OBSERVE WELL!

What is it we have asked of you? Nothing but peace, notwithstanding our present disturbed, situation—and if application should be made to you by any of the king's unwise and wicked ministers to join on their side, we only advise you to deliberate, with great caution, and in your wisdom look forward to the consequences of a compliance. For, if the king's troops take away our property, and destroy us who are of the same blood with themselves, what can you, who are Indians, expect from them afterwards?

Therefore, we say, brothers, take care—hold fast to your covenant chain. You now know our disposition towards you, the Six Nations of Indians, and your allies. Let this our good talk remain at Onondaga, your central council house. We depend upon you to send and acquaint your allies to the northward, the seven tribes on the river St. Lawrence, that you have this talk of ours at the great council fire of the Six Nations. And when they return, we invite your great men to come and converse farther with us at Albany, where we intend to re-kindle the council fire, which your and our ancestors sat round in great friendship.

Brothers and Friends!
We greet you all farewell.
(The large belt of intelligence and declaration.). . . .

Ordered, That a similar talk be prepared for the other Indian nations, preserving the tenor of the above, and altering it so as to suit the Indians in the several departments.

DOCUMENT NO. 9

GEORGE III ADDRESSES PARLIAMENT*

A copy of the king's speech, which announced his intention to wage war against colonies that refused to submit to his authority, arrived in Philadelphia on January 8, 1776. Some Americans still clung to the hope that, if they denied that they were seeking independence, the king might yet be persuaded to lead the way to reconciliation. Most, however, were convinced that the chance for peace had passed. Congress and the colonies made preparations to defend against the forces the king announced would be sent against them.

γ γ γ

October 27, 1775

My Lords and Gentlemen,

The present situation of America, and my constant desire to have your advice, concurrence, and assistance on every important occasion have determined me to call you thus early together.

Those who have long too successfully laboured to inflame my people in America by gross misrepresentations and to infuse into their minds a system of opinions, repugnant to the true constitution of the colonies, and to their subordinate relation to Great-Britain, now openly avow their revolt, hostility and rebellion. They have raised troups, and are collecting a naval force; they have seized the public revenue and assumed to themselves legislative, executive and judicial powers, which they already exercise in the most arbitrary manner, over the persons and property of their fellow-subjects: And altho' many of these unhappy people may still retain their loyalty, and may be too wise not to see the fatal consequence of this usurpation, and wish to resist it, yet the torrent of violence has been strong enough to compel their acquiescence, till a sufficient force shall appear to support them.

The authors and promoters of this desperate conspiracy have, in the conduct of it, derived great advantage from the difference of our intentions and theirs. They meant only to amuse by vague expressions of attachment to the Parent State, and the strongest protestations of loyalty to me, whilst they were preparing for a general revolt. On our part, though it was declared in your last session that a rebellion existed within

* *Pennsylvania Gazette*, January 10, 1776.

the province of the Massachusetts Bay, yet even that province we wished rather to reclaim than to subdue. The resolutions of Parliament breathed a spirit of moderation and forbearance; conciliatory propositions accompanied the measures taken to enforce authority; and the coercive acts were adapted to cases of criminal combinations amongst subjects not then in arms. I have acted with the same temper; anxious to prevent, if it had been possible the effusion of the blood of my subjects; and the calamities which are inseparable from a state of war; still hoping that my people in America would have discerned the traiterous views of their leaders, and have been convinced, that to be a subject of Great Britain, with all its consequences is to be the freest member of any civil society in the known world.

The rebellious war now levied is become more general, and is manifestly carried on for the purpose of establishing an independent empire. I need not dwell upon the fatal effects of the success of such a plan. The object is too important, the spirit of the British nation too high, the resources with which God hath blessed her too numerous, to give up so many colonies which she has planted with great industry, nursed with great tenderness, encouraged with many commercial advantages, and protected and defended at much expence of blood and treasure.

It is now become the part of wisdom, and (in its effects) of clemency, to put a speedy end to these disorders by the most decisive exertions. For this purpose, I have increased my naval establishment, and greatly augmented my land forces; but in such a manner as may be the least burthensome to my kingdoms.

I have also the satisfaction to inform you, that I have received the most friendly offers of foreign assistance, and if I shall make any treaties in consequence thereof, they shall be laid before you. . . .

When the unhappy and deluded multitude, against whom this force will be directed, shall become sensible of their error, I shall be ready to receive the misled with tenderness and mercy! And in order to prevent the inconveniences which may arise from the great distance of their situation, and to remove as soon as possible the calamities which they suffer, I shall give authority to certain persons upon the spot to grant general or particular pardons and indemnities, in such manner, and to such persons as they shall think fit, and to receive the submission of any Province of Colony which shall be disposed to return to its allegiance. It may be also proper to authorise the persons so commissioned to restore such Province or Colony, so returning to its allegiance, to the free

DOCUMENT NO. 10

*COMMON SENSE**

Thomas Paine's pamphlet was the most widely read and discussed tract of the American Revolution. In conjunction with the king's speech printed above, it immediately and dramatically changed the focus of the debate over relations with Great Britain from how Americans might persuade Parliament to redress their grievances to whether they should declare their independence.

γ γ γ

January, 1776

Thoughts on the Present State of American Affairs

... As much has been said of the advantages of reconciliation, which, like an agreeable dream, has passed away and left us as we were, it is but right that we should examine the contrary side of the argument, and inquire into some of the many material injuries which these colonies sustain, and always will sustain, by being connected with and dependent on Great Britain. To examine that connection and dependance, on the principles of nature and common sense, to see what we have to trust to, if separated, and what we are to expect, if dependant.

I have heard it asserted by some, that as America has flourished under her former connection with Great Britain, the same connection is necessary towards her future happiness, and will always have the same effect. Nothing can be more fallacious than this kind of argument. We may as well assert that because a child has thrived upon milk, that it is never to have meat, or that the first twenty years of our lives is to become a precedent for the next twenty. But even this is admitting more than is true; for I answer roundly, that America would have flourished as much, and probably much more, had no European power taken any notice of

---

* Moncure Daniel Conway, ed., *The Writings of Thomas Paine* (New York: Knickerbocker Press, 1894), 1: 85–89.

her. The commerce by which she hath enriched herself are the necessaries of life, and will always have a market while eating is the custom of Europe.

But she has protected us, say some. That she hath engrossed us is true, and defended the continent at our expense as well as her own, is admitted; and she would have defended Turkey from the same motive. *viz.* for the sake of trade and dominion.

Alas! we have been long led away by ancient prejudices and made large sacrifices to superstition. We have boasted the protection of Great Britain, without considering, that her motive was *interest* not *attachment*; and that she did not protect us from *our enemies* on *our account*: but from *her enemies* on *her own account*, from those who had no quarrel with us on any *other account*, and who will always be our enemies on the *same account*. Let Britain waive her pretensions to the continent, or the continent throw off the dependence, and we should be at peace with France and Spain, were they at war with Britain. The miseries of Hanover's last war ought to warn us against connections.

It hath lately been asserted in Parliament, that the colonies have no relation to each other but through the parent country, *i. e.* that Pennsylvania and the Jerseys, and so on for the rest, are sister colonies by the way of England; this is certainly a very roundabout way of proving relationship, but it is the nearest and only true way of proving enmity (or enemyship, if I may so call it.) France and Spain never were, nor perhaps ever will be, our enemies as *Americans*, but as our being the *subjects of Great Britain*.

But Britain is the parent country, say some. Then the more shame upon her conduct. Even brutes do not devour their young, nor savages make war upon their families; wherefore, the assertion, if true, turns to her reproach; but it happens not to be true, or only partly so, and the phrase *parent* or *mother country* hath been jesuitically adopted by the king and his parasites, with a low papistical design of gaining an unfair bias on the credulous weakness of our minds. Europe, and not England, is the parent country of America. This new world hath been the asylum for the persecuted lovers of civil and religious liberty from *every part* of Europe. Hither have they fled, not from the tender embraces of the mother, but from the cruelty of the monster; and it is so far true of England, that the same tyranny which drove the first emigrants from home, pursues their descendants still.

In this extensive quarter of the globe, we forget the narrow limits of three hundred and sixty miles (the extent of England) and carry our friendship on a larger scale; we claim brotherhood with every European Christian, and triumph in the generosity of the sentiment....

Much hath been said of the united strength of Britain and the colonies, that in conjunction they might bid defiance to the world. But this is mere presumption; the fate of war is uncertain, neither do the expressions mean any thing; for this continent would never suffer itself to be drained of inhabitants, to support the British arms in either Asia, Africa or Europe.

Besides, what have we to do with setting the world at defiance? Our plan is commerce, and that, well attended to, will secure us the peace and friendship of all Europe; because it is the interest of all Europe to have America a free port. Her trade will always be a protection, and her barrenness of gold and silver secure her from invaders.

I challenge the warmest advocate for reconciliation to show a single advantage that this continent can reap by being connected with Great Britain. I repeat the challenge; not a single advantage is derived. Our corn will fetch its price in any market in Europe, and our imported goods must be paid for, buy them where we will.

But the injuries and disadvantages which we sustain by that connection, are without number; and our duty to mankind at large, as well as to ourselves, instruct us to renounce the alliance: because, any submission to, or dependence on, Great Britain, tends directly to involve this continent in European wars and quarrels, and sets us at variance with nations who would otherwise seek our friendship, and against whom, we have neither anger nor complaint. As Europe is our market for trade, we ought to form no partial connection with any part of it. It is the true interest of America to steer clear of European contentions, which she never can do, while, by her dependence on Britain, she is made the makeweight in the scale of British politics.

Europe is too thickly planted with kingdoms to be long at peace, and whenever a war breaks out between England and any foreign power, the trade of America goes to ruin, *because of her connection with Britain.* The next war may not turn out like the last, and should it not, the advocates for reconciliation now will be wishing for separation then, because neutrality in that case would be a safer convoy than a man of war. Every thing that is right or reasonable pleads for separation. The blood of the slain, the weeping voice of nature cries, 'TIS TIME TO PART. Even the distance at which the Almighty hath placed England and America is a strong and natural proof that the authority of the one over the other, was never the design of heaven. The time likewise at which the continent was discovered, adds weight to the argument, and the manner in which it was peopled, encreases the force of it. The Reformation was preceded by the discovery of America: As if the Almighty graciously meant to open a sanctuary to the persecuted in future years, when home should afford neither friendship nor safety.

The authority of Great Britain over this continent, is a form of government, which sooner or later must have an end. And a serious mind can draw no true pleasure by looking forward, under the painful and positive conviction that what he calls "the present constitution" is merely temporary. As parents, we can have no joy, knowing that this government is not sufficiently lasting to insure any thing which we may bequeath to posterity. And by a plain method of argument, as we are running the next generation into debt, we ought to do the work of it, otherwise we use them meanly and pitifully. In order to discover the line of our duty rightly, we should take our children in our hand, and fix our station a few years farther into life; that eminence will present a prospect which a few present fears and prejudices conceal from our sight.

DOCUMENT NO. 11

THE DECLARATION OF INDEPENDENCE*

After six months of deliberation and debate, on July 2, 1776, the congressional delegations of twelve states voted to declare independence. The official proclamation Congress approved on July 4 justified its decision by cataloging and publicly denouncing the abuses Americans had suffered at the hands of the British government. The fine parchment copy of the Declaration Congress had ordered was signed by all the delegates attending Congress on August 2.

* Worthington Chauncey Ford, et al., eds. *Journals of the Continental Congress: 1774–1789.* 34 vols. (Washington, DC: U.S. Government Printing Office, 1904–1937), 5: 510–515.

γ　　　　　γ　　　　　γ

July 4, 1776

The unanimous Declaration of the thirteen United States of America.

When, in the Course of human events, it becomes necessary for one people to dissolve the political bands which have connected them with another, and to assume, among the Powers of the earth, the separate and equal station to which the Laws of Nature and of Nature's God entitle them, a decent respect to the opinions of mankind requires that they should declare the causes which impel them to the separation.

We hold these truths to be self-evident, that all men are created equal, that they are endowed by their Creator with certain unalienable Rights, that among these, are Life, Liberty, and the pursuit of Happiness. That, to secure these rights, Governments are instituted among Men, deriving their just Powers from the consent of the governed. That, whenever any form of Government becomes destructive of these ends, it is the Right of the People to alter or to abolish it, and to institute new Government, laying its foundation on such Principles, and organizing its Powers in such form, as to them shall seem most likely to effect their Safety and Happiness. Prudence, indeed, will dictate that Governments long established should not be changed for light and transient causes; and, accordingly, all experience hath shewn, that mankind are more disposed to suffer, while evils are sufferable, than to right themselves by abolishing the forms to which they are accustomed. But, when a long train of abuses and usurpations, pursuing invariably the same Object, evinces a design to reduce them under absolute Despotism, it is their right, it is their duty, to throw off such Government, and to provide new Guards for their future Security. Such has been the patient sufferance of these Colonies; and such is now the necessity which constrains them to alter their former Systems of Government. The history of the present King of Great Britain is a history of repeated injuries and usurpations, all having in direct object the establishment of an absolute Tyranny over these States. To prove this, let Facts be submitted to a candid world.

He has refused his Assent to Laws the most wholesome and necessary for the public good.

He has forbidden his Governors to pass Laws of immediate and pressing importance, unless suspended in their operation till his Assent

DECLARATION OF INDEPENDENCE

should be obtained; and when so suspended, he has utterly neglected to attend to them.

He has refused to pass other Laws for the accommodation of large districts of People, unless those People would relinquish the right of Representation in the legislature; a right inestimable to them and formidable to tyrants only.

He has called together legislative bodies at places unusual, uncomfortable, and distant from the depository of their Public Records, for the sole Purpose of fatiguing them into compliance with his measures.

He has dissolved Representative Houses repeatedly, for opposing, with manly firmness, his invasions on the rights of the People.

He has refused for a long time, after such dissolutions, to cause others to be elected; whereby the Legislative Powers, incapable of Annihilation, have returned to the People at large for their exercise; the State remaining in the mean time exposed to all the dangers of invasion from without, and convulsions within.

He has endeavoured to prevent the Population of these States; for that purpose obstructing the Laws for Naturalization of Foreigners; refusing to pass others to encourage their migrations hither, and raising the conditions of new Appropriations of Lands.

He has obstructed the Administration of Justice, by refusing his Assent to Laws for establishing Judiciary Powers.

He has made Judges dependent on his Will alone, for the tenure of their offices, and the amount and payment of their salaries.

He has erected a multitude of New Offices, and sent hither swarms of Officers to harrass our People, and eat out their substance.

He has kept among us, in times of Peace, Standing Armies, without the Consent of our legislatures.

He has affected to render the Military independent of and superior to the Civil Power.

He has combined with others to subject us to a jurisdiction foreign to our constitution, and unacknowledged by our laws; giving his Assent to their Acts of pretended Legislation:

For quartering large bodies of armed troops among us:

For protecting them, by a mock Trial, from Punishment for any Murders which they should commit on the Inhabitants of these States:

For cutting off our Trade with all parts of the world:

For imposing Taxes on us without our Consent:

For depriving us, in many cases, of the benefits of Trial by Jury:

For transporting us beyond Seas to be tried for pretended offences:

For abolishing the free System of English Laws in a neighbouring province, establishing therein an Arbitrary government, and enlarging its Boundaries, so as to render it at once an example and fit instrument for introducing the same absolute rule into these Colonies:

For taking away our Charters, abolishing our most valuable Laws, and altering fundamentally the Forms of our Governments:

For suspending our own Legislatures, and declaring themselves invested with Power to legislate for us in all cases whatsoever.

He has abdicated Government here, by declaring us out of his protection, and waging War against us.

He has plundered our seas, ravaged our Coasts, burnt our towns, and destroyed the Lives of our People.

He is at this time transporting large Armies of foreign Mercenaries to compleat the works of death, desolation and tyranny, already begun with circumstances of Cruelty and perfidy scarcely paralleled in the most barbarous ages, and totally unworthy the Head of a civilized nation.

He has constrained our fellow Citizens, taken Captive on the high Seas, to bear Arms against their Country, to become the executioners of their friends and Brethren, or to fall themselves by their Hands.

He has excited domestic insurrections amongst us, and has endeavoured to bring on the inhabitants of our frontiers, the merciless Indian Savages, whose known rule of warfare, is an undistinguished destruction of all ages, sexes and conditions.

In every stage of these Oppressions, We have Petitioned for Redress, in the most humble terms: Our repeated Petitions, have been answered only by repeated injury. A Prince, whose character is thus marked by every act which may define a Tyrant, is unfit to be the ruler of a free People.

Nor have We been wanting in attentions to our Brittish brethren. We have warned them from time to time of attempts by their legislature to extend an unwarrantable jurisdiction over us. We have reminded them of the circumstances of our emigration and settlement here. We have appealed to their native justice and magnanimity, and we have conjured them by the ties of our common kindred, to disavow these usurpations, which, would inevitably interrupt our connexions and correspondence. They too have been deaf to the voice of justice and of consanguinity.

We must, therefore, acquiesce in the necessity, which denounces our Separation, and hold them, as we bold the rest of mankind, Enemies in War, in Peace Friends.

We, therefore, the Representatives of the united States of America, in GENERAL CONGRESS assembled, appealing to the Supreme Judge of the World for the rectitude of our intentions, DO, in the Name, and by Authority of the good People of these Colonies, solemnly PUBLISH and DECLARE, That these United Colonies are, and of Right, ought to be Free and Independent States; that they are Absolved from all Allegiance to the British Crown, and that all political connexion between them and the State of Great Britain, is and ought to be totally dissolved; and that, as FREE and INDEPENDENT STATES, they have full Power to levy War, conclude Peace, contract Alliances, establish Commerce, and to do all other Acts and Things which INDEPENDENT STATES may of right do. AND for the support of this Declaration, with a firm reliance on the protection of divine Providence, we mutually pledge to each other our Lives, our Fortunes, and our sacred Honour.

DOCUMENT NO. 12

THE ARTICLES OF CONFEDERATION*

The Articles of Confederation were framed more to describe the limits of the central government's power than to create a government that would be capable of pursuing objectives vigorously. They established a government whose only branch was Congress—a coordinating committee that could make recommendations, set some policies, and issue directives. There was neither a fully empowered executive nor a true legislature. The Articles set some limits on activities states might engage in, but they did not provide any means other than persuasion that Congress might use to enforce its decisions on them.

γ   γ   γ

* Worthington Chauncey Ford, et al., eds. *Journals of the Continental Congress: 1774–1789*. 34 vols. (Washington, DC: U.S. Government Printing Office, 1904–1937), 19: 214–222.

March 1, 1781

Article I. The style of this Confederacy shall be "The United States of America."

Article II. Each State retains its sovereignty, freedom, and independence, and every Power, Jurisdiction and right, which is not by this Confederation expressly delegated to the United States, in Congress assembled.

Article III. The said states hereby severally enter into a firm league of friendship with each other, for their common defence, the security of their Liberties, and their mutual and general welfare, binding themselves to assist each other against all force offered to, or attacks made upon them, or any of them, on account of religion, sovereignty, trade, or any other pretence whatever.

Article IV. The better to secure and perpetuate mutual friendship and intercourse among the people of the different states in this union, the free inhabitants of each of these states, paupers, vagabonds and fugitives from justice excepted, shall be entitled to all privileges and immunities of free citizens in the several states, and the people of each state shall have free ingress and regress to and from any other state, and shall enjoy therein all the privileges of trade and commerce, subject to the same duties, impositions and restrictions as the inhabitants thereof respectively, provided that such restriction shall not extend so far as to prevent the removal of property imported into any state, to any other state of which the Owner is an inhabitant; provided also, that no imposition, duties or restriction shall be laid by any state, on the property of the united states, or either of them.

If any Person guilty of or charged with treason, felony, or other high misdemeanor in any state, shall flee from Justice, and be found in any of the united states, he shall, upon demand of the Governor or executive power, of the state from which he fled, be delivered up and removed to the state having jurisdiction of his offence.

Full faith and credit shall be given in each of these states to the records, acts, and judicial proceedings of the courts and magistrates of every other state.

Article V. For the more convenient management of the general interests of the united states, delegates shall be annually appointed in such manner as the legislature of each state shall direct, to meet in Congress on the first Monday in November, in every year, with a power reserved to each state to recall its delegates, or any of them, at any time within the year, and to send others in their stead, for the remainder of the Year.

No State shall be represented in Congress by less than two, nor by more than seven Members; and no person shall be capable of being a delegate for more than three years in any term of six years; nor shall any person, being a delegate, be capable of holding any office under the united states for which he, or another for his benefit receives any salary, fees or emolument of any kind.

Each state shall maintain its own delegates in a meeting of the states, and while they act as members of the committee of the states.

In determining questions in the united states, in Congress assembled, each state shall have one vote.

Freedom of speech and debate in Congress shall not be impeached or questioned in any court or place out of Congress, and the members of congress shall be protected in their persons from arrests and imprisonments, during the time of their going to or from, and attendance on congress, except for treason, felony, or breach of the peace.

Article VI. No State, without the Consent of the united states in congress assembled, shall send any embassy to, or receive any embassy from, or enter into any conference, agreement, alliance, or treaty with, any King prince or state; nor shall any person holding any office of profit or trust under the united states, or any of them, accept of any present, emolument, office, or title of any kind whatever from any king, prince or foreign state; nor shall the united states in congress assembled, or any of them, grant any title of nobility.

No two or more states shall enter into any treaty, confederation, or alliance whatever between them, without the consent of the united states in congress assembled, specifying accurately the purposes for which the same is to be entered into, and how long it shall continue.

No state shall lay any imposts or duties, which may interfere with any stipulations in treaties entered into by the united states in congress assembled, with any king, prince, or state, in pursuance of any treaties already proposed by congress, to the courts of France and Spain.

No vessels of war shall be kept in time of peace by any State, except such number only as shall be deemed necessary by the united states in congress assembled, for the defence of such state, or its trade; nor shall any body of forces be kept up by any state, in time of peace, except such number only as in the judgment of the united states in congress assembled, be deemed requisite to garrison the forts necessary for the defence of such state; but every state shall always keep up a well regulated and disciplined militia, sufficiently armed and accoutred, and shall provide and constantly have ready for use, in public stores, a due number of field pieces and tents, and a proper quantity of arms, ammunition and camp equipage.

No state shall engage in any war without the consent of the united states in congress assembled, unless such state be actually invaded by enemies, or shall have received certain advice of a resolution being formed by some nation of Indians to invade such state, and the danger is so imminent as not to admit of a delay till the united states in congress assembled can be consulted; nor shall any state grant commissions to any ships or vessels of war, nor letters of marque or reprisal, except it be after a declaration of war by the united states in congress assembled, and then only against the kingdom or state and the subjects thereof, against which war has been so declared, and under such regulations as shall be established by the united states in congress assembled, unless such State be infested by pirates, in which case vessels of war may be fitted out for that occasion, and kept so long as the danger shall continue, or until the united states in congress assembled, shall determine otherwise.

Article VII. When land-forces are raised by any state for the common defense, all officers of or under the rank of colonel, shall be appointed by the legislature of each state respectively, by whom such forces shall be raised, or in such manner as such state shall direct; and all vacancies shall be filled up by the State which first made the appointment.

Article VIII. All charges of war, and all other expenses that shall be incurred for the common defence or general welfare, and allowed by the united states in congress assembled, shall be defrayed out of a common treasury, which shall be supplied by the several states, in proportion to the value of all land within each state, granted to or surveyed for any Person, as such land and the buildings and improvements thereon shall be estimated according to such mode as the united states in congress assembled, shall from time to time direct and appoint. The taxes for paying that proportion shall be laid and levied by the authority and direction of the legislatures of the several states within the time agreed upon by the united states in congress assembled.

Article IX. The united states in congress assembled shall have the sole and exclusive right and power of determining on peace and war, except in the cases mentioned in the sixth article—of sending and receiving ambassadors—entering into treaties and alliances, provided that no treaty of commerce shall be made whereby the legislative power of the respective states shall be restrained from imposing such imposts and duties on foreigners, as their own people are subjected to, or from prohibiting the exportation or importation of any species of goods or commodities whatsoever—of establishing rules for deciding in all cases, what captures on land or water shall be legal, and in what manner prizes taken by land or naval forces in the service of the united states shall be divided or appropriated—of granting letters of marque and reprisal in times of peace—appointing courts for the trial of piracies and felonies committed on the high seas and establishing courts for receiving and determining finally appeals in all cases of captures, provided that no member of congress shall be appointed a judge of any of the said courts.

The united states in congress assembled shall also be the last resort on appeal in all disputes and differences now subsisting or that hereafter may arise between two or more states concerning boundary, jurisdiction, or any other cause whatever; which authority shall always be exercised in the manner following. . . .

The united states in congress assembled shall also have the sole and exclusive right and power of regulating the alloy and value of coin struck by their own authority, or by that of the respective states—fixing the standard of weights and measures throughout the united states—regulating the trade and managing all affairs with the Indians, not members of any of the states, provided that the legislative right of any state within its own limits be not infringed or violated—establishing and regulating post-offices from one state to another, throughout all the united states and exacting such postage on the papers passing thro' the same as may be requisite to defray the expenses of the said office—appointing all officers of the land forces, in the service of the united states, excepting regimental officers—appointing all the officers of the naval forces, and commissioning all officers whatever in the service of the united states—making rules for the government and regulation of the said land and naval forces, and directing their operations.

The united states in congress assembled shall have authority to appoint a committee, to sit in the recess of congress, to be denominated "A Committee of the States," and to consist of one delegate from each state; to appoint such other committees and civil officers as may be necessary for managing the general affairs of the united states under their direction—to appoint one of their number to preside, provided that no person be allowed to serve in the office of president more than one year in any term of three years; to ascertain the necessary sums of Money to be raised for the service of the united states, and to appropriate and apply the same for defraying the public expenses—to borrow money, or emit bills on the credit of the united states, transmitting every half-year to the respective states an account of the sums of money so borrowed or emitted,—to build and equip a navy—to agree upon the number of land forces, and to make requisitions from each state for its quota, in proportion to the number of white inhabitants in such state; which requisition shall be binding, . . .

The united states in congress assembled shall never engage in a war, nor grant letters of marque and reprisal in time of peace, nor enter into any treaties or alliances, nor coin money, nor regulate the value thereof, nor ascertain the sums and expenses necessary for the defence and welfare of the united states, or any of them, nor emit bills, nor borrow money on the credit of the united states, nor appropriate money, nor agree upon the number of vessels of war to be built or purchased, or the number of land or sea forces to be raised, nor appoint a commander-in-chief of the army or navy, unless nine states assent to the same; nor shall a question on any other point, except for adjourning from day to day, be determined, unless by the votes of a majority of the united states in congress assembled.

The congress of the united states shall have power to adjourn to any time within the year, and to any place within the united states, so that no period of adjournment be for a longer duration than the space of six Months, and shall publish the Journal of their proceedings monthly, except such parts thereof relating to treaties, alliances, or military operations, as in their judgment require secrecy; and the yeas and nays of the delegates of each state on any question shall be entered on the journal, when it is desired by any delegate; and the delegates of a state, or any of them, at his or their request, shall be furnished with a transcript of the said Journal, except such parts as are above excepted, to lay before the legislatures of the several states.

Article X. The committee of the states, or any nine of them, shall be authorized to execute, in the recess of congress, such of the powers of congress as the united states in congress assembled, by the consent of nine states, shall from time to time think expedient to vest them with:

provided that no power be delegated to the said committee, for the exercise of which, by the articles of confederation, the voice of nine states in the congress of the united states assembled is requisite.

Article XI. Canada, acceding to this confederation, and joining in the measures of the united states, shall be admitted into and entitled to all the advantages of this union; but no other colony shall be admitted into the same, unless such admission be agreed to by nine states.

Article XII. All bills of credit emitted, moneys borrowed, and debts contracted by or under the authority of congress, before the assembling of the united states in pursuance of the present confederation, shall be deemed and considered as a charge against the united states, for payment and satisfaction whereof the said united states, and the public faith are hereby solemnly pledged.

Article XIII. Every state shall abide by the determinations of the united states in congress assembled, on all questions which by this confederation are submitted to them. And the Articles of this confederation shall be inviolably observed by every state, and the union shall be perpetual; nor shall any alteration at any time hereafter be made in any of them; unless such alteration be agreed to in a congress of the united states, and be afterwards confirmed by the legislatures of every state.

And Whereas it hath pleased the Great Governor of the World to incline the hearts of the legislatures we respectfully represent in congress, to approve of and to authorize us to ratify the said articles of confederation and perpetual union. Know Ye that we, the undersigned delegates, by virtue of the power and authority to us given for that purpose, do by these presents, in the name and in behalf of our respective constituents, fully and entirely ratify and confirm each and every of the said articles of confederation and perpetual union, and all and singular the matters and things therein contained: And we do further solemnly plight and engage the faith of our respective constituents, that they shall abide by the determinations of the united states in congress assembled, on all questions, which by the said confederation are submitted to them. And that the articles thereof shall be inviolably observed by the states we respectively represent, and the union shall be perpetual. In Witness whereof we have hereunto set our hands in Congress. Done at Philadelphia in the state of Pennsylvania the ninth day of July, in the Year of our Lord one Thousand seven Hundred and Seventy-eight, and in the third year of the independence of America.

DOCUMENT NO. 13

A PLAN OF TREATIES*

The plan reflects the aspirations of an emerging nation and its most entrepreneurial citizens to play a significant role in the international economy. Before this objective could be realized, however, American negotiators would have to persuade European nations to lower mercantilist trade barriers and move in the direction of freer trade. Expectations that they would be able to penetrate powerful, long-established national monopolies, convince European nations to revise trade regulations, and to protect American commerce were brashly optimistic. They were, however, correctly founded on the assumption that Europe and her colonies needed the commodities the United States produced and the markets her dynamically growing population afforded.

γ γ γ

September 17, 1776

There shall be a firm, inviolable, and universal Peace, and a true and sincere Friendship between A. and B. and the Subjects of A. and of B. and between the Countries, Islands, Cities, and Towns situate under the Jurisdiction of A. and of B. and the People and Inhabitants thereof of every degree; with out Exception of Persons or Places; and the Terms herein after mentioned shall be perpetual between A. and B.

Art. I. The Subjects of the most Christian King shall pay no other Duties or Imposts in the Ports, Havens, Roads, Countries, Islands, Cities, or Towns of the said united States, or any of them, than the Natives thereof, or any Commercial Companies established by them or any of them, shall pay, but shall enjoy all other the Rights, Liberties, Priviledges, Immunities, and Exemptions in Trade, Navigation and Commerce in passing from one Part thereof to another, and in going to and from the same, from and to any Part of the World, which the said Natives, or Companies enjoy.

Art. II. The Subjects, People and Inhabitants of the said united States, and every of them, shall pay no other Duties, or Imposts in the Ports, Havens, Roads, Countries, Islands, Cities, or Towns of the most

---

* Worthington Chauncey Ford, et al., eds. *Journals of the Continental Congress: 1774–1789.* 34 vols. (Washington, DC: U.S. Government Printing Office, 1904–1937), 5: 768–779.

A PLAN OF TREATIES 161

Christian King, than the Natives of such Countries, Islands, Cities, or Towns of France, or any commercial Companies established by the most Christian King shall pay, but shall enjoy all other the Rights, Liberties, Priviledges, Immunities and Exemptions in Trade, Navigation and Commerce, in passing from one port [Part] thereof to another, and in going to and from the same, from and to any Part of the World, which the said Natives, or Companies enjoy.

Art. III. His most Christian Majesty shall retain the same Rights of Fishery on the Banks of Newfoundland, and all other Rights relating to any of the said Islands, which he is entitled to by virtue of the Treaty of Paris.

Art. IV. The most Christian King shall endeavour, by all the Means in his Power to protect and defend all Vessels, and the Effects belonging to the Subjects, People, or Inhabitants of the said united States, or any of them, being in his Ports, Havens, or Roads, or on the Seas, near to his Countries, Islands, Cities, or Towns, and to recover and to restore, to the right owners, their Agents or Attornies, all such Vessels, and Effects, which shall be taken, within his Jurisdiction; and his Ships of War, or any Convoys sailing under his Authority, shall upon all occasions, take under their Protection all Vessels belonging to the Subjects, People or Inhabitants of the said United States, or any of them, and holding the same Course, or going the same Way, and, shall defend such Vessells as long as they hold the same Course, or go the same Way, against all Attacks, Force, and Violence, in the same manner, as they ought to protect and defend Vessells belonging to the Subjects of the most Christian King.

Art. V. In like manner the said United States, and their Ships of War and Convoys sailing under their Authority shall protect and defend all Vessels and Effects belonging to the Subjects of the most Christian King, and endeavour to recover and restore them, if taken within the Jurisdiction of the said United States, or any of them.

Art. VIII. If, in Consequence of this Treaty, the King of Great Britain, should declare War, against the most Christian King, the said United States shall not assist Great Britain, in such War, with Men, Money, Ships, or any of the Articles in this treaty denominated Contraband Goods.

Art. XI. If in any War, the most Christian King, shall conquer, or get Possession of the Islands in the West Indies, now under the Jurisdiction of the King or Crown of Great Britain, or any of them, or any Dominions of the said King or Crown in any other Parts of the World, the Subjects, People and Inhabitants of the said United States, and every of them, shall enjoy the same Rights, Liberties, Priviledges, Immunities and Exemptions in Trade, Commerce and Navigation, to and from the said Islands, and Dominions, that are mentioned in the Second Article of this Treaty.

Art. XII. It is the true Intent and Meaning of this Treaty, that no higher or other Duties shall be imposed on the Exportation of any Thing of the Growth, Production, or Manufacture of the Islands in the West Indies now belonging or which may hereafter belong to the most Christian King, to the said United States, or any of them, than the lowest that are or shall be imposed on the Exportation thereof to France or to any other Part of the World.

Art. XXVII. This Liberty of Navigation and Commerce shall extend to all Kinds of Merchandizes, excepting those only which are distinguished by the Name of Contraband: and under this Name of Contraband, or prohibited Goods, shall be comprehended Arms, Great Guns, . . . and all other war like Instruments whatsoever. . . .

DOCUMENT NO. 14

THE ARMY CELEBRATES A THANKSGIVING AT VALLEY FORGE*

Joseph Plumb Martin, a young Connecticut lad, enlisted in the Continental army in 1776 and served throughout the war. At age seventy, he set down his recollections of his service so that Americans who had not experienced the war would know what the army suffered as it fought to secure independence. Martin's story begins several months after Washington's army was defeated by the British at Germantown.

γ γ γ

December, 1777

Starvation seemed to be entailed upon the army and every animal connected with it. The oxen, brought from New England for draught,

---

* Joseph Plumb Martin, *Private Yankee Doodle, Being a Narrative of Some of the Adventures, Dangers and Sufferings of a Revolutionary Soldier*, George F. Scheer, ed., (Boston: Little, Brown, 1962), 99–102.

all died, and the southern horses fared no better; even the wild animals that had any concern with us suffered. A poor little squirrel, who had the ill luck to get off from the woods and fixing himself on a tree standing alone and surrounded by several of the soldier's huts, sat upon the tree until he starved to death and fell off the tree. He, however, got rid of his misery soon. He did not live to starve by piecemeal six or seven years. . . .

Soon after the British had quit their position on Chestnut Hill, we left this place and after marching and countermarching back and forward some days, we crossed the Schuylkill in a cold, rainy and snowy night [December 12] upon a bridge of wagons set end to end and joined together by boards and planks. And after a few days more maneuvering we at last settled down at a place called "the Gulf" (so named on account of a remarkable chasm in the hills); and here we encamped some time, and here we had liked to have encamped forever—for starvation here *rioted* in its glory. But lest the reader should be disgusted at hearing so much said about "starvation," I will give him something that, perhaps, may in some measure alleviate his ill humor.

While we lay here there was a Continental Thanksgiving ordered by Congress; and as the army had all the cause in the world to be particularly thankful, if not for being well off, at least that it was no worse, we were ordered to participate in it. We had nothing to eat for two or three days previous, except what the trees of the fields and forests afforded us. But we must now have what Congress said, a sumptuous Thanksgiving to close the year of high living we had now nearly seen brought to a close. Well, to add something extraordinary to our present stock of provisions, our country, ever mindful of its suffering army, opened her sympathizing heart so wide, upon this occasion, as to give us something to make the world stare. And what do you think it was, reader? Guess. You cannot guess, be you as much of a Yankee as you will. I will tell you; it gave each and every man *half* a *gill* of rice and a *tablespoonful* of vinegar!!

After we had made sure of this extraordinary superabundant donation, we were ordered out to attend a meeting and hear a sermon delivered upon the happy occasion. We accordingly went, for we could not help it. I heard a sermon, a "thanksgiving sermon," what sort of one I do not know now, nor did I at the time I heard it. I had something else to think upon. My belly put me in remembrance of the fine Thanksgiving dinner I was to partake of when I could get it. I remember the text, like an attentive lad at church. I can *still* remember that it was this, "And the soldiers said unto him, And what shall we do? And he said unto them, Do violence to no man, nor accuse anyone falsely." The preacher ought to have added the remainder of the sentence to have made it complete, "And be content with your wages." But that would not do, it would be too apropos. However, he heard it as soon as the service was over, it was shouted from a hundred tongues. Well, we had got through the services of the day and had nothing to do but to return in good order to our tents and fare as we could. As we returned to our camp, we passed by our commissary's quarters. All his stores, consisting of a barrel about two-thirds full of hocks of fresh beef, stood directly in our way, but there was a sentinel guarding even that. However, one of my messmates purloined a piece of it, four or five pounds perhaps. I was exceeding glad to see him take it; I thought it might help to eke out our Thanksgiving supper, but alas! how soon my expectations were blasted! The sentinel saw him have it as soon as I did and obliged him to return it to the barrel again. So I had nothing else to do but to go home and make out my supper as usual, upon a leg of nothing and no turnips.

The army was now not only starved but naked. The greatest part were not only shirtless and barefoot, but destitute of all other clothing, especially blankets. I procured a small piece of raw cowhide and made myself a pair of moccasins, which kept my feet (while they lasted) from the frozen ground, although, as I well remember, the hard edges so galled my ankles, while on a march, that it was with much difficulty and pain that I could wear them afterwards; but the only alternative I had was to endure this inconvenience or to go barefoot, as hundreds of my companions had to, till they might be tracked by their blood upon the rough frozen ground. But hunger, nakedness and sore shins were not the only difficulties we had at that time to encounter; we had hard duty to perform and little or no strength to perform it with.

DOCUMENT NO. 15

WOMEN'S AND LOYALISTS' EXPERIENCE OF THE WAR*

Even women in elite circles, like Mary Morris, wife of Robert Morris, and her friend, Kitty Livingston, sister-in-law to John Jay and member of

* MS: Matthew Ridley Papers, *Courtesy of the Massachusetts Historical Society*.

one of New York's most prominent families, felt the effects of the war and saw how harshly it treated the less fortunate. Pennsylvania's laws against loyalists brought great suffering to women whose families' allegiances were divided. Elizabeth Graeme Ferguson was an outstanding patriot—but her inheritance became liable to confiscation because her husband was a loyalist. Mary also describes how the Ladies Association in Philadelphia collected funds to alleviate the privation suffered by soldiers in the Continental army. Women in New Jersey, Maryland, and Virginia formed similar organizations.

γ γ γ

Mary Morris to Catharine Wilhelmina Livingston

[the Hills?] June 10th. [1780]

Thrice welcome my dear is your last letter, I find Myself much relieved from my Apprehensions about you being informed were you are, that you are well, & as yet safe from the insults of your Victoryous foe; I made anxious enquiry of every Person I saw wether they had heard anything respecting Your Family, & requested Mr. Morris to do the same but to no purpose till yours Arrived last Evening Dicteated by reall Friendship, which is desireous to releive an anxious friend tho their own Situation claim all their attention. . . .

I write this in the green House, which room far exceeds our expectations in beauty, & Conveniance, The stilness, coolness, Shade & harmony which the little Songsters afford that inhabit the grove that runs to the back of it, all of these as it shoud seem, shoud dispose my mind to tranquility, & fill my Imagination with a variety of such pleaseing Subjects as would afford you an amusing Epistle; but quite otherways is my Situation, this delightfull retreat cannot prevent my feelings being wounded for the sufferings of a Number of my Sex in this State, who are compeld to leave it, by that Cruell Edict of our Counsels a resolve which oblidges all the women whose Husbands are with the enemy, & Children whose parents are there, to repair to *them* Immediately; a determination like this which admits of no Exceptions, is unjust & cruell, they are bound by law to Contribute towards the support of those Women & there is many whose conduct has not Merited it, tho there is Others that have, Yet why not discriminate between the Innocent & guilty. The destress of many of those poor Sufferers are such & their Relations, as would melt your Simpathetick Heart; Mrs. Furgerson is determind not to go, She says they may take her life, but shall never banish her from Her Country, This Ladys uncommon good Sense, and great virtues, has allways distinguished her as the first with us. poor Mrs. Gansey to be torn from the friend of her Infancy (Mrs. Swift) to whose more than paternal Arms She returnd in her Widowd state for an assilum. There are others, were fortune fond, had not built there Nest on high but yet are still greater Objects of our Pity whose cottage is renderd happyer by the banishment of a worthless Husband and who by honest industry gains a Subsistence for themselves & Children to be torn from it to perish; I dare say you have heard of the Ladys plan for raiseing a Subscription for the Army. I will enclose you one of them but there is an Alterration taken place instead of waiting for the Donations being sent the ladys of each Ward go from dore to dore & collect them. I am one of those, Honourd with this business. Yesterday we began our tour of duty & had the Satisfaction of being very Successful. There was two lady that were very liberal One 8000 dollars & 10000. There is company in Sight. Adieu. I shall seal this and Send it by the first opertunity.

MM

DOCUMENT NO. 16

THE FORT WILSON RIOT*

Social and political tensions had been building in Pennsylvania before the conflict with Britain began. Philadelphia's working class was well organized, politically active, patriotic, and militant in defense of Pennsylvania's Constitution and of its own interests. Mechanics and artisans did not hesitate to confront members of the political elite, many of whom they regarded as tories because they profited from wartime trade while soldiers and patriots experienced want and hunger.

William Paca was a Maryland delegate to Congress from 1774 to 1779, and governor of the state from 1782 to 1785. William Hemsley was a planter who represented Maryland in Congress from 1782–1783.

γ   γ   γ

* Revolutionary War Collection, MS. 1814, Manuscripts Department, Maryland Historical Society Library, reprinted in Paul H. Smith, Gerard W. Gawalt, Ronald M. Gephart, et al., eds. *Letters of Delegates to Congress: 1774–1789* (Washington, DC: Library of Congress, 1976–1998), 4: 45–46.

William Paca to William Hemsley

Dear Sir   7 Octo. 1779

Yours by the Post was just now delivered to me. . . .

On Monday last we have a great riot in this city. A body of two hundred militia assembled for the purpose of expelling all such as they considered Tories: among these they considered Mr. Morris, Mr. Wilson, Gen. Higbee . . . and included all such who had distinguished themselves in opposition to the present Constitution and Code of Pennsylvania. Apprized of the design of the militia those gentlemen collected their friends and armed themselves and took post in Mr. Wilson's House. The militia assembled in the Commons and dismissed their officer . . . not being obedient enough to their orders: they now marched into the City to Mr. Wilson's House where a formal engagement took place. The militia firing in platoons at Wilson's windows & the other Party firing from the windows: four of the militia I hear were killed & ten wounded: one of the other party was killed & four wounded. Happily for both parties Governor Reed headed the light horse of the City and in a lucky moment just as Wilson's doors were broken down charged with drawn swords on the armed militia, wounded several, took many prisoners & put the rest to flight. The next day the militia again assembled but without arms & obliged the Justices to commit to jail several of Wilson's party. Gov. Reed being absent with the lighthorse at Germantown this day. On the Governors return they were released. This day the Governor and Counsel met at the State House to investigate the affair & both parties are to be heard. . . .

                                                                Yr, Wm Paca

DOCUMENT NO. 17

"AN AMERICAN" ARGUES THE CASE FOR AN UNREGULATED ECONOMY*

In this essay Gouverneur Morris, a member of James Wilson's circle, argued that the very price regulations and tender laws that the Philadelphia militia championed in the Fort Wilson Riot were a major cause of their dif-

---

* *Pennsylvania Packet* (Philadelphia), March 23, 1780.

ficulties and the chaos which bedeviled attempts to supply the army and brought it to the point of mutiny. (See Doc. No. 18.) Free enterprise, fiscal responsibility, and privatization, he insisted, were the only remedies that would set the economy on the path to recovery.

Gouverneur Morris had served as a New York delegate to Congress. In 1781 he was appointed Robert Morris's assistant in the Office of Finance, and drafted many of its arguments in favor of free trade. The essay which follows is one of a series he wrote to answer three anonymous pieces entitled "On Appreciation" which appeared at the end of January in the Pennsylvania Packet. *Their author viewed currency depreciation as a democratic form of taxation that spread the cost of the war equitably among all classes, and argued against attempts to "appreciate" or raise the value of the Continental currency. To this, Gouverneur Morris replied that the young American republic would lose its credibility if it failed to do justice to patriots who had accepted Congress's pledge that it would redeem the Continental currency at face value. The lower classes, however, continued to believe that currency depreciation, tender laws, and price regulations were the best means of correcting what they considered to be the unfair advantages the commercial classes enjoyed.*

γ γ γ

To the INHABITANTS of AMERICA.

[Philadelphia, March 23, 1780]

MY COUNTRYMEN,

... When this war began, we were so much opposed to the tyranny of Great-Britain, and so much disgusted with the abuses of her administration, that, by a very natural progress of the human mind, we felt a repugnance even against those useful institutions which our enemies had adopted. It was therefore a kind of merit to do every thing the reverse of what they did. A general rule to which many and great exceptions ought undoubtedly to be made.

A dislike to contracts and contractors was among the number of those which were then imbibed. Whether the Rulers of America were themselves tinctured with the prevailing prejudice, or whether they thought it was wise to give way to the popular stream, is not worth an inquiry. Certain it is, that they might at that time have made as many contracts as they pleased, upon very good terms, and thereby secured every necessary article, stipulating no other payment than their paper. I shall not now state the many advantages which would have resulted from adopt-

THE CASE FOR AN UNREGULATED ECONOMY 169

ing that mode of obtaining supplies, because men are pretty generally convinced of them. I shall simply observe, that it had been sanctioned by the constant practice of all wise nations, particularly by the King of Prussia, the greatest œconomist in Europe; and that if we had followed their example, it would have been the interest of the contractors with all their Agents and deputies to keep down prices, or in other words, to keep up the value of the paper. I mean not to draw invidious comparisons, but I must be permitted to say, that there is wisdom in rendering private interest subservient to the public welfare. Let me add, that had contracts been made, there would not have been even the appearance of necessity to render the paper a lawful tender, or to regulate prices.

Another and a capital error, was the prohibition laid on all commerce. By this the use of money was lessened, at the moment when the quantity of it was increased. America, deprived of manufactures from abroad, was compelled to make them at home, in a season when the demand for labor was increased by the demand of men for the army. The merchant was obliged to sell his ships, and dismiss his seamen in foreign countries, when ships and seamen were necessary to distress the enemy. And the farmer being deprived of a market, had no longer any incitement to his industry, from which must necessarily follow a scarcity of his productions.

A third great error, in the line of finance, was the regulation of prices. Its operation on the money has already been mentioned, but this was only one among many evils. It disgusted the people at a time when their good will and affection was most necessary. It gave a woeful impression of the new governments, by laying down a violation of the rights of property as the corner stone on which they were to be erected. It discouraged commerce, manufactures and agriculture, or rather it left to the husbandman, tradesman and merchant no encouragement at all. It tended to lock up all commodities, compelling the whole community to become monopolizers. It introduced the tedious and expensive mode of trading by barter. And it sapped the foundations of civil authority, for the temptation of interest to contravene or elude the law was too great to be resisted. Hence the breach of it became general, and that taught the dangerous lesson, that laws may be broken with impunity. Of consequence, the legislature fell into contempt, because it was made manifest that they were not possessed of this superior wisdom and power, which are the sources of reverence and respect.

From the breach of regulations of the first kind arose a contest between the government and the people. A contest always dangerous, but particularly so at such times as those in which it happened. This contest produced regulations of the second kind, enforcing the former by pains and penalties, and empowering persons to seize at limited prices. As the legislatures felt a necessity of assigning reasons for these laws they pretty generally agreed to *whereas it is necessary to carry on this just and necessary war, and whereas it is necessary to support the army who are engaged in it.* From such recitals followed, first, a very disagreeable impression of the justice of a war which was to be maintained by injustice, instead of fair, equal and general taxation; and secondly, a variance between the people and the army, or at least an abatement of their warm and cordial affection towards each other. For on the one hand, the people felt a degree of coldness for those who were held up as the cause why their property was wrested from them; and on the other hand, the army could not but be disgusted at a people who would not otherwise than by force give bread to their protectors. Besides all this, the British were greatly encouraged to carry on the war, by a hope of obtaining that assistance among us which their refugee adherents had promised. . . .

These second regulations were the worst children in the whole family of regulations. The tyranny of the former laws now appeared in its proper garb. The invasion of the rights of property was clothed with every necessary circumstance of violence. And the industrious men who bro't from abroad or produced at home those things which we stood in need of, were subjected to all the insult, and no little degree of the infamy of felons. Good God! What should we think of a legislator who would declare, that it was a crime to procure bread for the hungry, or clothes for the naked, and enact, that those who should in future commit that crime, should have their houses and barns and stores broken open, their property seized, their persons insulted, and their reputation stigmatized with the odious appellations of Monopolizer and Tory? Change but the terms, and we have had such laws. We have had them, even in the hour of our wants and distresses.

Here let us pause, and ask of plain common sense, what must be the necessary effect of this strange policy. The answer is short. Dearth and dearness. . . .

These are the appendages on a system of regulations. These are the fruits of that notable system, which in spite of reason and of history was adopted, and in spite of feeling and experience adhered to. A system of injustice, where injury is sharpened by insult. . . .

But what are these regulations in the event? Are they not a tax, and a very unequal one? They certainly are intended to operate a tax, and on those near to the seat of war, who already suffer enough of its disadvantages. A tax levied on every man in proportion to his industry, and with every circumstance of rigorous injustice. A penalty on commerce, an incitement to engrossing, a discouragement to labor, a reward of indolence. What can such a system produce, except want and distress? Ask of the farmer, why notwithstanding the regulations, he ploughed and sowed, or the merchant, why he imported, their answer is the same, a hope that, by the next harvest or the next arrival, the regulations would be no more; and a confidence that, at the worst, all regulations might be eluded. . . .

By the fruit we may know the tree, and sad fruit indeed hath this tree borne. Who would have suspected three years ago that, in the midst of a war against the greatest naval power, our native productions should become dearer than foreign commodities? Yet even this thing hath come to pass. The whole system of commerce hath been inverted, the laws of property invaded, the laws of justice infringed, every absurdity practiced, and every impossibility tried, to get a little beef and a little bread, which would almost have come forward of themselves if things had been left to their natural course, if honest labor had been permitted to heap the blushing clusters of plenty in the lap of freedom. And now, after straining and working this cumbrous machinery of grinding regulations for three long tedious and oppressive years, what at last have we squeezed from it to recompense our toil? What but the dry husks of penury? Nothing! Nay worse than nothing. For it is notorious that, when we began this war, our country was full of provisions, that our annual exportation and consumption have been much less than they used to be, and that at present we are miserably poor and bare. . . .

AN AMERICAN.

DOCUMENT NO. 18

MUTINY IN THE CONNECTICUT LINE*

In the two and a half years since the austere thanksgiving celebration Joseph Plumb Martin described the army had continued to experience every

---

* Joseph Plumb Martin, *Private Yankee Doodle, Being a Narrative of Some of the Adventures, Dangers and Sufferings of a Revolutionary Soldier,* George F. Scheer, ed., (Boston: Little, Brown, 1962), 182–187.

sort of privation. Martin did not try to identify who or what was most to blame for the army's plight—unwise regulations, incompetence, or greedy speculators. He only knew that his country had failed its defenders miserably. The soldiers' decision to march under arms in defiance of orders was a potent symbol of exasperation at their country's failure to supply them with the most basic necessities. Actual violence was minimal, but neither army officers nor civilian officials underestimated the seriousness of the threat the mutiny implied. Lack of food, clothing and pay were persistent irritants throughout the war. The mutiny of the Connecticut line was by no means the largest or most threatening protest that occurred.

γ γ γ

New Jersey, May 25, 1780

We left Westfield about the twenty-fifth of May and went to Basking Ridge to our old winter cantonments. We did not reoccupy the huts which we built, but some others that the troops had left, upon what account I have forgotten. Here, the monster Hunger, still attended us. He was not be shaken off by any efforts we could use, for here was the old story of starving, as rife as ever. We had entertained some hopes that when we had left the lines and joined the main army, we should fare a little better, but we found that there was no betterment in the case. For several days after we rejoined the army, we got a little musty bread and a little beef, about every other day, but this lasted only a short time and then we got nothing at all. The men were now exasperated beyond endurance; they could not stand it any longer. They saw no other alternative but to starve to death, or break up the army, give all up and go home. This was a hard matter for the soldiers to think upon. They were truly patriotic, they loved their country, and they had already suffered everything short of death in its cause; and now, after such extreme hardships to give up all was too much, but to starve to death was too much also. What to be done? Here was the army starved and naked, and there their country sitting still and expecting the army to do notable things while fainting from sheer starvation. All things considered, the army was not to be blamed. Reader, suffer what we did and you will say so, too.

We had borne as long as human nature could endure, and to bear longer we considered folly. Accordingly, one pleasant day, the men spent the most of their time upon the parade, growling like soreheaded dogs. At evening roll call they began to show their dissatisfaction by snapping

MUTINY IN THE CONNECTICUT LINE

at the officers and acting contrary to their orders. After their dismissal from the parade, the officers went, as usual, to their quarters, except the adjutant, who happened to remain, giving details for next day's duty to the orderly sergeants, or some other business, when the men, none of whom had left the parade began to make him sensible that they had something in train. He said something that did not altogether accord with the soldiers' ideas of propriety, one of the men retorted; the adjutant called him a mutinous rascal, or some such epithet, and then left the parade. This man, then stamping the butt of his musket upon the ground, as much as to say, I am in a passion, called out, "Who will parade with me?" The whole regiment immediately fell in and formed.

We had made no plans for our future operations, but while we were consulting how to proceed, the Fourth Regiment, which lay on our left, formed, and came and paraded with us. We now concluded to go in a body to the other two regiments [the Third and Sixth] that belonged to our brigade and induce them to join with us. These regiments lay forty or fifty rods in front of us, with a brook and bushes between. We did not wish to have anyone in particular to command, lest he might be singled out for a court-martial to exercise its demency [thus in text, probably "clemency"] upon. We therefore gave directions to the drummers to give certain signals on the drums; at the first signal we shouldered our arms, at the second we faced, at the third we began our march to join with the other two regiments, and went off with music playing.

By this time our officers had obtained knowledge of our military maneuvering and some of them had run across the brook, by a nearer way than we had taken, it being now quite dark, and informed the officers of those regiments of our approach and supposed intentions. The officers ordered their men to parade as quick as possible *without* arms. When that was done, they stationed a camp guard, that happened to be near at hand, between the men and their huts, which prevented them from entering and taking their arms, which they were very anxious to do. Colonel [Return Jonathan] Meigs, of the Sixth Regiment, exerted himself to prevent his men from obtaining their arms until he received a severe wound in his side by a bayonet in the scuffle, which cooled his courage at the time. He said he had always considered himself the soldier's friend and thought the soldiers regarded him as such, but had reason now to conclude he might be mistaken. Colonel Meigs was truly an excellent man and a brave officer. The man, whoever he was, that wounded him, doubtless had no particular grudge against him; it was dark and the wound was given, it is probable, altogether unintentionally. Colonel Meigs ['s son] was afterwards Governor of Ohio and Postmaster General.

When we found the officers had been too crafty for us we returned with grumbling instead of music, the officers following in the rear growling in concert. One of the men in the rear calling out, "Halt in front," the officers seized upon him like wolves on a sheep and dragged him out of the ranks, intending to make an example of him for being a "mutinous rascal," but the bayonets of the men pointing at their breasts as thick as hatchel teeth, compelled them quickly to relinquish their hold of him. We marched back to our own parade and then formed again. The officers now began to coax us to disperse to our quarters, but that had no more effect upon us than their threats. One of them slipped away into the bushes, and after a short time returned, counterfeiting to have come directly from headquarters. Said he, "There is good news for you, boys, there has just arrived a large drove of cattle for the army." But this piece of finesse would not avail. All the answer he received for his labor was, "Go and butcher them," or some such slight expression. The lieutenant colonel of the Fourth Regiment [John Sumner] now came on to the parade. He could persuade *his* men, he said, to go peaceably to their quarters. After a good deal of palaver, he ordered them to shoulder their arms, but the men taking no notice of him or his order, he fell into a violent passion, threatening them with the bitterest punishment if they did not immediately obey his orders. After spending a whole quiver of the arrows of his rhetoric, he again ordered them to shoulder their arms, but he met with the same success that he did at the first trial. He therefore gave up the contest as hopeless and left us and walked off to his quarters, chewing the cud of resentment all the way, and how much longer I neither knew nor cared. The rest of the officers, after they found that they were likely to meet with no better success than the colonel, walked off likewise to their huts.

While we were under arms, the Pennsylvania troops, who lay not far from us, were ordered under arms and marched off their parades upon, as they were told, a secret expedition. They had surrounded us, unknown to either us or themselves (except the officers). At length, getting an item of what was going forward, they inquired of some of the stragglers what was going on among the Yankees. Being informed that they had mutinied on account of the scarcity of provisions, "Let us join them," said they. "Let us join the Yankees; they are good fellows, and

MUTINY IN THE CONNECTICUT LINE

have no notion of lying here like fools and starving." Their officers needed no further hinting. The troops were quickly ordered back to their quarters, from fear that they would join in the same song with the Yankees. We knew nothing of all this for some time afterwards.

After our officers had left us to our own option, we dispersed to our huts and laid by our arms of our own accord, but the worm of hunger gnawing so keen kept us from being entirely quiet. We therefore still kept upon the parade in groups, venting our spleen at our country and government, then at our officers, and then at ourselves for our imbecility in staying there and starving in detail for an ungrateful people who did not care what became of us, so they could enjoy themselves while we were keeping a cruel enemy from them. While we were thus venting our gall against we knew not who, Colonel [Walter] Stewart of the Pennsylvania Line, with two or three other officers of that Line, came to us and questioned us respecting our unsoldierlike conduct (as he termed it). We told him he needed not to be informed of the cause of our present conduct, but that we had borne till we considered further forbearance pusillanimity; that the times, instead of mending, were growing worse; and finally, that we were determined not to bear or forbear much longer. We were unwilling to desert the cause of our country, when in distress; that we knew her cause involved our own, but what signified our perishing in the act of saving her, when that very act would inevitably destroy us, and she must finally perish with us.

"Why do you not go to your officers," said he, "and complain in a regular manner?" We told him we had repeatedly complained to them, but they would not hear us. "Your officers," said he, "are gentlemen, they *will* attend to you. I know them; they cannot refuse to hear you. But," said he, "your officers suffer as much as you do. We all suffer. The officers have no money to purchase supplies with any more than the private men have, and if there is nothing in the public store we must fare as hard as you. I have no other resources than you have to depend upon. I had not a sixpence to purchase a partridge that was offered me the other day. Besides," said he, "you know not how much you injure your own characters by such conduct. You Connecticut troops have won immortal honor to yourselves the winter past, by your perseverance, patience, and bravery, and now you are shaking it off at your heels. But I will go and see your officers, and talk with them myself." He went, but what the result was, I never knew. This Colonel Stewart was an excellent officer, much beloved and respected by the troops of the line he belonged to. He possessed great personal beauty; the Philadelphia ladies styled him *the Irish Beauty.*

Our stir did us some good in the end, for we had provisions directly after, so we had no great cause for complaint for some time.

DOCUMENT NO. 19

CONGRESS APPROVES A TAX ON TRADE*

Proposals for an impost (tax on trade) raised some ideologically charged questions: who should have the authority to levy and collect it, Congress or the states; what purposes should its revenues be used for; how long should it remain in effect? Congressman John Witherspoon suggested giving Congress broad powers to tax and to regulate both domestic and foreign commerce. His resolution provided that the impost would be in effect when approved by nine states, not the thirteen required to amend the Articles (not yet in effect). These suggestions, if accepted, would have created a very different kind of central government than the one the Articles described. Congress's journal reveals none of the passion which must have characterized the debate. The resolution finally approved asked the states to give Congress the power to levy the impost. Its proceeds were assigned solely to pay off the war debt, after which it would cease to be in effect.

γ γ γ

Saturday, February 3, 1781

The order of the day was called for, when a motion was made by Mr. [John] Witherspoon, seconded by Mr. [Thomas] Burke,

That it is indispensably necessary that the United States in Congress assembled, should be vested with a right of superintending the commercial regulations of every State, that none may take place that shall be partial or contrary to the common interest; and that they should be vested with the exclusive right of laying duties upon all imported articles, no restriction to be valid, and no such duty to be laid, but with

* Worthington Chauncey Ford, et al., eds. *Journals of the Continental Congress: 1774–1789.* 34 vols. (Washington, DC: U.S. Government Printing Office, 1904–1937), 19: 110–113.

the consent of nine states. Provided, that all duties and imposts laid by the United States in Congress assembled, shall always be a certain proportion of the value of the article or articles on which the same shall be laid; and the same article shall bear the same duty and impost throughout the said states without exemption: and provided that all such duties and imposts shall be for the perfecting of certain specified purposes, which purposes being perfected, the said duties and imposts so appropriated, shall cease: provided also, that the United States in Congress assembled, shall not be empowered to appropriate any duties or imposts for perpetual annuities, or other perpetual or indefinite interests, or for annuities for more than three lives at the same time in being, or for a longer term than _____ years . . . ~~and provided that when any duty or impost shall be laid on any article of the growth or produce of any state, or upon any article not imported into the United States, the net proceeds of such duties and imposts shall be placed to the credit of the State producing, the said article or paying the said duty or impost; and such duties and imposts shall cease to operate in the states respectively so soon as their respective quotas of the appropriated fund shall be discharged.~~

On the question to agree to this, the yeas and nays being required by Mr. [John] Mathews:
So it passed in the negative. . . .

The report from the Committee of the Whole, being amended, was agreed to as follows:

Resolved, That it be recommended to the several states, as indispensably necessary, that they ~~pass laws granting to~~ vest a power in Congress, to levy for the use of the United States, a duty of five per cent. *ad valorem*, at the time and place of importation, upon all goods, wares and merchandises of foreign growth and manufactures, which may be imported into any of the said states from any foreign port, island or plantation, after the first day of May, 1781; except arms, ammunition, cloathing and other articles imported on account of the United States, or any of them; . . .
~~That the monies arising from the said duties be paid quarterly into the hands of such persons as Congress shall appoint to receive the same.~~
That the monies arising from the said duties be appropriated to the

discharge of the principal and interest of the debts already contracted, or which may be contracted, on the faith of the United States, for supporting the present war:

That the said ~~laws be continued in force and the~~ duties ~~aforesaid collected and paid as aforesaid~~ be continued until the said debts shall be fully and finally discharged.

DOCUMENT NO. 20

THOUGHTS ON THE CHARACTERS OF AMERICAN MINISTERS*

Gouverneur Morris advocated strengthening the central government by creating executive departments. His unpublished "thoughts" were intended to persuade his audience that ministers would enable the government to function more effectively and to convince those who feared executive power that Congress would appoint qualified men who had the "virtue" republicans required of office holders. Morris described candidates he had in mind. His choice for financier was Robert Morris. Soon after Robert was appointed, he named Gouverneur as his assistant. For the war department, Gouverneur favored Nathanael Greene, who had served as Quartermaster General and who had replaced Benjamin Lincoln as commander of the southern department after Lincoln surrendered to the British at Charleston. Congress chose Lincoln, not Greene. It selected Gouverneur's close friend, New York lawyer Robert R. Livingston, over Arthur Lee as secretary for foreign affairs. When it could not find anyone willing to head the marine department, it asked Robert Morris to manage this department as well.

γ γ γ

[Philadelphia, 1780–1781]

To determine who should be appointed Minister either of the Finances, of War, of the Marine, or of foreign Affairs, may be very difficult; but it may not be so difficult to determine the Qualities necessary in each of these Departments, and having thereby established a Rule, the proper Persons will be more easily ascertained: These Qualities may

---

* MS: Gouverneur Morris Papers, Rare Book and Manuscript Library, Columbia University.

be classed under the different Heads of Genius, Temper, Knowlege, Education, Principles, Manners, and Circumstances.

Our Minister of the Finances should have a strong Understanding, be persevering, industrious, and severe in exacting from all a rigid Compliance with their Duties. He should possess a Knowlege of Mankind, and of the Culture and Commerce, Produce and Resources, Temper and Manners, of the different States. He should be Habituated to Business, on the most extensive Scale particularly with that which is usually denominated *Money Matters* and He should, therefore, be not only a regular bred Merchant, but also one who hath been long and deeply engaged in that Profession. At the same Time he should be practically acquainted with our political Affairs, and the Management of public Business. He should be warmly and thoroughly attached to America, not bigotted to any particular State; and his Attachment should be founded, not on Whim, Caprice, Resentment, or a weak Compliance with the Current of Opinion, but on a manly and rational Conviction of the Benefits of Independence. His Manners should be plain and simple, sincere and honest, his Morals pure, his Integrity unblemished, and he should enjoy general Credit and Reputation, both at Home and abroad.

Our Minister of War should have a Mind penetrating, clear, methodical, and comprehensive, joined to a firm and indefatigable Spirit. He should be thoroughly acquainted with the Soldiery, Know the Resources of the Country, be most intimately informed of the Geography of America, and the Means of marching and subsisting Armies in every Part of it. He should be taken from the Army and he should have acted, at some time or other, as a Quarter Master General, if not as a Commander in a seperate Department. He should be attached to the civil Head of the Empire, and not envious of the Glory of others, but ambitious of honest Fame. His Manners should be those of a generous Soldier, and not of an intriguing Politician. He should be disagreeable to no considerable Body or Denomination of Men, and he should by all Means be agreeable to the Commander in Chief.

A Minister of the Marine should be a Man of plain good Sense, and a good Oeconomist, firm but not harsh. He should be well acquainted with Sea Affairs, such as the Construction, fitting and victualling Ships, the Conduct of Manœvres on a Cruize and in Action, the nautical Face of the Earth, and maritime Phenomena. He should also know, the Temper Manners and Disposition of Sailors, for all which Purposes, it is proper that he should have been bred to that Business, and have followed it, in Peace and in War, in a military and commercial Capacity. His Principles and Manners should be absolutely republican and his Circumstances not indigent.

A Minister of foreign Affairs should have a Genius quick, lively penetrating. He should write, on all Occasions, with Clearness and Perspicuity, be capable of expressing the Sentiments of the Sovereign with Dignity, and conveying strong Sense and Argument, in easy and agreable Diction. His Temper should be mild, cool, and placid; he should be festive, insinuating, and pliant, yet obstinate; communicative and yet reserved. He should know the human Face and Heart, and the Connections between them; He should be versed in the Laws of Nature and Nations and not ignorant of the civil and municipal Law. He should know Something of the History of Europe and of the Interests, Views, Commerce; and Productions, of the commercial and maritime Powers. He should know the Interests and Commerce of America, understand the french and spanish Languages, at least the forms, and he should be acquainted with the Modes and Forms of public Business. He should be a Man educated more in the World than in the Closet and more to public, than to private Business, that by Use, as well as by Nature, he may have proper Attention to great Objects and proper Contempt for small ones. He should be attached to the Independence of America, and the Alliance with France, as the great Pillars of our Politicks; and this Attachment should not be slight and accidental, but regular, consistent, and founded in strong Conviction. His Manners should be gentle and polite, above all Things he should be honest, and least of all Things avaricious. His Circumstances and Connections should be such, as to give solid Pledges for his Fidelity and he should by no Means be disagreable to the Prince with whom we are in Alliance, his Ministers, or Subjects.

DOCUMENT NO. 21

NEW INSTRUCTIONS FOR THE AMERICAN PEACE COMMISSIONERS*

Congress first specified the terms that it would accept as a basis for a peace settlement on August 14, 1779. The "great object" of the war and a precon-

---

* Worthington Chauncey Ford, et al., eds. *Journals of the Continental Congress: 1774-1789.* 34 vols. (Washington, DC: U.S. Government Printing Office, 1904-1937), 20: 651-652.

dition for any negotiation, it said, was British recognition of American independence. Congress then instructed its commissioners to claim the Mississippi River south to the 31st parallel as the new nation's western and southern boundaries, but gave them latitude to negotiate. Although it also wished to obtain all of Canada and Nova Scotia, and recognition of Americans' "equal common" right to fish traditional grounds off Newfoundland and in the Gulf of St. Lawrence, Congress refrained from making either acquisition an "ultimatum" so as not to prolong the war. In the revised instructions printed below, Congress expressed much more willingness to allow France great influence over which, if any, of its secondary but "desirable" objectives would be achieved in the peace settlement.

γ γ γ

[Philadelphia, June 15, 1781]

Instructions to the honourable. John Adams, Benjamin Franklin, John Jay, Henry Laurens and Thomas Jefferson, Ministers plenipotentiary on behalf of the United States to negotiate a treaty of Peace.

You are hereby authorised and instructed to concur, in behalf of these United States, with his Most Christian Majesty, in accepting the mediation proposed by the Empress of Russia and the Emperor of Germany:

You are to accede to no treaty of peace which shall not be such as may 1st. effectually secure the independence and sovereignty of the thirteen states, according to the form and effect of the treaties subsisting between the said states and his Most Christian Majesty; and 2d. in which the said treaties shall not be left in their full force & validity.

As to disputed boundaries and other particulars, we refer you to the Instructions given to Mr. Adams, dated 14 August, 1779, and 18 October, 1780, from which you will easily perceive the desires and expectations of Congress; but we think it unsafe, at this distance to tie you up by absolute and peremptory directions upon any other subject than the two essential articles above mentioned. You are therefore at liberty to secure the interest of the United States in such manner as circumstances may direct, and as the state of the belligerent and disposition of the mediating powers may require. For this purpose, you are to make the most candid and confidential communications upon all subjects to the ministers of our generous ally, the King of France; to undertake nothing in the negotiations for peace or truce without their knowledge and concurrence; and ultimately to govern yourselves by their advice and opinion, endeavouring in your whole conduct to make them sensible how much we rely upon his Majesty's influence for effectual support in every thing that may be necessary to the present security, or future prosperity of the United States of America.

If a difficulty should arise in the course of the negotiation for peace, from the backwardness of Britain to make a formal acknowledgment of our independence you are at liberty to agree to a truce, or to make such other concessions as may not affect the substance of what we contend for; and provided that Great Britain be not left in possession of any part of the thirteen United States.

DOCUMENT NO. 22

POLITICAL ARGUMENTS AGAINST THE IMPOST*

Rhode Island Congressmen Jonathan Arnold and David Howell cast Congress in the role the British government had played in the years before the revolution, and sounded classic republican themes which resonate as much today as they did in the eighteenth century. The letter printed below reached its destination in time to be read to the Rhode Island Assembly just before it voted—against ratifying the impost amendment on November 1.

γ γ γ

Rhode Island Delegates (Jonathan Arnold and David Howell)
to the Governor of Rhode Island (William Greene)

Philadelphia Octr. 15th. 1782.

Sir:

On this all important occasion we cannot be silent. A moment remains before the post sets off, the last which can arrive at Providence, before the October Session of Assembly.

The object of a seven year's war has been to preserve the liberties of this country, and not to assume into our own hands the power of governing tyrannically.

* William R. Staples, *Rhode Island in the Continental Congress: 1765–1790.* ed. Reuben A. Guild (Providence, RI, 1870), 394–398.

POLITICAL ARGUMENTS AGAINST THE IMPOST

It has been on our part a contest for freedom—not for power! This has been the prize for which we so nobly contended. This, the goal, for which our course, so unremittingly pursued, has been directed. This the sacred palladium of all our hopes. We know your early, continued, and persevering zeal in your country's cause. We cannot doubt your firmness. To quicken your memory, awaken your feelings, and to fix your attention is the object of this letter.

Congress has demanded of you an immediate answer, in regard to the impost.... A perpetual grant is demanded of you. We say perpetual, for that it will eventually be, such is as clear as the meridian sun. It is to be granted to Congress until all their debts are paid. They have power to contract as many debts as they please, and are not to account with you for their conduct. Will not half pay, pensions, and other pretexts, perpetually involve you deeper and deeper in debt, and render it still more necessary to continue this grant to perpetuity, than it is to make it in the first instance! Consult the voice of nature; consult the histories of mankind. Nay, consult your own experience and give an answer, and let that answer govern your vote on this occasion.

This being the case, permit us, Sir, to demand of you, what right you have to make a perpetual grant of money? Will not succeeding assemblies discover that you have invaded their rights? Will not posterity complain that you have given away their money, which, on every principle of the present revolution, they would be entitled to do themselves? ... Is not this a bold attack on the liberties of the people at large? ... Did America resist the power of Britain to avoid only three pence on a pound in tea, or was it their claims, their unlimited claims, and the tendency of their measures? Was it not rather oppression and violence apprehended and which existed in our well grounded fears and reasonable jealousy, that brought on the present war, than the great weight of present injuries.

A system was formed which, if carried into effect,—and it would have been by degrees,—would have deprived us of all that is valuable in life. This approach of tyranny was resisted, and with good reason, and hitherto by the blessing of Heaven with good success. Tyranny is to be resisted most easily and effectually in its first approaches, and at a distance. When its standard is planted, it will have numerous adherents, and power to protect and gratify them. ...

The bribes of half-pay officers, pensioners, and public creditors, whose number and influence might be increased from time to time, at the pleasure of Congress, would enlarge, extend and increase their power, and soon induce the necessity of pursuing the remaining parts of the plan, by adopting the land tax, the poll tax, and the excise. After which the bonds of Union, to use the phrase of the advocates of these measures, would be complete; and we will add, the yoke of tyranny fixed on all the states, and the chains riveted.

The great system of government is established by the Confederation. This was a work of time and great wisdom. The eighth Article points out the method of ascertaining the quotas of the states in all pecuniary requisitions, the equality and justice of the mode is not contested. But it is said, annual taxation in this mode does not give sufficient security to the public creditors. In reply it may be observed that this was all the security they had a right to expect when they became creditors, of the public. This was the ancient and only approved method of raising money, before the Confederation was adopted. The creditors, therefore, who trusted the public before that period, have no right to demand a greater security, for it was not promised them, in the contract.

And by the sixth and ninth Articles of Confederation, the power of imposing duties is expressly retained by the states in their individual capacities. The public creditors, therefore, cannot claim a right to a Continental impost, as a security for their money, in virtue of the Confederation, which in so many words, would entirely blast all hopes of that kind, had they been previously indulged. On what ground then, can they demand greater security than they have by annual taxation? On none whatever. They ought, however, to be paid, and we make no doubt they will be paid to the extent of their just demands, and that in a Continental way, and no other.

But it is further said, the impost is necessary to give us further credit, and to procure loans. The contrary is fact. We have drawn from Europe by loans or gratuity already, thirty seven millions of livers, and a large loan is now negotiating there, and has in part succeeded, and will no doubt be filled up, without the security of mortgaging an impost, or any promise of the kind. Posterity, instead of regretting that our credit was not better established, will rather admire at its extent when they feel the weight of the burthen thereby transmitted down upon them.

It is not necessary, therefore, to enable us to procure loans abroad, but rather to be avoided on that account as a temptation to incur an extravagant foreign debt, and endangering a more lavish expenditure of public moneys. On what footing, then, is the measure necessary? No plighted faith requires it; no reasons of finance can induce it; no policy of state can justify it; no principle of our Constitution can warrant it. The glorious fabric of freedom erected in this new world is the admiration of all civilized nations. May it long remain unimpaired. The structure of its several parts deserves attention, and constitutes its symmetry and elegance.

The weight of Congress rests and bears only on the several states; the states bear only on the several counties, in some states and the counties on the towns, and, in others, the states bear immediately on the towns, and the towns, in all, on the individuals,—the broad basis of power,—which reared and supports the whole fabric.

The impost would break in upon this beautiful proportion and empower Congress, by their own officers, to bear with their own weight directly on individuals. This would disturb the general harmony, derange the elegant proportion, and endanger the welfare of the whole building.

The Continental Treasury is to be supplied from the several states, agreeable to Article eight, by successive requisitions. When a new requisition is made, the purposes for which it is to be appropriated are to be pointed out to you; and it is to be accompanied with particular estimates. You are, at the same time, to be informed what has been done, with your last quota, and, on a full consideration of the representation so made to you, you are to grant your money like freemen, from time to time, bound only, as a sovereign and independent State, by your sentiments of justice, of virtue and by your sacred honor. This is the voice of the Confederation. . . .

We cannot doubt but the measure will be postponed, or finally rejected by a large majority of the virtuous and patriotic Legislature of Our State, which has from its first settlement preserved its liberties entire; been foremost in the present glorious revolution, and by a decided opinion on this important occasion, will preserve the liberties of the United States and transmit them to posterity, and thereby erect to themselves a monument more durable than brass.

With sentiments of the highest esteem we have the honor to be
    Your Excellency's very humble servants,
                              Jonathan Arnold,
                              David Howell

DOCUMENT NO. 23

THE SUPERINTENDENT OF FINANCE RESIGNS*

When Robert Morris agreed to serve as Financier he argued that paying past debts, like the back pay owed to the army, would eat up revenues that were needed for current expenses. Nevertheless, he knew that he had to convince the public's creditors that the United States was fiscally responsible and would take measures to pay what it owned as soon as possible after the war was over. Defeat of the impost amendment made this highly unlikely and limited the prospect for more foreign loans. This short letter announcing his provisional resignation appears to have been designed to jolt Congress into approving a comprehensive revenue plan and to encourage both civilian and military public creditors to provide the political leverage needed to persuade all the states to ratify it. Publication of Morris's letter on March 1 set the stage for the Newburgh conspiracy and for a "republican" reaction to Morris's insistence that the central government had to be given the power to levy a tax.

γ γ γ

Robert Morris to the President of Congress (Elias Boudinot)

Office of Finance 24th. January 1783

Sir

As Nothing but the public Danger would have induced me to accept my Office, so I was determined to hold it, until the Danger was past, or else to meet my Ruin in the common Wreck. Under greater Difficulties than were apprehended by the most timid, and with less Support than was expected by the least sanguine, the generous Confidence of the Public accomplished more than I presumed to hope.

Congress will recollect, that I expressly stipulated to take no Part in past Transactions. My Attention to the public Debts, therefore, arose from the Conviction that funding them on solid Revenues was the last essential Work of our glorious Revolution. The Accomplishment of

---

* *Independent Gazetteer* (Philadelphia), March 1, 1783; reprinted in E. James Ferguson, et al., eds., *The Papers of Robert Morris* (Pittsburgh: University of Pittsburgh Press, 1973-1999), 7: 368.

this necessary Work, is among the Objects nearest my Heart; and to effect it, I would continue to sacrafice Time, Property, and domestic Bliss.

Many late Circumstances have so far lessened our Apprehensions from the common Enemy, that my original Motives have almost ceased to operate. But other Circumstances have postponed the Establishment of public Credit in such Manner, that I fear it will never be made. To encrease our Debts while the Prospect of paying them diminishes, does not consist with my Ideas of Integrity. I must therefore quit a Situation which becomes utterly insupportable. But lest the Public Measures might be deranged by any Precipitation, I will continue to serve until the End of May. If effectual Measures are not taken by that Period, to make permanent Provision for the public Debts, of every Kind, Congress will be pleased to appoint some other Man to be the Superintendant of their Finances. I should be unworthy of the Confidence reposed in me by my fellow Citizens, If I did not explicitly declare, that I will never be the Minister of Injustice. With perfect Esteem and Respect I have the Honor to be Sir your Excellency's most obedient and humble Servant.

Robt Morris

His Excellency The President of Congress

DOCUMENT NO. 24

CONGRESS CONFRONTS A GROWING CRISIS*

The remarkable peace treaty the American commissioners had negotiated in defiance of their instructions to obtain France's prior approval reached Philadelphia on March 12. Madison's notes show that Congress was focused, not on the victory Americans had won, but on the problems that remained to be solved before her triumph was complete.

γ γ γ

* The Papers of James Madison, DLC; reprinted in William T. Hutchinson and William M. E. Rachal, et al., eds. *The Papers of James Madison, Congressional Series*, (Chicago and Charlottesville, VA., 1962–1991) 6: 348.

Monday March 17 [1783].

A letter was rcd. from Genl Washington inclosing two anonymous & inflammatory exhortations to the army to assemble for the purpose of seeking by other means, that justice which their country shewed no disposition to afford them. The steps taken by the Genl. to avert the gathering storm & his professions of inflexible adherence to his duty to Congress & to his country, excited the most affectionate sentiments towards him. By private letters from the army & other circumstances there appeared good ground for suspecting that the Civil Creditors were intriguing in order to inflame the army into such desperation as wd. produce a general provision for the public debts. These papers were committed to Mr. Gilman, Mr. Dyer, Mr. Clark, Mr. Rutlidge & Mr. Mercer. The appt. of These gentlemen was brought about by a few members who wished to saddle with this embarrassment the men who had opposed the measures necessary for satisfying the army viz, the half pay & permanent funds, agst. one or other of which the individuals in question had voted.

This alarming intelligence from the army added to the critical situation to wch our affairs in Europe were reduced by the variance of our ministers with our ally, and to the difficulty of establishing the means of fulfilling the Engagemts. & securing the harmony of the U.S. & to the confusions apprehended from the approaching resignation of the Superintt. of Finance, gave peculiar awe & solemnity to the present moment, & oppressed the minds of Congs. with an anxiety & distress which had been scarcely felt in any period of the revolution.

DOCUMENT NO. 25

"LUCIUS" ATTACKS THE FINANCIER*

"Lucius" has never been definitively identified. The five essays which appeared under this pseudonym in the spring of 1783 may or may not be the work of a single author. Arthur Lee, a strident critic of Robert Morris and

---

* *Freeman's Journal* (Philadelphia), March 12, 1783; reprinted in E. James Ferguson, et al., eds., *The Papers of Robert Morris* (Pittsburgh: University of Pittsburgh Press, 1973–1999), 7: 559–561.

an ally of leading republicans in Massachusetts, was widely believed to have been either directly or indirectly responsible for most or all of them. "Lucius" challenged Morris's motives for insisting that the central government had to be given powers to raise a revenue to pay the public debt in terms very similar to those used by John Adams against Governor Bernard and his "junto" in his "Novanglus" essay.

In their totality, the "Lucius" essays reprised the full range of issues related to taxation, the central government, executive power, influence, and corruption that had generated the revolution and remained central to republican ideology. Where once the context of the debate was imperial, now it clearly had national relevance and focus. The "Lucius" essays were reprinted in New York City by James Rivington, a loyalist printer, and in Massachusetts and Rhode Island, where, republicans hoped, they would sustain opposition to the impost.

γ γ γ

[Philadelphia, March 12, 1783]

To ROBERT MORRIS, Esq.

"I Have done the deed!" you may cry out like Macbeth, and with equal horror—"I have murdered public credit as she slept—I have murdered her, being my guest!" To your guardianship, sir, she was committed. Where is she now? Does she exist? Has not your announcing to the public, that nothing but the most *insupportable injustice govern[e]d the councils of this nation—that we are most dishonestly* increasing our *debts, as the prospect of* paying them *diminishes*, stab'd her to the heart? If the public give any credit to your assertions, if they do not judge, and such judgment would be right, that *the man who is capable of betraying the high secrets of his office, is unworthy of credit*, who is it that will henceforth trust a single shilling to the United States of America?

Was this a time, sir, when a persuasion of the impracticability of succeeding had so balanced with the enemy the injury of losing us, that the scales of war and peace hung even—was this a time to make such a disclosure of our weakness to that enemy? Did your tory friends deem it necessary to throw this into the scale of war, that all its horrors might be renewed upon us? That the enemy might be tempted to try once more, what force combined with seduction may do, against a people deprived of credit abroad by you, and thrown into convulsions at home? The able, the artful Carleton, stands ready for the purpose.

Could you, sir, be ignorant that *these must be the effects of your publication?* You cannot say you were. Ignorance made drunk could not but foresee it. Where then will your conduct find apology or atonement?

But what will the public think of you, when I shew that your imputations are not founded in truth. Will you deny, sir, that at the time of your publication, Congress had resolved, that funding the public debts was proper; and that they were employed in preparing such a plan for it, as might be admissible in the states? Will you deny, that the payments from the respective states have been increasing as their abilities increased, and that the pressure of the war, and the almost total abolition of commerce, are the real reasons why their contributions are not fully adequate to satisfy the public demands? With what truth then could you say, that they are increasing their debts as the prospect of paying them diminishes; and that their minister must be the minister of injustice? Though I am not in the secrets of government, yet I have such information that I defy you to contradict those facts.

Your partisans will say, you had a right to resign and to publish your reasons for it. In some measure this is true. But had you a *right to calumniate Congress* and *deceive* the *public?* I have shewn that you have attempted both, and, as far as the secrets of the heart are disclosed by actions, you appear to have done it with the most malignant view.

Let us suppose, for I am willing to give you every advantage, that your opinion, with regard to the most proper method of paying the public debt, had not been adopted, would that warrant your accusing Congress or the states of dishonesty and artifice? Can you say with truth, that any state, or portion of a state, has shewn the smallest inclination to defraud the public creditors? On what foundation then do your imputations rest? That your sovereign will should be received as law; that submission to your absolute dictation should be the only rule of government, are manifestly your sentiments. So much has a sudden and enormous acquisition of wealth, by speculating on the distresses of the war, pampered your pride and inebriated your understanding. Remember, sir, what you *were* and think what you *may be.* This admonition is the salutary admonition of a friend. There was a time, sir, and it is not long past, when you were compelled to atone, not only to Congress, but to individuals, by the most abject submission, for the injurious insolence of your conduct. Beware of a similar humiliation.

Whether this system of permanent funds, the establishment of which you demand in the tone of a sovereign more than a servant, be eligible,

I shall not at present enquire. But as this system, however *near your heart*, did not originate with you, since you expressly stipulated to have no part in past transactions, it seems unaccountable that these actions should be made the reason of your resignation. Why should you now be so anxious about these debts, which you stipulated to have no concern with at your entrance into office. Is it that you are engaged in those deep speculations, that have been made in loan office certificates. Must these speculations be secured in the possession of princely fortunes, or the United States be thrown into convulsions, and, as far as you can effect it, their credit ruined? Your former speculations had nearly ruined the worthy citizens of Boston; your present ones strike at the whole union. Perhaps then it will be found that all this boast of honesty and patriotism, is prompted solely by the interest you and your friends have in these certificates, not as *original subscribers*, but as *purchasers* from the *distressed possessors*, at an *immense depreciation*.

But whether folly, or faction, or private interest, or public enmity, were the real motives of your publication, the act itself is so replete with mischief that it ought to destroy you for ever in the opinion of a discerning people.

LUCIUS

DOCUMENT NO. 26

DAVID RAMSAY'S ACCOUNT OF THE NEWBURGH AFFAIR*

This and the following account present two contrasting interpretations of the Newburgh affair written by authors who were alive at the time, had access to different sources of information, and held different perspectives on the type of government that was needed to preserve the benefits of the Revolution. David Ramsay had been a physician in the Continental army and was a South Carolina delegate to Congress when the officers' protest occurred. He published his history of the Revolution in 1789, shortly after George Washington took office as president under the Constitution of the United

---

* David Ramsay, *The History of the American Revolution*, Lester Cohen, ed., (Indianapolis: Liberty*Classics*, 1990), 639–641.

States. Ramsay, an enthusiastic supporter of the new government, celebrates Washington's critical role in preventing the Newburgh affair from getting out of hand. He stresses the army's sufferings and its virtues, not its anger. He would have been well aware of rumors about civilian conspirators but does not mention them. Instead, he portrays the Newburgh affair as largely the work of the author of the Newburgh address. He minimizes the protests made by soldiers as they returned to their home states, and claims instead that they were easily reintegrated into their former occupations.

γ γ γ

1789

WHILE THE CITIZENS OF THE United States were anticipating the blessings of peace, their army which had successfully stemmed the tide of British victories, was unrewarded for its services. The States which had been rescued by their exertions from slavery, were in no condition to pay them their stipulated due. To dismiss officers and soldiers, who had spent the prime of their days in serving their country, without an equivalent for their labors, or even a sufficiency to enable them to gain a decent living, was a hard but unavoidable case. An attempt was made by anonymous and seditious publications to inflame the minds of the officers and soldiers, and induce them to unite in redressing their own grievances, while they had arms in their hands. As soon as General Washington was informed of the nature of these papers, he requested the General and field officers, with one officer from each company, and a proper representation from the staff of the army, to assemble on an early day. He rightly judged that it would be much easier to divert from a wrong to a right path, than to recal fatal and hasty steps, after they had once been taken. The period, previously to the meeting of the officers, was improved in preparing them for the adoption of moderate measures. Gen. Washington sent for one officer after another, and enlarged in private, on the fatal consequences, and particularly on the loss of character to the whole army, which would result from intemperate resolutions. When the officers were convened the commander in chief addressed them in a speech well calculated to calm their mind. He also pledged himself to exert all his abilities and influence in their favor, and requested them to rely on the faith of their country, and conjured them "as they valued their honor—as they respected the rights of humanity, and as they regarded the military and national character of

America, to express their utmost detestation of the man, who was attempting to open the floodgates of civil discord, and deluge their rising empire with blood." Gen. Washington then retired. The minds of those who had heard him were in such an irritable state, that nothing but their most ardent patriotism and his unbounded influence, prevented the proposal of rash resolutions which if adopted, would have sullied the glory of seven years service. No reply whatever was made to the General's Speech. The happy moment was seized, while the minds of the officers softened by the eloquence of their beloved commander, were in a yielding state, and a resolution was unanimously adopted by which they declared "that no circumstances of distress or danger, should induce a conduct that might tend to sully the reputation and glory they had acquired, that the army continued to have an unshaken confidence, in the justice of Congress and their country. That they viewed with abhorrence and rejected with disdain, the infamous propositions in the late anonymous address to the officers of the army.["] Too much praise cannot be given to Gen. Washington, for the patriotism and decision which marked his conduct, in the whole of this serious transaction. Perhaps in no instance did the United States receive from heaven a more signal deliverance, through the hands of the commander in chief.

Soon after these events, Congress completed a resolution which had been for some time pending, that the officers of their army, who preferred a sum in gross to an annuity, should be entitled to receive to the amount of five years full pay, in money or securities at six per cent. per annum, instead of the half pay for life, which had been previously promised to them.

To avoid the inconveniences of dismissing a great number of soldiers in a body, furloughs were freely granted to individuals, and after their dispersion they were not enjoined to return. By this arrangement a critical moment was got over. A great part of an unpaid army, was disbanded and dispersed over the States, without tumult or disorder. The privates generally betook themselves to labor, and crowned the merit of being good soldiers, by becoming good citizens. Several of the American officers, who had been bred mechanics resumed their trades. In old countries the disbanding a single regiment, even though fully paid, has often produced serious consequences, but in America where arms had been taken up for self defence, they were peaceably laid down as soon as they became unnecessary. As soldiers had been easily and speedily formed in 1775, out of farmers, planters, and mechanics, with equal ease and expedition in the year 1783, they dropped their adventitious character, and resumed their former occupations.

DOCUMENT NO. 27

MERCY OTIS WARREN'S ACCOUNT OF THE NEWBURGH AFFAIR*

Mercy Otis Warren was a member of prominent Boston families that traced their ancestry back to the earliest settlers in Massachusetts. Both Otises and Warrens distinguished themselves as patriots from the early days of the Revolution and were closely connected to many important Massachusetts republicans, including Samuel, John and Abigail Adams, and Elbridge Gerry.

*Mercy did not accurately report details of the army's demands or Congress's actions on them. Her access to information on this aspect of the conspiracy was not as good as Ramsay's and she was much more interested in civilian involvement in it. Here, her sources included the first two "Lucius" essays, copies of which her husband had received from Arthur Lee. She would also have read Gerry's letter on the Society of Cincinnati (*See Doc. No. 28*). Mercy held the civilian conspirators she believed to have been involved in the Newburgh Conspiracy responsible for the many objections that she raised to the Constitution of the United States.*

γ γ γ

1805

We have seen through the narration of events during the war, the armies of the American states suffering hunger and cold, nakedness, fatigue, and danger, with unparalleled patience and valor. A due sense of the importance of the contest in which they were engaged, and the certain ruin and disgrace in which themselves and their children would be involved on the defeat of their object, was a strong stimulus to patient suffering. An attachment to their commanding officers, a confidence in

---

* Mercy Otis Warren, *History of the Rise, Progress and Termination of the American Revolution* (Boston, 1805), Lester H. Cohen, ed., (Indianapolis: Liberty*Classics*, 1988), 610–612.

the faith of congress, and the sober principles of independence, equity, and equality, in which the most of them had been nurtured, all united to quiet any temporary murmurs that might arise from present feelings, and to command the fidelity of soldiers contending for personal freedom, and the liberties of their country.

The deranged state of the American finances from a depreciating currency, the difficulty of obtaining loans of monies, and various other causes, had sufficiently impressed them with the danger that threatened the great object, the independence of the United States of America. These circumstances had led the army to submit to a delay of payment of their equitable dues, notwithstanding their personal sufferings, and to wait the effects of more efficient stipulations for adequate rewards in some future day.

But on the certain intelligence that peace was at hand, that it had been proposed to disband the army by furloughs, and that there was no appearance of a speedy liquidation of the public debts, many of both officers and soldiers grew loud in their complaints, and bold in their demands. They required an immediate payment of all arrearages; and insisted on the security of the commutation engaged by congress some time before, on the recommendation of general Washington: he had requested, that the officers of the army might be assured of receiving seven years' whole pay, instead of half pay for life, which had been stipulated before: this, after reducing the term to five years, congress had engaged.

They also demanded a settlement for rations, clothing, and proper consideration for the delay of payment of just debts, which had long been due, and an obligation from congress for *compensation,* or immediate payment. They chose general M'Dougal, colonel Brooks, and colonel Ogden, a committee from the army to wait on congress, to represent the general uneasiness, and to lay the complaints of the army before them, and to enforce the requests of the officers, most of whom were supposed to have been concerned in the business. Anonymous addresses were scattered among the troops; poisonous suggestions whispered, and the most inflammatory resolutions drawn up, and disseminated through the army: these were written with ingenuity and spirit, but the authors were not discovered.

Reports were every where circulated, that the military department would do itself justice; that the army would not disband until congress had acceded to all their demands; and that they would keep their arms in their hands, until they had compelled the delinquent states to a settlement, and congress to a compliance with all the claims of the public creditors.

These alarming appearances were conducted with much art and intrigue. It was said, and doubtless it was true, that some persons not belonging to the army, and who were very *adroit* in fiscal management, had their full share in ripening the rupture.

Deeply involved in public contracts, some of the largest public creditors on the continent were particularly suspected of fomenting a spirit, and encouraging views, inconsistent with the principles and professions of the friends to the revolution. These were disgusted at the rejection of the late five per cent. impost, which had been contemplated: they were thought to have been busy in ripening projects, which might bring forward measures for the speedy liquidation of the public demands. The private embarrassments and expenses of some of this class, had frequently prompted them to ill-digested systems for relief to themselves, in which the public were also involved, from the confidence placed in them by men of the first consideration: but their expedients and their adventures ended in the complete ruin of some individuals.

Those gentlemen, however, most particularly implicated in the public opinion, sustained a character pure, and morals correct, when viewed in comparison with others who were looking forward to projects of extensive speculation, to the establishment of banks and funding systems, and to the erecting a government for the United States, in which should be introduced ranks, privileged orders, and arbitrary powers. Several of these were deep, designing instruments of mischief; characters able, artful, and insinuating; who were undoubtedly engaged in the manoeuvres of the army; and though their designs were not fully comprehended, it was generally believed, that they secretly encouraged the discontents and the attempts of the disaffected soldiery.

In answer to the address of the officers of the army, congress endeavoured to quiet by palliatives, and by expressions of kindness, encouragement, and hope. Several months passed in this uneasy situation: the people anxious, the officers restless, the army instigated by them, and by ambitious and interested men in other departments, proceeded to the most pernicious resolutions, and to measures of a very dangerous nature.

In the mean time, general Washington, both as commander in chief, and as a man who had the peace of his country at heart, did every thing in his power to quiet complaint, to urge to patience, and to dissipate the mutinous spirit that prevailed in the army. By his assiduity, prudence, and judgment, the embers were slightly covered, but the fire was not extinguished: the secret murmurs that had rankled for several months, and had alternately been smothered in the sullen bosom, or blazed high in the sanguine, now broke out into open insurrection. [Here Warren begins to discuss the mutiny of the Pennsylvania line which broke out in Philadelphia in June 1783.]

DOCUMENT NO. 28

THE SOCIETY OF THE CINCINNATI*

The New England states were hot-points of opposition to army pensions and to the Society of Cincinnati, which, republicans believed, might easily evolve into a conspiratorial machine that would, like the "junto" Novanglus had condemned, prey on and destroy republican government. Elbridge Gerry, currently a Massachusetts delegate to Congress, presents the case against the Society to Stephen Higginson. Higginson, a member of the state's delegation in 1783, had been denied reelection because, under pressure of the Newburgh affair, he had voted to approve the plan to provide army officers with pensions equivalent to five years full pay.

Gerry's discussion of the Cincinnati constituted a single, very long, paragraph in his letter. To enhance readability, additional paragraphing is provided, and missing letters have been supplied over blanks in the original. Samuel Adams revised and published the letter in Boston's Independent Chronicle *(April 22 and 29, 1784.) He masked Gerry's criticism of the commander in chief by substituting "influential men" for "General Washington" in the passage which speculates on the role he might play in any movement toward establishing a monarchy. Adams also omitted the passage which suggested that military men should recognize that civilians accepted equal or greater risks, and should acknowledge that the militia's contribution was as significant as that of the "standing" army.*

---

* MS: Samuel Adams Papers, Manuscripts Division, The New York Public Library, Astor, Lenox and Tilden Foundations; reprinted in Paul H. Smith, Gerard W. Gawalt, Ronald M. Gephart, et al., eds. *Letters of Delegates to Congress: 1774–1789* (Washington, DC: Library of Congress, 1976–1998), 21: 407–411.

γ   γ   γ

Elbridge Gerry to Stephen Higginson

Annapolis 4th March 1784

My dear Sir

... I am clearly convinced in my own Mind of the Rectitude of the Intentions of the Officers in general, respecting the Cincinnati. I have a great Opinion of those vertuous Men, & am very desirous to reward their Services.

It is well known our Treasury, is, like those of most Nations after a War, much deranged; & the *professed* Design of that Institution, is to secure the payment of the publick Debt. Formed for such a purpose, the officers may by degrees be sensibly drawn into Measures; which they would now shudder at the thot of, & which I have no Doubt will be the result, unless, this political Monster is crushed in Embryo. ...

General Washington, I am well informed, has to my great astonishment, written a Circular Letter, directing a Meeting of the representative Officers, of the State Cincinnatis, in May next, at Philadelphia, which will be the first Meeting of the Cincinnati *Congress*—in Gods Name, may it be the last. The *General* in his last address, if I recollect right, to the Army urged them to use their *Influence* to increase the powers of Congress, or in other Words to *alter* the fœderal Government. It is not improbable then that this will be an object of *Deliberation* with the cincinnati Congress. It cannot be denied, that if the Meeting thereof is permitted to pass unnoticed, they may agitate that or any other Subject, & that they cannot fail in carrying any continental Measure which they may undertake & conduct with prudence. No other precautions are necessary, than Gentleness & a little patience in the Beginning, & perseverance in the prosecution—all which are habitual Accomplishments of military Characters.

When any plan or object is agreed on in the Cincinnati Congress, it will of course be communicated to the Cincinnati Conventions in each state, & the Members thereof, who have been trained to Subordination, without which they never could have attained such Reputation as they merit in their military profession, will undoubtedly consider themselves rather as an executive than a deliberative Body, & readily pledge themselves to carry the Decissions of their Congress into Effect, more especially as they honestly suppose the only object is to obtain payment of their arrearages & Commutation. The Convention being thus prepared with the Arrets of their Congress, will return to their Towns & Counties, & use their Influence with the Representatives & Senators of their Acquaintance to promote the Measure whether to increase the power of Congress, or for other objects in the Legislatures of the several States.

. . . the same Influence, at the next Election of Members for the Legislature, may be & undoubtedly will be used (*successfully* in many Instances) to send the Members of the Cincinnati as Representatives or Senators to the General Assembly—in each State this Body should consist of a tenth part of those Members, whose object is fixed, & whose Exertions will be *incessantly* exerted to attain it, their Address, Ingenuity, perseverance, & prowess, will undoubtedly, if We consider the Manner of conducting Business in such Bodies, secure them Success. There may be some little Difficulty in the Beginning, but this will daily decrease. . . .

We have only reasoned on the presumption of a tenth part of the Members of the General Assemblies, being of the Cincinnati, but the probability is that the proportion will in a short Time be much greater, & the Influence of Consequence increased. The Assemblies being thus prepared, your Republican Congress will of course be soon filled with Members of the Cincinnati, having already five of this Order, & the fœderal powers will be enlarged. Whatever is proposed in the Cincinnati Congress, under such Circumstances, will be immediately adopted by the republican Congress & ratified by the Legislatures; & then you may bid adieu, a lasting & final adieu, to republican principles.

You would probably see the government of the united States first consisting of three Branches, under the humble Denominations of Governor General, Council & House, but with all the powers of King, Lords & Commons; & after a short Time you may be told that to support the Dignity of Government, it is necessary to take these Titles, & that no Disadvantage can result from the Measure, because it may be adopted without any additional Powers, or with such an addition as is of no great Consequence. Thus my Friend may We loose the advantages of a severe Conflict, which after an amazing expence of the Blood & Treasure of our Country, has so happily terminated in its independence.

If it be said that *General Washington* has given us too strong proofs of his patriotism, to admit of a Jealousy that he would permit such an Event; the Answer is easy & natural. It may be in his power to put such a Machine in Motion, but not to stop its progress. But admitting he could, is it certain that he would have such a Disposition? He is subject to Errors, as well as another person, & finding himself at the Head of a Society, which are attached by every Tye of Friendship to his person, & for a long Time been subject to his Nod; if he supposes the publick Interest may be promoted by a Change of Government, is it not probable that he will attempt it; & is not the undertaking such, that if once made, it must either terminate successfully or in his Ruin. Moreover, when a Crown is in View, who will answer for the patriotism of any Man? Who dare be responsible for it? If *any person* is so unwise as to offer himself a pledge, for the self denial of another to a Throne, or of a great Number of enterprizing Men to peerdoms, under such powerful Temptations, *that person* may be generous in his Disposition, but I will venture to pronounce him in point of Sagacity, as being unfit, & unqualified for a Statesman.

It is well known, that altho a Monarch being in Alliance with a republick, if he has artful Ministers, may clog & embarrass the Measures thereof: but it is not so easy to *carry* points in a popular assembly as to *defeat* them. It is therefore for the Interest of a certain Court, in order to make America subserve their purposes, to effect a Change of Government; & I have not the least Doubt, that, if an Attempt should be made to accomplish this, not only Money, but Troops of a foreign power, commanded by officers thereof who are honored with the Title of Cincinnati, would be furnished, to assist in the accomplishment of a plan, so evidently calculated as it would appear to them, to promote the Happiness of America. What a Situation should We then be in? What Rivers of Blood would thus flow from the harmless Fountain of the Cincinnati?

If it be said that all these Apprehensions, exist only in Imagination, I answer, that it is now in the power of America to prevent their having any other Existence; but can any person be sure that she will have this power long, if she suffers such a System, directly in the Face of the Confederation, to be formed & carried on? . . .

Besides the Dangerous Tendency pointed out, it is very extraordinary, that the military Gentlemen should be so vain as to suppose they have all the Merit of effecting the revolution. Very few of them were concerned in the early opposition to the Measures of the british Ministry, & the Opposers thereof risked more, or at least, as much, as any Citizens of America, whether civil or military. Indeed those Who have conducted the civil Departments have been proscribed, whilst the Military Gentlemen were proferred pardons; & the Fatigues & Hardships of the first have been very great altho undoubtedly exceeded by those of the Camp.

Again have the Militia no part of the Honor of this Revolution? I will venture to say, that without them We should have been inevitably, a conquered people, & that they would have defended this Country if the Army had been unfortunately cut off. Can it be supposed, that ten or fifteen thousand veterans would have defended the Country, & that 500,000 Militia would have resigned their Liberties? Surely not. If a Monarch looses his army he is undone, but the loss of a republican Army, generally produces Exertions that furnish double or treble the Number. . . .

I shall not mention the Influence which the Body would further acquire, by a Connection with the Treasury, & the Officers of the great Departments of Congress; for the latter of which, military Gentlemen are Candidates, & shall only observe, that the most Effectual Mode of stopping the progress of the Cincinnati plan, will be, for the Towns to assemble on the Occasion & instruct their Representatives to discountenance it in the Legislature, & to publish their Resolves: at the same Time requesting the officers within their Districts, to disavow the Institution, or in Case of Refusal, to inform them, they cannot expect the Suffrages of their Countrymen, for the civil offices of Government in future. . . .

DOCUMENT NO. 29

A PLAN FOR A TEMPORARY GOVERNMENT OF THE WESTERN TERRITORY*

Jefferson's plan presumes that all the western territory ceded by Britain would eventually enter the national domain, even if it had not yet been acquired from the Indians. His paramount objective was to devise means by which a temporary government, properly republican and chosen by free male settlers rather than dictated by Congress, could be quickly put into place. He also wanted to ensure that the new territories would remain in the union, recognize Congress's right to dispose of the national domain, and help to pay off the war debt. Jefferson told Madison in a letter of April 25 that the ban

---

* Worthington Chauncey Ford, et al., eds. *Journals of the Continental Congress: 1774–1789.* 34 vols. (Washington, DC: U.S. Government Printing Office, 1904–1937), 26: 275–279.

on slavery had been "lost by an individual vote only," and that, while Congress did not approve of hereditary titles, it considered the plan an "improper place" to raise the issue.

γ γ γ

April 23, 1784

Resolved, That so much of the territory ceded or to be ceded by individual states to the United States, as is already purchased or shall be purchased of the Indian inhabitants, and offered for sale by Congress, shall be divided into distinct states, in the following manner, as nearly as such cessions will admit; that is to say, by parallels of latitude, . . .

That the settlers on any territory so purchased, and offered for sale, shall, either on their own petition or on the order of Congress, receive authority from them, with appointments of time and place, for their free males of full age within the limits of their State to meet together, for the purpose of establishing a temporary government, to adopt the constitution and laws of any one of the original States; so that such laws nevertheless shall be subject to alteration by their ordinary legislature; and to erect, subject to a like alteration, counties, townships, or other divisions, for the election of members for their legislature.

. . . [That when any such State shall have acquired twenty thousand free inhabitants, on] giving due proof thereof to Congress, they shall receive from them authority with appointments of time and place, to call a convention of representatives to establish a permanent constitution and government for themselves. Provided that both the temporary and permanent governments be established on these principles as their basis:

First. That they shall for ever remain a part of this confederacy of the United States of America.

Second. That . . . they shall be subject to . . . to the Articles of Confederation in all those cases in which the original states shall be so subject, [and to all the acts and ordinances of the United States in Congress assembled, conformable thereto.

Third. That they in no case shall interfere with the primary disposal of the soil by the United States in Congress assembled, nor with the ordinances and regulations which Congress may find necessary, for securing the title in such soil to the bona fide purchasers.]

A PLAN FOR A TEMPORARY GOVERNMENT

Fourth. That they shall be subject to pay a part of the federal debts contracted or to be contracted, to be apportioned on them by Congress, according to the same common rule and measure by which apportionments thereof shall be made on the other states.

Fifth. That no tax shall be imposed on lands, the property of the United States.

Sixth. That their respective governments shall be ~~in republican forms, and shall admit no person to be a citizen who holds any hereditary title. That after the year 1800 of the Christian era, there shall be neither slavery nor involuntary servitude in any of the said states, otherwise than in punishment of crimes, whereof the party shall have been convicted to have been personally guilty,~~ republican.

Seventh. . . . That whensoever any of the said states shall have, of free inhabitants, as many as shall then be in any one the least numerous of the thirteen Original states, such State shall be admitted by its delegates into the Congress of the United States, on an equal footing with the said original states; provided . . . the consent of so many states in Congress is first obtained as may at the time be competent to such admission. And in order to adapt the said Articles of Confederation to the state of Congress when its numbers shall be thus increased, it shall be proposed to the legislatures of the states, originally parties thereto, to require the assent of two-thirds of the United States in Congress assembled, in all those cases wherein, by the said articles, the assent of nine states is now required, which being agreed to by them, shall be binding on the new states. Until such admission by their delegates into Congress, any of the said states, after the establishment of their temporary government, shall have authority to keep a member in Congress, with a right of debating but not of voting.

[That measures not inconsistent with the principles of the Confederation, and necessary for the preservation of peace and good order among the settlers in any of the said new states, until they shall assume a temporary government as aforesaid, may, from time to time, be taken by the United States in Congress assembled.]

That the preceding articles shall be formed into a charter of compact; shall be duly executed by the President of the United States in Congress assembled, under his hand, and the seal of the United States; shall be promulgated; and shall stand as fundamental constitutions between the thirteen original states, and each of the several states now newly described, unalterable [from and after the sale of any part of the territory of such State, pursuant to this resolve] but by the joint consent of the United States in Congress assembled, and of the particular State within which such alteration is proposed to be made. . . .

DOCUMENT NO. 30

BILLEY STAYS IN PENNSYLVANIA*

In this letter to his father, James Madison, Sr., Madison describes the impact of life in Philadelphia on his personal slave. The editors of the Madison Papers conclude that Madison may have sold Billey into indentured servitude in Pennsylvania as a means of recovering some of his worth and of providing him with a path to eventual freedom.

γ γ γ

Hond Sir

Philada. Sepr. 8. 1783.

. . . . I shall return to Princeton tomorrow; my final leaving of which will depend on events, but can not now be at any very great distance. On a view of all circumstances I have judged it most prudent not to force Billey back to Va. even if could be done; and have accordingly taken measures for his final separation from me. I am persuaded his mind is too thoroughly tainted to be a fit companion for fellow slaves in Virga. The laws here do not admit of his being sold for more than 7 years. I do not expect to get near the worth of him; but cannot think of punishing him by transportation merely for coveting that liberty for which we have paid the price of so much blood, and have proclaimed so often to be the right, & worthy the pursuit, of every human being.

[James Madison]

* The Papers of James Madison, DLC; reprinted in William T. Hutchinson and William M. E. Rachal, et al., eds. *The Papers of James Madison, Congressional Series*, (Chicago and Charlottesville, VA., 1962–1991) 7: 304.

DOCUMENT NO. 31

WHO QUALIFIES AS A VOTER?*

When republican thinkers contemplated the Society of the Cincinnati they worried that republican government could be undermined by a politically powerful elite. Adams here points to dangers from below and justifies withholding the full benefits of citizenship from many members of society. A serious uprising of men who, even though they were voters, felt themselves excluded from full participation in Massachusetts's political process helped to convince many that the Articles of Confederation had to be amended to create a government strong enough to withstand challenges from men who did not have a "sufficient" stake in republican society. (See Doc. No. 34 and Doc. No. 35)

γ γ γ

John Adams to James Sullivan

Philadelphia May. 26. 1776

Dear Sir

... Our worthy Friend, Mr. Gerry has put into my Hand, a Letter from you, of the Sixth of May, in which you consider the Principles of Representation and Legislation, and give us Hints of Some Alterations, which you Seem to think necessary, in the Qualification of Voters. ...

It is certain in Theory, that the only moral Foundation of Government is the Consent of the People. But to what an Extent Shall We carry this Principle? Shall We Say, that every Individual of the Community, old and young, male and female, as well as rich and poor, must consent, expressly to every Act of Legislation? No, you will Say. This is impossible. How then does the Right arise in the Majority to govern the Minority, against their Will? Whence arises the Right of the Men to govern Women, without their Consent? Whence the Right of the old to bind the Young, without theirs.

---

* Reprinted by permission of the publishers from THE PAPERS OF JOHN ADAMS: VOLUME 4 ed. Robert J. Taylor, Gregg L. Lint and Celeste Walker, Cambridge, Mass.: The Belknap Press of Harvard University Press, Copyright © 1979 by the Massachusetts Historical Society.

But let us first Suppose, that the whole Community of every Age, Rank, Sex, and Condition, has a Right to vote. This Community, is assembled—a Motion is made and carried by a Majority of one Voice. The Minority will not agree to this. Whence arises the Right of the Majority to govern, and the Obligation of the Minority to obey? from Necessity, you will Say, because there can be no other Rule. But why exclude Women? You will Say, because their Delicacy renders them unfit for Practice and Experience, in the great Business of Life, and the hardy Enterprizes of War, as well as the arduous Cares of State. Besides, their attention is So much engaged with the necessary Nurture of their Children, that Nature has made them fittest for domestic Cares. And Children have not Judgment or Will of their own. True. But will not these Reasons apply to others? Is it not equally true, that Men in general in every Society, who are wholly destitute of Property, are also too little acquainted with public Affairs to form a Right judgment, and too dependent upon other Men to have a Will of their own? If this is a Fact, if you give to every Man, who has no Property, a Vote, will you not make a fine encouraging Provision for Corruption by your fundamental Law? Such is the Frailty of the human Heart, that very few Men, who have no Property, have any judgment of their own. They talk and vote as they are directed by Some Man of Property, who has attached their Minds to his Interest.

Upon my Word, sir, I have long thought an Army, a Piece of Clock Work and to be governed only by Principles and Maxims, as fixed as any in Mechanicks, and by all that I have read in the History of Mankind, and in Authors, who have Speculated upon Society and Government, I am much inclined to think, a Government must manage a Society in the Same manner; and that this is Machinery too.

Harrington has Shewn that Power always follows Property. This I believe to be as infallible a Maxim, in Politicks, as, that Action and Reaction are equal, is in Mechanicks. Nay I believe We may advance one Step farther and affirm that the Ballance of Power in a Society, accompanies the Ballance of Property in Land. The only possible Way then of preserving the Ballance of Power on the side of equal Liberty and public Virtue, is to make the Acquisition of Land easy to every Member of Society: to make a Division of the Land into Small Quantities, So that the Multitude may be possessed of landed Estates. If the Multitude is possessed of the Ballance of real Estate, the Multitude will have the Ballance of Power, and in that Case the Multitude will take Care of the

Liberty, Virtue, and Interest of the Multitude in all Acts of Government.

I believe these Principles have been felt, if not understood in the Massachusetts Bay, from the Beginning: And therefore I Should think that Wisdom and Policy would dictate in these Times, to be very cautious of making Alterations. Our people have never been very rigid in Scrutinizing into the Qualifications of Voters, and I presume they will not now begin to be so. But I would not advise them to make any alteration in the Laws, at present, respecting the Qualifications of Voters.

Your Idea, that those Laws, which affect the Lives and personal Liberty of all, or which inflict corporal Punishment, affect those, who are not qualified to vote, as well as those who are, is just. But, So they do Women, as well as Men, Children as well as Adults. What Reason Should there be, for excluding a Man of Twenty years, Eleven Months and twenty-seven days old, from a Vote when you admit one, who is twenty one? The Reason is, you must fix upon Some Period in Life, when the Understanding and Will of Men in general is fit to be trusted by the Public. Will not the Same Reason justify the State in fixing upon Some certain Quantity of Property, as a Qualification.

The Same Reasoning, which will induce you to admit all Men, who have no Property, to vote, with those who have, for those Laws, which affect the Person will prove that you ought to admit Women and Children: for generally Speaking, Women and Children, have as good Judgment, and as independent Minds as those Men who are wholly destitute of Property: these last being to all Intents and Purposes as much dependent upon others, who will please to feed, cloath, and employ them, as Women are upon their Husbands, or Children on their Parents.

As to your Idea, of proportioning the Votes of Men in Money Matters, to the Property they hold, it is utterly impracticable. There is no possible Way of Ascertaining, at any one Time, how much every Man in a Community, is worth; and if there was, So fluctuating is Trade and Property, that this State of it, would change in half an Hour. The Property of the whole Community, is Shifting every Hour, and no Record can be kept of the Changes.

Society can be governed only by general Rules. Government cannot accommodate itself to every particular Case, as it happens, nor to the Circumstances of particular Persons. It must establish general, comprehensive Regulations for Cases and Persons. The only Question is, which general Rule, will accommodate most Cases and most Persons.

Depend upon it, sir, it is dangerous to open So fruitfull a Source of Controversy and Altercation, as would be opened by attempting to alter the Qualifications of Voters. There will be no End of it. New Claims will arise. Women will demand a Vote. Lads from 12 to 21 will think their Rights not enough attended to, and every Man, who has not a Farthing, will demand an equal Voice with any other in all Acts of State. It tends to confound and destroy all Distinctions, and prostrate all Ranks, to one common Levell. I am &c.

DOCUMENT NO. 32

LORD SHEFFIELD'S OBSERVATIONS ON THE COMMERCE OF THE AMERICAN STATES*

Lord Sheffield, a principal architect of Britain's postwar trade policy with its former colonies, completely rejected American arguments that free trade would increase the wealth and strength of all nations that participated in it. There is credible but not definitive evidence that he derived some of his ideas from Silas Deane. Deane had become disillusioned with the American cause after the bitter conflict over settlement of his accounts. By the end of the war, he was residing in England, where he became Sheffield's friend.

γ γ γ

[1783]

As a sudden revolution, an unprecedented case, a momentous change, the independence of America, has bewildered our reason, and encouraged the wildest sallies of imagination, systems have been preferred to experience, rash theory to successful practice, and the navigation Act itself, the guardian of the prosperity of Britain, has been almost abandoned by the levity or ignorance of those who have never seriously examined the spirit or the consequence of ancient rules. Our calmer reflections will soon discover, that such great sacrifices are neither requisite nor expedient; and the knowledge of the exports and imports of the American States will afford us facts and principles to ascertain the value

---

* John Baker Holroyd, Lord Sheffield. *Observations on the Commerce of the American States with Europe and the West Indies; Including the several Articles of Import and Export and on the Tendency of a Bill now depending in Parliament.* (London: J. Debrett, 1783), 1–4.

of their trade, to foresee their true interest and probable conduct, and to choose the wisest measures (the wisest are always the most simple) for securing and improving the benefits of a commercial intercourse with this foreign and independent nation. For it is in the light of a foreign country that America must henceforward be viewed; it is the situation she herself has chosen by asserting her independence, and the whimsical definition of a people *sui generis*, is either a figure of rhetoric which conveys no distinct idea, or the effort of cunning to unite at the same time the advantages of two inconsistent characters. By asserting their independence, the Americans have renounced the privileges, as well as the duties of British subjects. If in some instances, as in the loss of the carrying trade, they feel the inconvenience of their choice, they can no longer complain; but if they are placed on the footing of the most favoured nation, they must surely applaud our liberality and friendship, without expecting that, for their emolument, we should sacrifice the navigation and the naval power of Great Britain. By this simple, if only temporary expedient, we shall escape the unknown mischiefs of crude and precipitate systems, we shall avoid the rashness of hasty and pernicious concessions, which can never be resumed without provoking the jealousy, and perhaps not without an entire commercial breach, with the American States.

In the youthful ardour of grasping the advantages of the American trade, a bill, still depending, was first introduced into parliament. Had it passed into a law, it would have affected our most essential interests in every branch of commerce, and to every part of the world; it would have endangered the repose of Ireland, and excited the just indignation of Russia and other countries, and the West India planters would have been the only subjects of Britain who could derive any benefit, however partial, from their open intercourse directly with the American States, and indirectly with the rest of the world. Fortunately some delays have intervened, and if we diligently use the opportunity of reflection, the future welfare of our country may depend on this salutary pause.

Our natural impatience to pre-occupy the American market, should perhaps be rather checked than encouraged. The same eagerness has been indulged by our rival nations; they have vied with each other in pouring their manufactures into America, and the country is already stocked, most probably overstocked, with European commodities. It is experience alone that can demonstrate to the French, or Dutch trader, the fallacy of his eager hopes, and *that* experience will operate each day in favour of the British merchant. He alone is able and willing to grant that liberal credit which must be extorted from his competitors by the rashness of their early ventures; they will soon discover that America has neither money or sufficient produce to send in return, and cannot have for some time; and not intending or being able to give credit, their funds will be exhausted, their agents will never return, and the ruin of the first creditors will serve as a lasting warning to their countrymen. The solid power of supplying the wants of America, of receiving her produce, and of waiting her convenience, belongs almost exclusively to our own merchants. If we can abstain from mischievous precipitation, we may now learn what we shall hereafter feel, that the industry of Britain will encounter little competition in the American market. We shall observe with pleasure, that, among the maritime states, France, our hereditary foe, will derive the smallest benefits from the commercial independence of America. She may exult in the dismemberment of the British empire, but if we are true to ourselves, and to the wisdom of our ancestors, there is still life and vigour left to disappoint her hopes, and to controul her ambition.

DOCUMENT NO. 33

"GOVERNMENTS AS IMPERFECT AS OURS ARE"*

By September 1786, Americans had experienced three years as an independent nation under the government of the Articles of Confederation. Republican thinkers may have been pleased that the menace of executive tyranny and taxation by the central government had been avoided, but more and more congressmen were confronting the nation's inability to identify and implement solutions for its political, constitutional, commercial, and diplomatic problems. Rufus King, a Massachusetts delegate to Congress, clearly conveys to Jackson, a former delegate, his sense that the system republicans had struggled to maintain was deeply flawed and needed to be extensively

* Lee Family Papers, *Courtesy of the Massachusetts Historical Society*; reprinted in Paul H. Smith, Gerard W. Gawalt, Ronald M. Gephart, et al., eds. *Letters of Delegates to Congress: 1774–1789* (Washington, DC: Library of Congress, 1976–1998), 23: 541-543.

revised. Such feelings would soon be intensified by domestic insurrection in western Massachusetts.

γ γ γ

Rufus King to Jonathan Jackson

New York 3. Sep. 1786

Dear Sir,

.... A Treaty with Spain is at this Time a desirable Event; If the present situation is preferable to a rupture with Spain a Treaty between us must not be long delayed—the boundaries of their and our Territories, remain to be ascertained; they claim extensive Tracts of country within the Limits of the united States as fixed by the Treaty of Peace & Freindship with Great Britain; we insist on the right of freely navigating the Missisippi from its source to the Ocean. They deny this right and refuse us the navigation where both banks are in the possession of Spain—the Rapid Settlement of the western country, more particularly on the Ohio and that Part of Georgia, which is adjacent to the Missisippi, urges a decision of these interfering claims and Pretensions. As Time is more favorable to young than old nations, policy would warrant Delay—but these western adventurers will not suffer it—they at this time hold a bold language, are yearly making almost incredible accessions of Strength, and their own particular interest is to them as to all others the active principle of their Conduct. If therefore our Disputes with Spain are not settled, we shall be obliged either wholly to give up the western Settlers or join *them* in an issue of Force with the Catholic King: the latter we are in no condition to think of, the former would be impolitic for many Reasons, and cannot with Safety be *now* admitted, although very few men who have examined the subject will refuse their assent to the Opinion that every Citizen of the Atlantic States, who emigrates to the westward of the Allegany is a total Loss to our confederacy.

Nature has severed the two countries by a vast and extensive chain of mountains, interest and convenience will keep them separate, and the feeble policy of our disjointed Government will not be able to unite them. For these reasons I have ever been opposed to encouragements of western emigrants—the States situated on the Atlantic are not sufficiently populous, and loosing our men, is loosing our greatest Source of wealth.

But what is wealth in Governments imperfect as ours are? indeed my

Dr. Sir, your opinions on this subject are but too well founded—and you may be assured that the ablest and most discerning men in these States, are anxiously affected with the Difficulties which you so feelingly & properly describe. What can be done is the Question—the answer is various. Some say, and the opinion is extensive, infuse a new portion of Strength into the confederation and all will be well. But it should be remembered that the pressure of a common Calamity which induced the present confederation is now removed, that the individual States are governed by their particular Interests; these stand, or are supposed to stand, in Opposition to each other, and, so long as the Idea obtains, will prevent Unanimity in any Opinion concerning the Corroboration of the Federal Constitution.

Others, and by no means the least respectable, answer, that nothing can be done in our present Form; that the Error lies in the original plan. Diminish say they, the Number of States—let those which are to be Established be nearly equal. Reform their Constitutions, give their Governments more Energy—the Laws more Stability, the Magistrates greater Authority and Responsibility—Let the State Governments be confined to concerns merely internal: and let there be a federal Government with a vigourous Executive, wise Legislative, and independent Judicial—they tell you that a League or confederation between so many small, and unequal, Sovereignties never did, or can, answer the views of its Patrons—they illustrate, by affirming that the Greek Republics were finally melted down, and united, under one Head—that in France and Spain, which were formerly each divided into as many independent States or Sovereignties, as they now contain Provinces, the People did not find their Happiness in these small Divisions, but sought it under their present form—that the Heptarchy, or seven Saxon Kingdoms, of England were finally united by Egbert, and that peace & Happiness then succeeded to Treasons, insurrections, & Wars, which made up the History of that famed Confederacy.

It must not be understood that these Remarks authorize an Opinion that a monarchy would promote the Happiness of the people of America —far, very far, from it. But they show this; if wise & prudent men discerning the Imperfections of the present Governments, do not in Season and without Fear, repose suitable Remedies, the causes which changed the Governments alluded to may, and probably will, change those of America. Since a convention must assemble at Annapolis I am glad that Delegates will attend from Massachusetts. I hope extraordinary as the measure is, that it may issue more favorably than I have ever expected.

Neither Chancellor Livingston nor Mr. Duane will attend; they are very little concerned in the politicks of the present Times. Mr. Madison of Virginia has been here for some Time past, he will attend the convention. He does not discover or propose any other Plan than that of investing congress with full powers for the Regulation of commerce Foreign, & domestic. But this power will run deep into the Authorities of the individual States, and can never be well exercised without a federal Judicial—the reform must necessarily be extensive.

I will not add on these subjects. We must wait Events. . . .

Rufus King

DOCUMENT NO. 34

PROCEEDINGS OF THE CONVENTION HELD IN HAMPSHIRE COUNTY, MASSACHUSETTS*

Although the assemblies which met in Anson County, North Carolina and Hampshire County, Massachusetts, were seventeen years apart, the grievances both sets of frontier people complained about were very similar and were expressed with equal force. Heavy tax burdens coupled with specie and currency shortages, extortionate practices by those connected with the law, and an unrepresentative government led to popular uprisings which bracketed the Revolution at either end. Clearly, Hampshire folk did not see their state government as much of an improvement over colonial rule. To achieve their objectives, they employed the same tactics which had brought the colonies to independence: conventions, petitions, correspondence committees, mob activity, and, eventually, armed resistance to duly constituted authority. They sustained their effort long enough to convince many of the Revolution's established leaders that the Confederation had to be strengthened to enable it to meet the threat of domestic insurrection.

γ γ γ

* George Richards Minot, *The History of the Insurrections in Massachusetts* (1788), pp. 34–37.

August 22-25, 1786

At a meeting of delegates from fifty towns in the county of *Hampshire*, in convention held at *Hatfield*, in said county, on Tuesday the 22d day of *August* instant, and continued by adjournments until the twenty fifth, &c.
Voted, that this meeting is constitutional.

The convention from a thorough conviction of great uneasiness, subsisting among the people of this county and Commonwealth, then went into an inquiry for the cause; and, upon mature consideration, deliberation and debate, were of opinion, that many grievances and unnecessary burdens now lying upon the people, are the sources of that discontent so evidently discoverable throughout this Commonwealth. Among which the following articles were voted as such, viz.

1st. The existence of the Senate.

2d. The present mode of representation.

3d. The officers of government not being annually dependent on the representatives of the people, in General Court assembled, for their salaries.

4th. All the civil officers of government, not being annually elected by the Representatives of the people, in General Court assembled.

5th. The existence of the Courts of Common Pleas, and General Sessions of the Peace.

6th. The Fee Table as it now stands.

7th. The present mode of appropriating the impost and excise.

8th. The unreasonable grants made to some of the officers of government.

9th. The supplementary aid.

10th. The present mode of paying the governmental securities.

11th. The present mode adopted for the payment and speedy collection of the last tax.

12th. The present mode of taxation as it operates unequally between the polls and estates, and between landed and mercantile interests.

13th. The present method of practice of the attornies at law.

14th. The want of a sufficient medium of trade, to remedy the mischiefs arising from the scarcity of money.

15th. The General Court sitting in the town of *Boston*.

16th. The present embarrassments on the press.

17th. The neglect of the settlement of important matters depending between the Commonwealth and Congress, relating to monies and averages.

18th. Voted, This convention recommend to the several towns in this county, that they instruct their Representatives, to use their influence in the next General Court, to have emitted a bank of paper money, subject to a depreciation; making it a tender in all payments, equal to silver and gold, to be issued in order to call in the Commonwealth's securities.

19th. Voted, That whereas several of the above articles of grievances, arise from defects in the constitution; therefore a revision of the same ought to take place.

20th. Voted, That it be recommended by this convention to the several towns in this county, that they petition the Governour to call the General Court immediately together, in order that the other grievances complained of, may by the legislature, be redressed.

21st. Voted, That this convention recommend it to the inhabitants of this county, that they abstain from all mobs and unlawful assemblies, until a constitutional method of redress can be obtained.

22d. Voted, That Mr. *Caleb West* be desired to transmit a copy of the proceedings of this convention to the convention of the county of *Worcester*.

23d. Voted, That the chairman of this convention be desired to transmit a copy of the proceedings of this convention to the county of *Berkshire*.

24th. Voted, That the chairman of this convention be directed to notify a county convention, upon any motion made to him for that purpose, if he judge the reasons offered be sufficient, giving such notice, together with the reasons therefor, in the publick papers of this county.

25th. Voted, That a copy of the proceedings of this convention be sent to the press in *Springfield* for publication.

DOCUMENT NO. 35

A REPORT ON SHAYS'S REBELLION*

Charles Pettit, a businessman who had served in the Quartermaster Department during the war, was currently representing Pennsylvania in Con-

---

* MS: Benjamin Franklin Papers, American Philosophical Society; reprinted in Paul H. Smith, Gerard W. Gawalt, Ronald M. Gephart, et al., eds. *Letters of Delegates to Congress: 1774–1789* (Washington, DC: Library of Congress, 1976–1998), 23: 603–604.

gress. He was also a public creditor, and therefore personally interested in seeing that government debts were paid at full value. The inability of the central government to respond quickly and effectively to the general unrest he describes and fears that British agents were encouraging and supporting it gave strength to calls for a convention to revise the Articles of Confederation.

γ γ γ

Charles Pettit to Benjamin Franklin

Sir, New York 18th. October 1786

I have to acknowledge the Receipt of your Excellency's Letter of the 10th Instant. Time will not at present permit me to make any Observations on the Subjects therein mentioned. The immediate Object of giving you the Trouble of this is a fresh Communication from the Eastward which represents the State of Massachusets as in a most dangerous & critical Situation; the Danger indeed extends immediatly to all the Eastern States and the Consequences cannot be unimportant to the other States in the Union. Till very lately the Insurrections in Massachusets were considered as the ebulitions of Discontent arising from the transient Inconveniences they suffer from the Stagnation of Commerce & the other usual Effects of changing from the diffusive circulation of Money in War to the Habits of Frugality and Oeconnomy adapted to Peace. But the Discontents now assume a more alarming Aspect, and take Root in a variety of Causes which were hardly supposed to have Existence in America. A total Abolition of all Debts both public and Private, and even a general Distribution of Property are not without Advocates. Men who have respectable Standings & Characters & possessed of decent Shares of Property are said to countenance the general Insurgency tho' they avowedly claim less Reform (as they call it) than the others, but even they propose to reliquidate the public Debts & then pay them off in a Paper Money to be created without Funds & to make it a legal Tender. Strange as it may appear, it is said that five Counties containing more than half the Free men of the State have large Majorities, & some are almost unanimous in the Measures of Insurgency. It is conjectured, & the Conjecture is founded in at least plausible Circumstances, that foreign Influence has no little weight in their Councils— that they have a great Degree of Systematic Order in their Measures, and are ready on an Alarm to come forth an organized Army of not less than 10,000 Men armed & Officered.

Whether these alarming Circumstances are magnified or not Time must discover, but these Communications are from high Authority. Prudence however requires that they be made a discreet use of. Your Excellency's known Prudence & judgment can only justify me in the Communication I am now making, & at present I trust you will not extend it as it is under a Seal of Secrecy in Congress. Some Resolutions will probably issue for an Augmentation of Troops, the Reasons assigned for which may be our Intelligence respecting the Western Indians; but in Fact this Augmentation seems to be necessary to the preservation of interior Government. . . .

Cha. Pettit

BIBLIOGRAPHY

DOCUMENTARY EDITIONS

Balderston, Marion, and Syrett, David. *The Lost War: Letters from British Officers during the American Revolution.* (New York: Horizon Press, 1975).
Boyd, Julian P., et al., eds. *The Papers of Thomas Jefferson.* 27 vols. to date. (Princeton, NJ: Princeton University Press, 1950–).
Butterfield, Lyman H., Taylor, Robert J., et al, eds., *The Papers of John Adams.* 11 vols. to date. *Adams Family Correspondence.* 6 vols. (Cambridge, MA, and London: Belknap Press of Harvard University, 1977–; 1963-1993).
Chase, Philander D., ed. *The Papers of George Washington: Revolutionary War Series.* 10 vols. to date. Abbot, William W., Twohig, Dorothy, et al., eds. *The Papers of George Washington: Confederation Series.* 6 vols. (Charlottesville: University of Virginia Press, 1992-1997; 1985–).
Clark, William Bell, et al., eds. *Naval Documents of the American Revolution.* 10. vols. to date. (Washington, DC: U.S. Government Printing Office, 1964–).
Crane, Elaine Forman, et al., eds. *The Diary of Elizabeth Drinker.* 3 vols. (Boston: Northeastern University Press, 1991).
Dickinson, John. *Letters from a Farmer in Pennsylvania, to the Inhabitants of the British Colonies.* (New York: Outlook Company, 1903).
Duffy, John J., et al., eds. *Ethan Allen and His Kin: Correspondence, 1772-1819.* 2 vols. (Hanover, NH: University of New England Press, 1998).
Ferguson, E. James, et al., eds. *The Papers of Robert Morris.* (Pittsburgh: University of Pittsburgh Press, 1973-1999).
Foner, Philip S., ed. *The Complete Writings of Thomas Paine.* 2 vols. (New York: The Citadel Press, 1945).
Ford, Worthington Chauncey, et al., eds. *Journals of the Continental Congress: 1774-1789.* 34 vols. (Washington, DC: U.S. Government Printing Office, 1904-1937).
Giunta, Mary A., et al., eds. *The Emerging Nation: A Documentary History of the Foreign Relations of the United States under the Articles of Confederation, 1780-1789.* 3 vols. (Washington, DC: National Historical Publications and Records Commission, 1996).
Greene, Jack P. ed., *Colonies to Nation: 1763-1789: A Documentary History of the American Revolution.* (New York and London: Norton, 1967).
Hamer, Philip M., Chesnutt, David R., Taylor, C. James, et al., eds. *The Papers of Henry Laurens.* 14 vols. to date, (Columbia: University of South Carolina Press, 1968–).
Holroyd, John Baker, Lord Sheffied, *Observations on the Commerce of the American States with Europe and the West Indies; Including the several Articles of*

Import and Export; and On the Tendency of a Bill now depending in Parliament. (London: J. Debrett, 1783).

Hutchinson, William T., Rutland, Robert A., et al., eds. *The Papers of James Madison, Congressional Series.* 17 vols. (Chicago: University of Chicago Press, 1962–1977; and Charlottesville: University of Virginia Press, 1977–1991).

Idzerda, Stanley J. et al., eds. *Lafayette in the Age of the American Revolution: Selected Letters and Papers, 1776–1790.* 5 vols. (Ithaca, NY, and London: Cornell University Press, 1977–1983).

Jensen, Merrill, et al., eds. *The Documentary History of the Ratification of the Constitution.* (Madison: State Historical Society of Wisconsin, 1976–).

Labaree, Leonard W., et al., eds., *The Papers of Benjamin Franklin.* 35 vols. to date (New Haven, CT and London: Yale University Press, 1959–).

Martin, Joseph Plumb. *Private Yankee Doodle, Being a Narrative of Some of the Adventures, Dangers and Sufferings of a Revolutionary Soldier.* George E. Scheer, ed. (Boston: Little, Brown, 1962).

Morris, Richard B. et al., eds., *John Jay, the Making of a Revolutionary: Unpublished papers, 1745–1780,* and *John Jay, The Winning of the Peace: Unpublished Papers, 1780–1784.* (New York: Harper and Row, 1975, 1980).

Peckham, Howard H., ed. *The Sources of American Independence: Selected Manuscripts from the Collections of the William L. Clements Library.* 2 vols. (Chicago and London: University of Chicago Press, 1978).

Showman, Richard K. et al., eds. *The Papers of Nathanael Greene.* 10 vols. to date. (Chapel Hill: University of North Carolina Press, 1976–).

Smith, Paul H., Gawalt, Gerard W., Gephart, Ronald M., et al., eds. *Letters of Delegates to Congress: 1774–1789.* 25 vols. (Washington, DC: Library of Congress, 1976–1998).

Syrett, Harold C., Cooke, Jacob E., et al., eds. *The Papers of Alexander Hamilton.* 27 vols. (New York: 1961–1987).

Thorpe, Francis Newton, ed. *The Federal and State Constitutions, Colonial Charters, and Other Organic Laws of the States, Territories, and Colonies now or Heretofore Forming the United States of America.* 7 vols. (Washington, DC, Government Printing Office 1909).

Van Schreeven, William J., comp., and Scribner, Robert L., ed. *Revolutionary Virginia: The Road to Independence.* 7 vols. (Charlottesville: University Press of Virginia, 1973).

Wheatley, Phillis. *Poems on Various Subjects, Religious and Moral.* (London: A. Bell, 1773).

MONOGRAPHS

Ahlstrom, Sydney E. *A Religious History of the American People.* (New Haven, CT, and London: Yale University Press, 1972).

BIBLIOGRAPHY

Bailyn, Bernard. *The Ideological Origins of the American Revolution: Enlarged Edition.* (Cambridge, MA, and London, England: Belknap Press of Harvard University Press, 1992).

Berlin, Ira, and Hoffman, Ronald. eds., *Slavery and Freedom in the Age of the American Revolution.* (Urbana: University of Illinois Press, 1983).

Bonwick, Colin. *The American Revolution.* (Charlottesville: University Press of Virginia, 1991).

Brewer, John. *The Sinews of Power: War, Money and the English State, 1688–1783.* (New York: Knopf, 1989).

Buel, Joy Day, and Richard, Jr. *The Way of Duty: A Woman and Her Family in Revolutionary America.* (New York and London: Norton, 1984).

Buel, Richard, Jr. *In Irons: Britain's Naval Supremacy and the American Revolutionary Economy.* (New Haven, CT, and London: Yale University Press, 1998).

Butler, Jon. *Awash in a Sea of Faith: Christianizing the American People.* (Cambridge, MA, and London: Harvard University Press, 1990).

Carp, E. Wayne. *To Starve the Army at Pleasure: Continental Army Administration and American Political Culture, 1775–1783.* (Chapel Hill: University of North Carolina Press, 1963).

Cooke, Jacob Ernest. et al., eds. *Encyclopedia of the North American Colonies.* (New York and Toronto: Charles Scribner's Sons, 1993).

Davis, David Brion. *The Problem of Slavery in the Age of Revolution, 1770–1823.* (New York: Oxford University Press, 1975).

Dull, Jonathan. *A Diplomatic History of the American Revolution.* (New Haven, CT: Yale University Press, 1985).

Ferguson, E. James. *The Power of the Purse: A History of American Public Finance, 1776–1790.* (Chapel Hill: University of North Carolina Press, 1961).

Franklin, John Hope. *From Slavery to Freedom: A History of Negro Americans.* (New York: Knopf, 1967).

Gipson, Lawrence Henry. *The British Empire before the American Revolution.* 15 vols. (New York: Caxton Printers, 1936–1970).

Graymont, Barbara. *The Iroquois in the American Revolution.* (Syracuse, NY: Syracuse University Press, 1972).

Greene, Jack P., and Pole, J. R., eds. *The Blackwell Encyclopedia of the American Revolution.* (Oxford and Cambridge, MA: Basil Blackwell, 1991).

Henderson, H. James. *Party Politics in the Continental Congress.* (New York: McGraw-Hill, 1974).

Higginbotham, Don. *War and Society in Revolutionary America: The Wider Dimensions of the Conflict.* (Columbia: University of South Carolina Press, 1988).

Jennings, Francis, ed., *American Indians and the American Revolution.* (Chicago: Newberry Library, 1983).

Jensen, Merrill. *The New Nation: A History of the United States During the Confederation, 1781–1789.* (New York: Vintage, 1965).

Kennedy, Paul. *The Rise and Fall of the Great Powers: Economic Change and Military Conflict from 1500 to 2000.* (New York: Random House, 1987).

Kerber, Linda K. *Women of the Republic: Intellect and Ideology in Revolutionary America.* (New York: Norton, 1980).

Lutz, Donald S. *The Origins of American Constitutionalism.* (Baton Rouge and London: Louisiana State University Press, 1988).

McCusker, John J., and Menard. Russell R. *The Economy of British America: 1607–1789.* (Chapel Hill and London: University of North Carolina Press, 1991).

Maier, Pauline. *From Resistance to Revolution: Colonial Radicals and the Development of American Opposition to Britain, 1765–1776.* (New York: Vintage, 1972).

Marks, Frederick W., III. *Independence on Trial: Foreign Affairs and the Making of the Constitution.* (Baton Rouge: Louisiana State University Press, 1973).

Mattern, David B. *Benjamin Lincoln and the American Revolution.* (Columbia: University of South Carolina Press, 1995).

Middlekauff, Robert. *The Glorious Cause: The American Revolution, 1763–1789.* (New York and Oxford: Oxford University Press, 1982).

Morgan, Edmund S., and Helen M. *The Stamp Act Crisis.* (New York and London: Collier Books, 1965).

Morris, Richard B. *The Forging of the Union, 1781–1789.* (New York: Harper and Row, 1987).

Myers, Minor, Jr., *Liberty without Anarchy: A History of the Society of the Cincinnati.* (Charlottesville: University of Virginia Press, 1983).

Nash, Gary B. *The Urban Crucible: Social Change, Political Consciousness, and the Origins of the American Revolution.* (Cambridge, MA, and London: Harvard University Press, 1979).

Norton, Mary Beth. *Liberty's Daughters: The Revolutionary Experience of American Women, 1750–1800.* (Boston: Little, Brown, 1980).

Nuxoll, Elizabeth Miles. *Congress and the Munitions Merchants: The Secret Committee of Trade during the American Revolution.* (New York and London: Garland, 1985).

Quarles, Benjamin. *The Negro in the American Revolution.* (New York: Norton, 1961)

Rakove, Jack N. *The Beginnings of National Politics: An Interpretive History of the Continental Congress.* (New York: Knopf, 1979).

Rakove, Jack N. *Original Meanings: Politics and Ideas in the Making of the Constitution.* (New York: Knopf, 1997).

Ramsay, David, M. D. *The History of the American Revolution.* (Indianapolis: Liberty*Classics*, 1990).

Rogers, Alan. *Empire and Liberty: American Resistance to British Authority, 1755-1763.* (Berkeley, Los Angeles, and London: University of California Press, 1974).

Rosswurm, Steven. *Arms, Country, and Class: The Philadelphia Militia and the "Lower Sort" During the American Revolution.* (New Brunswick, NJ: Rutgers University Press, 1987).

Royster, Charles. *A Revolutionary People at War: The Continental Army and American Character.* (New York: Norton, 1979).

Sanders, Jennings B. *Evolution of Executive Departments of the Continental Congress, 1774-1789.* (Chapel Hill: University of North Carolina Press, 1935).

Shy, John. *A People Numerous and Armed: Reflections on the Military Struggle for American Independence.* (Ann Arbor: University of Michigan Press, 1976).

Staples, William R. *Rhode Island in the Continental Congress: 1765-1790.* ed., Reuben A. Guild. (Providence, RI: 1870).

Stinchcombe, William. *The American Revolution and the French Alliance.* (Syracuse, NY: Syracuse University Press, 1969).

Thomas, Peter D. G. *British Politics and the Stamp Act Crisis: The First Phase of the American Revolution, 1763-1767.* (Oxford: Clarendon Press, 1975).

Thomas, Peter D. G. *The Townshend Duties Crisis: The Second Phase of the American Revolution, 1767-1773.* (Oxford: Clarendon Press, 1987).

Ver Steeg, Clarence L. *Robert Morris, Revolutionary Financier, with an Analysis of His Earlier Career.* (Philadelphia: Octagon Books, 1954).

Ward, Harry M. *"Unite or Die": Intercolony Relations 1690-1763.* (Port Washington, NY, and London: Kennikat Press, 1971).

Warren, Mercy Otis. *History of the Rise, Progress and Termination of the American Revolution.* 2 vols. (Indianapolis: LibertyClassics, 1988).

Wood, Gordon S. *The Creation of the American Republic, 1776-1787.* (New York and London: Norton, 1993).

Wright, Robert K., Jr. *The Continental Army.* (Washington, DC: Center of Military History, 1983).

INDEX

Adams, Abigail, 111–12, 194
Adams, John, 26, 28, 34, 36, 51, 60, 61, 62, 112, 118, 121, 194
 and diplomacy, 68–69, 76, 93
 writings of, 136–37, 189, 205–8
Adams, Samuel, 34, 57, 58, 59, 194, 197
Albany Plan, 8–10, 36, 54
Allen, Ethan, 45–46
Annapolis Convention, 116, 212–13
Anson County, N.C., 127–29, 213
Aranjuez Convention, 73, 75, 76
aristocracy, 196, 199, 202, 203
Armstrong, John (Jr.), 192, 195
army, Continental, 47–48, 64–65, 71–72, 79, 90–91, 110, 118, 155–56, 157, 198, 200–201
 mutinies in, 81–82, 101, 171–76, 192–97
 supplies for, 59, 78, 95, 97, 162–64, 165–66, 168–69, 170
army, standing, 5, 118, 151, 197
Arnold, Benedict, 45–46, 52, 63, 72, 78, 84, 90
Arnold, Jonathan, 97, 182–85
Articles of Confederation, 62, 65–67, 68, 85, 103, 114, 120, 153–59, 184, 202
 amendment of, 86–87, 94–95, 106, 115–16, 176–78, 205, 210–13, 216

Bank of North America, 86, 89, 196
Barney, Joshua, 100
Barras, Jacques Melchoir Saint-Laurent, Comte de, 90, 91
Barrington, William Wildman, 2nd Viscount, 15, 26, 44

Beaumarchais, Pierre Augustin Caron de, 71
Bernard, Francis, 20–21, 136–37, 189,
Billey, 204
Bland, Richard, 16–17, 38
Board of Trade, 6, 8, 9
Bonvouloir, Julian-Alexandre Achard de, 59
Boston Massacre, 24–25, 26
Boston Tea Party, 30
Boudinot, Elias, 186
Bunker Hill, 49–50
bureaucracy, 85–86, 96, 98, 151
 salaries for, 19–20, 23, 27–29, 88, 137, 213
Burgoyne, John, 49, 71–72
Burke, Edmund, 43, 62
Burke, Thomas, 176

Canada, 40, 52, 63, 76, 100, 159, 181
Carleton, Guy, 52, 63
Carlisle Commission, 74–75
Charleston, S.C., 22, 63–64, 76
children, 206–8
Cincinnati, Society of, 103–4, 194, 197–201
citizenship, 154, 205–8
civil rights, 151
Clinton, Henry, 49, 63–64, 72, 74, 76, 82, 90
Coercive Acts, 30–33, 34, 38, 41, 42
colonies, 9, 47, 59, 61, 144–46
Committee of the States, 157–59
Common Sense, 56–58, 146–49
Concord, Mass., 44–45, 46
Congress, Continental, 46, 51, 55–56, 57, 59, 60, 61, 65–67, 71–

225

72, 85–86, 89, 93–94, 111, 119, 149–53, 154–59
  and army, 47–48, 81–82, 97–99, 101–2, 103, 193, 194, 195–96
  and diplomacy, 68–69, 70–71, 73, 74–76, 100, 180–82, 187–88
  and executive departments, 87–88, 105–6, 178
  First Continental, 33–42
  and Indians, 52–53, 108, 140–43, 157
  powers of, 67, 95–97, 101, 176–78, 183–85, 190
  and public debt, 48–49, 69, 80–81, 84, 86–87, 94–95, 106, 168, 186–87, 196, 198
  and trade, 54–55, 59–60, 78, 113, 115–16, 157, 213
  and west, 107–8, 201–4
Connecticut, 46, 81, 171–76
Constitution, United States, 119, 120–22, 194
Continental Association, 39, 40, 55
contracts, military, 89–90, 97, 168–69, 196
Cornwallis, Charles, 76, 90–91, 110
corruption, 69–70, 88, 96, 104–5, 189
Cromwell, Oliver, 4
Crown Point, 45, 52
currency, Continental, 48–49, 79, 80–81, 84, 168, 195

Dartmouth, William Legge, 2nd Earl, 26, 134–36
Dawes, William, 44
Deane, Silas, 69–70, 84, 208
debt, public, 107, 117, 119, 216
Declaration and Resolves, 39, 42
Declaration of Causes and Necessity of Taking up Arms, 50–51
Declaration of Independence, 32, 149–53

Declaratory Act, 18–19, 21
Delaware, 57, 62, 95–96
Dickinson, John, 19–20, 40, 50–52, 58, 62, 121
Digby, Robert, 92
Drummond, Thomas Lundin, Lord, 58
Duane, James, 91, 213
Dunmore, John Murray, Lord, 56, 58, 110

East India Company, British, 19–20, 29–30
economy, American, 78, 117, 167–71
Estaing, Jean Baptiste Charles Henri Hector Théodat, Comte d', 74, 75, 76

farmers, 78, 79–80, 93, 169
Fauquier, Francis, 21–22
Ferguson, Elizabeth Graeme, 165–66
fisheries, 76, 93, 161, 181
Fort Ticonderoga, 45–47, 52
Fort Wilson riot, 80, 166–67
France, 3, 83, 103, 147, 200
  and American trade, 92, 114, 209–10
  diplomacy of, 59, 68–74, 93–94, 100, 160–62, 181–82, 187–88
  loans from, 88–89, 91, 96–97, 106
Franklin, Benjamin, 18, 26, 29, 30, 51, 54, 57, 62, 121, 129, 215–17
  and Albany Plan, 8–10, 34–35, 125–26
  and confederation, ix, 54, 66, 120, 138
  as diplomat, 70, 71, 76, 88, 93, 99–100
Franklin, William, ix
French and Indian War, 10
frontier, 11–12, 64, 77, 117, 152
  grievances of, 127–29, 213–15, 216

INDEX

Gadsden, Christopher, 38
Gage, Thomas, 15, 26, 27, 34, 42, 43–44, 45, 49, 52,
Galloway, Joseph, 33, 36–37, 38, 46, 138–40
Gaspée incident, 26–27
Gates, Horatio, 63, 72, 77, 99
George III, 42, 56, 144–46, 150–52
Georgia, 55, 76
Gérard, Conrad Alexandre, 74, 75–76
Gerry, Elbridge, 121, 194, 197–201, 205
government, central, x, 3, 5, 9, 14, 53–54, 59, 65, 118, 125–26, 189, 216
    powers of, 102, 104–5, 106, 199, 205, 210–13. *See also* Articles of Confederation; Constitution, United States; Galloway, Joseph
Grasse, François Joseph Paul, Comte de, 91, 92
Graves, Samuel, 55
Great Britain, 5–6, 8–9, 41, 52–53, 58, 70–71, 74–75, 100, 108, 110, 118, 137, 138–40, 144–53, 161, 216
    and American trade, 12–14, 22–24, 26–27, 29–31, 37–40, 58, 60, 91–92, 113–15, 208–10
Greene, Nathanael, 77, 90, 178
Greene, William, 96–97
Grenville, George, 13, 14, 49, 129

Halifax, George Montagu Dunk, Earl of, 6
Hamilton, Alexander, 116, 121
Hampshire County, Mass., 117, 213–15
Hancock, John, 21, 34, 95–96, 134
Hemsley, William, 166–67
Henry, Patrick, 16–17, 38
Higginson, Stephen, 197–201

Hillsborough, Wills Hill, 2nd Viscount, 20–21, 23, 26
Howe, Richard, 64, 71, 75
Howe, William, 49, 64, 71–72
Howell, David, 96–97, 105, 182–85
Hutchinson, Thomas, 24, 27–29, 30, 134, 136–37

impost, 67, 86–87, 95–97, 99, 101, 176–78, 182–85, 186, 189, 196
independence, 46–47, 57, 61–62, 63, 83, 146, 208–9
Indians, xi, 8, 12, 44, 52–53, 56, 64, 66, 71–72, 108, 140–43, 152, 201

Jackson, Jonathan, 210–13
Jay, John, 40, 46, 76, 88, 93, 164
Jefferson, Thomas, 38, 50–52, 62, 93–94, 107–10, 118, 121, 201–4

King, Rufus, 121, 210–13
Kirkland, Samuel, 52–53

Lafayette, Marie Joseph Paul Yves Roch Gilbert du Motier, Marquis de, 75
La Luzerne, Anne César, Chevalier de, 93, 98
Laurens, Eleanor, 132–34
Laurens, Henry, 47, 76, 94, 110, 132–34
Laurens, John, 47, 88–89
Lee, Arthur, 53, 70, 178, 189, 194
Lee, Charles, 64
Lee, Richard Henry, 51, 61
Lexington, Mass., 44–46
Lincoln, Benjamin, 76, 117, 178
Livingston, Catharine Wilhelmina, 164–66
Livingston, Robert R., 62, 178, 213

Loudoun, John Campbell, Earl of, 10
loyalists, 64, 74, 77–78, 106–7, 164–66
"Lucius," 100–1, 188–91, 194

Madison, James, 100, 110, 121, 187–88, 201, 204, 213
Martin, Joseph Plumb, 45, 162–64, 171–76
Maryland, 57, 62, 67, 68, 84–85, 95–96
Mason, George, 121
Massachusetts, 8, 14, 17, 20, 27–29, 30, 32–34, 43, 44, 45, 47, 68, 89, 95–96, 111, 116–19, 145, 206–7, 216
mercantilism, x, xi, 4, 69, 160–62, 208–10
merchants, 17, 18, 22, 23, 33, 80, 93, 169
militia, 72, 80, 167, 197, 201
Mississippi River, 76, 181, 211
Model Treaty, 68–69, 115, 160–62
Morgan, Daniel, 77, 90
Morris, Gouverneur, 121, 167–71, 178–80
Morris, Mary, 164–66
Morris, Robert, 69–70, 74, 103, 121, 164, 167, 201
  as Superintendent of Finance, 87–88, 89, 91, 96, 97, 98–99, 101, 105–6, 168, 178, 186–87, 188–91
Moultrie, William, 64

Navy, American, 55–56, 92, 157
navy, British, 55, 78, 92, 93
navy, French, 75, 76
Netherlands, 88, 96–97
Newburgh affair, 98, 99, 100, 186, 191–97
New England, 13–14, 23, 38, 43, 51, 216

New Hampshire, 111, 118
New Jersey, 57, 62, 64, 65, 82, 106, 112
New York, 15–16, 22, 23, 30, 31, 40, 47, 62, 64, 71–72, 101, 112
North, Frederick, 7th Baron, 23–24, 26, 29, 43, 49, 51, 92
North Carolina, 12, 47, 61, 63–64, 76, 90, 112, 127–29
Northwest Ordinance, 107–8, 111

Olive Branch Petition, 51, 56
Oliver, Andrew, 29, 30, 134, 136–37
Oliver, Peter, 28–29
Oswald, Richard, 100

Paca, William, 166–67
Paine, Thomas, 57–58, 116, 146–49
paper money, 6–7, 26, 79, 117, 118, 128, 168, 215, 216
Parker, Peter, 63–64
Parliament, 7, 13, 15–16, 42–43, 55, 58, 60, 138–40, 144–46
  powers of, 22, 28–29, 35–36, 38
  taxes colonies, ix–x, 14, 19–20, 25, 51, 129–30
peace, 75–76, 93, 94, 99–100, 110, 180–82, 195
Pendleton, Edmund, 61
Penet, J. Pierre, 59
Pennsylvania, 8, 12, 23, 57, 89, 112, 165, 174–75, 204
  constitution of, 57, 61, 68, 166–67
  mutinies of troops from, 81–82, 95, 101, 104, 174–75
pensions, 183, 193, 195, 197, 198
Pettit, Charles, 215–17
Philadelphia, 22, 30, 71, 74, 104–5, 166–67
Pitt, William (the elder), 10–11, 18, 42
Pliarne, Emmanuel de, 59
Pollock, Oliver, 70

privateers, 60
Proclamation of 1763, 12

Quartering Acts, 15–16, 32, 151
Quebec Act, 32, 40, 152

Ramsay, David, 16, 56, 191–94
Randolph, Edmund, 121
Randolph, Peyton, 33
Reed, Esther DeBerdt, 81
Reed, Joseph, 74, 82, 167
regulators, 12, 127–29
religion, 32, 77, 109–10, 163–64
republicanism, 5, 27–28, 87, 97, 100–6, 117, 118, 121, 122, 136–37, 182–85, 188–91, 194–201, 205–8, 210–13
requisitions, 14, 18, 25, 49, 66–67, 86, 97, 101–2, 106, 121, 129, 156, 184
Revere, Paul, 34, 44
Rhode Island, 56, 95–97, 98–99, 101, 182–85, 189
Rochambeau, Jean Baptiste Donatien de Vimeur, Comte de, 90–91
Rockingham, Charles Watson-Wentworth, Marquis of, 17, 92–93
Roderigue Hortalez and Company, 71
Rodney, George, 92
Rush, Benjamin, 57

St. Leger, Barry, 71–72
Saratoga, 71–72
Schuyler, Philip, 52
Secret Committee of Trade, 55, 59, 69–70
Shays's Rebellion, 116–19, 205–11, 215–17
Sheffield, John Baker Holroyd, 1st Earl of, 114, 208–10

Shelburne, William Petty, Earl, 92–93, 113
slavery, 44, 110–11, 134–36, 202, 203, 204
slaves, xi, 24, 53, 56, 90, 110, 152
Sons of Liberty, 17, 24, 30
South, 53, 60–61, 64, 74, 76–77, 90–91, 111
South Carolina, 12, 38, 40, 47, 53, 76, 77, 90
Spain, 3, 10, 73, 76, 115, 116, 147, 211
specie, 3, 100
  shortage of, x, 6–7, 13, 79, 86, 89, 91, 92, 129, 148, 213
  taxation in, 15, 17, 25, 117
Stamp Act, 14–18, 49, 129–34
States, 65–68, 106–7, 112, 113–14, 115–16, 118, 120, 121–22, 153–56, 202–4, 212, 215
  and army, 81–82, 84, 90, 199
  economic regulations of, 79, 169–70
  and revenue, 97, 98–99, 101, 106, 117, 184–85, 190
Suffolk County Resolves, 34, 42
Sugar Act, 13–14
Sullivan, James, 112, 118, 205–8
Sullivan, John, 63, 75, 93

taxation, x, 5, 9, 80, 90, 102, 126, 128–29, 170–71, 213–14
  and representation, 14, 16–17, 18, 19–20, 21, 129–31, 137, 141, 151
tea, 22–23, 140
  tax on, 19–20, 27, 29–30, 41, 183
Thomson, Charles, 33, 48
Townshend Acts, 19–21, 23
trade, American, ix, 59–60, 147–48, 190
  postwar, 113–15, 117, 208–10, 216
  regulation of, x, 3, 26–27, 37–39, 54–55, 213

restrictions on, 10, 51, 61, 73, 91–92, 129, 151, 167–71
taxation of, ix, 12–13, 19–20, 22, 29–30, 67, 68, 86, 176–78
Treaty of Paris (1783), 11, 99–100, 113, 211

Vergennes, Charles Gravier, Comte de, 59, 69, 71, 72–74, 75, 93, 100
Vice Admiralty Courts, 13
Virginia, 21–22, 27, 40, 47, 61, 67, 85, 90, 97, 116
and Stamp Act, 14, 16–17, 129–31

Warren, Mercy Otis, 112, 118, 194–97

Washington, George, 10, 62, 67, 88, 89, 98, 103–4, 121, 162, 199–200
as commander in chief, 48, 55, 64–65, 71, 75, 81, 90–91, 95, 97, 195
and Newburgh affair, 99, 188, 191–93, 196–97
western lands, 66, 67, 106, 107–8, 201–4, 211
West Indies, 10, 13, 42–43, 73, 114, 115, 161–62, 209
Wheatley, Phillis, 26, 134–36
Wilson, James, 58, 80, 121, 167
women, xi, 79, 81, 111–13, 164–66, 206–8

Yorktown, 91